Private Lives and Public Responses

Private Lives and Public Responses

Edited by

Reuben Ford and Jane Millar

Policy Studies Institute

The publishing imprint of the independent
POLICY STUDIES INSTITUTE
100 Park Village East, London NW1 3SR
Tel. 0171 468 0468 Fax. 0171 388 0914

ISBN 0 85374 736 9
PSI Report 851

Cover design by Andrew Corbett
Typeset by Oxford Publishing Services, Oxford
**Printed and bound in Great Britain by
Athenaeum Press Ltd, Gateshead, Tyne & Wear.**

Contents

Contents

Acronyms and Abbreviations

AFDC	aid to families with dependent children
BHPS	British Household Panel Survey
CF	couple family
CHS	Continuous Household Survey
CPAG	Child Poverty Action Group
CSA	Child Support Agency
CSO	Central Statistical Office
DHSS	Department of Health and Social Security
DHSS (NI)	Department of Health and Social Services (Northern Ireland)
DSS	Department of Social Security
ECHP	European Community Household Panel
EOC	Equal Opportunities Commission
EOCNI	Equal Opportunities Commission Northern Ireland
ESRC	Economic and Social Research Council
EU	European Union
FC	family credit
FES	Family Expenditure Survey
FRS	Family Resources Survey
GAIN	Greater Avenues for Independence
GHQ	general health questionnaire
GHS	General Household Survey
HBAI	households below average income
IS	income support
JET	Jobs, Education and Training
JRF	Joseph Rowntree Foundation
LFS	Labour Force Survey
LP	lone parent
NACAB	National Association of Citizens Advice Bureaux
NHS	National Health Service
OECD	Organization for Economic Cooperation and Development
OPCS	Office of Population Censuses and Surveys
OPF	one-parent family
OSM	Original sample member
PRILIF	Programme of Research into Low Income Families

PSI	Policy Studies Institute
QoL	quality of life
SCELI	Social Change and Economic Life Initiative
SLS	Servicing the Legal System
SSAC	Social Security Advisory Committee
STICERD	Suntory–Toyota International Centre for Economics and Related Disciplines

Acknowledgements

The chapters in this volume were originally presented as papers at the 'Private Lives and Public Responses' policy seminar held at the University of Bath on 5–6 June 1997. At the university, we are grateful especially to Donna Davies for her help in organizing the seminar, and to the recorders: Sarah Harkcom, Nicki Liles and Tess Ridge. A special thank you is owed to Nicki Liles at the University of Bath, and Selina Cohen at Oxford Publishing Services, for their assistance in preparing the text that appears here.

Thanks are due, of course, to the authors of the papers, and to the seminar discussants who helped synthesize the key messages emerging from research in each strand of the seminar: Kath Kiernan, Fran Bennett, Robert Walker, Rosalind Edwards and Ruth Lister. We must extend our thanks also to all those who attended the seminar and contributed to the discussions.

The seminar would not have been possible without the support of the Joseph Rowntree Foundation, and valued advice and encouragement were received from Barbara Ballard. The DSS has kindly given permission for the use of its data sets in Chapters 10, 11 and 12. Responsibility for the views expressed here rests with the respective authors.

Reuben Ford
Policy Studies Institute

Jane Millar
University of Bath

January 1998

Contributors

KARL ASHWORTH is a research fellow at the Centre for Research in Social Policy, Loughborough University. His research interests include childhood poverty, social security benefits, unemployment and work. Relevant publications include K Ashworth, M Hill and R Walker (1994) 'Patterns of Childhood Poverty: New Challenges for Policy', *Journal of Poliçy Analysis and Management*; K Ashworth, M Hill and R Walker (1993) 'A New Approach to Poverty Dynamics', *Bulletin de Methodologie sociologique*; R Walker with K Ashworth (1994) *Poverty Dynamics: Issues and Examples*, Aldershot: Avebury.

JONATHAN BRADSHAW is Professor of Social Policy at the University of York. He is director of the Institute for Research in the Social Sciences, associate director of the Social Policy Research Unit and co-director of the European Observatory on National Family Policies. His research includes Bradshaw and Kennedy et al (1996) *The Employment of Lone Parents: A Comparison of Policy in 20 Countries,* London: HMSO; and with Stimson et al (forthcoming) *Non Resident Fathers in Britain*.

ALEX BRYSON is a senior fellow at the Policy Studies Institute. His research interests span industrial relations through to social policy and labour economics. Recent publications include A Bryson and S McKay (1997) 'What about the Workers?' in R Jowell, A Park, L Brook, K Thomson and C Bryson, *British Social Attitudes: The 14th Report*, Aldershot: Dartmouth; A Bryson, R Ford and M White (1997) *Making Work Pay: Lone Mothers' Employment and Wellbeing*, York: Joseph Rowntree Foundation; and A Bryson and A Marsh (1996) *Leaving Family Credit*, London: HMSO.

KAREN CLARKE is Lecturer in Social Policy at the University of Manchester. Her current research interests are changing family forms, gender roles and work–family relations and the development of family support policies. Recent publications include K Clarke, C Glendinning and G Craig (1996) *Losing Support: Lone Mothers and the Child Support Act*, Family Policy Studies Centre; and K Clarke, C Glendinning and G Craig

(1996) *Children's Views on Child Support. Parents, Families and Responsibilities*, Children's Society.

GARY CRAIG is head of the Policy Studies Research Centre and Professor of Social Policy at the University of Lincolnshire and Humberside. His current research interests include the impact of local government reorganization on social services work, anti-poverty community development and family policy. He is co-editor of *Social Policy Reviews nos 8 and 9*, Social Policy Association 1996 and 1997; *Community Empowerment* (Zed Books, 1995) and co-author of *Combating Local Poverty,* Local Government Management Board, 1995.

EILEEN EVASON is Professor in Social Administration and Policy at the University of Ulster. She has published extensively on poverty and social security. Recent publications include E Evason and R Woods (1995) 'Poverty, Deregulation of the Labour Market and Benefit Fraud', *Social Policy and Administration*; E Evason (1995) 'Social Security Law in Northern Ireland', in B Dickson and D McBride (eds) *Digest of Northern Ireland Law*, SLS Publications, Queen's University Belfast.

REUBEN FORD is a senior research fellow at the Policy Studies Institute, working in family finances and social security research. His interests span labour migration, life course change and family structure and work incentives among families with children. He has written four major reports while at PSI (*Childcare in the Balance, What Happens to Lone Parents, Changes in Lone Parenthood* and *Relative Needs*) and has recently finished a longitudinal study of lone parents' well-being for the JRF *Making Work Pay* project.

LOUISE FINLAYSON is a research fellow at the Policy Studies Institute. Her current research interests include lone parents and employment; women and the labour market; and welfare-to-work policies. She is author, with A Marsh and R Ford (1997) of *Lone Parents, Work and Benefits*, The Stationery Office, and, with J Nazroo (forthcoming 1998), of *Gender Inequalities in Nursing Careers*, PSI.

CAROLINE GLENDINNING is currently senior research fellow, National Primary Care Research and Development Centre, University of Manchester. Prior to this she was senior research fellow, Department of Social Policy and Social Work, University of Manchester, where she collaborated with Karen Clarke and Gary Craig on a series of studies on the impact of the Child Support Act.

xii

Contributors

JOHN HASKEY is a statistician/demographer who heads the Social Statistics Unit within the Office for National Statistics. He has written on a variety of demographic subjects, including marriage and divorce; families – including one-parent families and stepfamilies – households; and the ethnic minority and overseas-born populations. (He also has an interest in the socio-economic and socio-legal aspects of these subjects.) Besides publishing a number of articles and papers on these topics, he has also contributed chapters to various books, including Grahame Crowe and Michael Hardey (eds) (1991) *Lone Parenthood: Coping with Constraints and Making Opportunities*, Hemel Hempstead: Harvester/Wheatsheaf; A H Bittles and D F Roberts (eds) (1992) *Minority Populations: Genetics, Demography and Health*, London: Macmillan Press in association with the Galton Institute; *European Population* (1993) *Volume 2*, INED, Paris; and Peter Caterall and Virginia Preston (1995 and 1996) *Contemporary Britain: An Annual Review*, London: Institute of Contemporary British History.

SARAH JARVIS is a researcher in the ESRC Research Centre on Micro-social Change at the University of Essex. Her current research interests include income and poverty dynamics, savings and investment behaviour and social security reform in the former socialist economies of central and eastern Europe. Recent publications include Sarah Jarvis and Stephen P Jenkins (1997) 'Income Dynamics in Britain: New evidence from the British Household Panel Survey', in Paul Gregg (ed) *Jobs, Wages and Poverty: Patterns of Persistence and Mobility in the new Flexible Labour Market*, January; and Sarah Jarvis and Gerry Redmond (1997) 'Child Poverty, Economic Transition and Welfare State Regimes in the UK and Hungary', *Journal of European Social Policy*.

STEPHEN P. JENKINS is a professor in the ESRC Research Centre on Micro-social Change at the University of Essex. An applied economist, his current research focuses on longitudinal dimensions of the distribution of income, the labour market and social security benefits. His recent publications include Stephen Jenkins and Peter Lambert (1997) 'Three "I"s of poverty curves, with an analysis of UK poverty trends', *Oxford Economic Papers*; Stephen Jenkins and Sarah Jarvis (1997) 'Low income dynamics in 1990s Britain', *Fiscal Studies*; and S Jenkins, A Shaw, R Walker, K Ashworth and K Middleton (1996) *Moving Off Income Support: Barriers and Bridges*, DSS Research Report Series, Report No 53.

STEPHEN McKAY is a research fellow at the Centre for Research in Social Policy at Loughborough University. Previous publications include Stephen

McKay and Alan Marsh (1994) *Lone Parents and Work,* London: PSI; and Stephen McKay, Alan Marsh and Reuben Ford (1995) *Changes in Lone Parenthood,* London: HMSO. His current research includes studies of young people and benefits, and a comparative analysis of social exclusion and the dynamics of family change.

JOHN McKENDRICK is a geographer at the Department of Social Sciences at Glasgow Caledonian University. He has published on the geographies of poverty, the family and children in work conducted for the ESRC, Tommy's Campaign and Barnado's. His current research includes the private sector provision of leisure space for young children (part of the ESRC 5–16 programme) and the community–poverty interface.

MAVIS MACLEAN is a senior research fellow at the Centre for Socio-Legal Studies at Wolfson College, Oxford and academic advisor for the Lord Chancellor's Department. Recent publications include M Maclean and J Eekelaar (1997) *The Parental Obligation,* Oxford: Hart Publishing.

ALAN MARSH is a programme director at the Policy Studies Institute where he leads a programme of research into Britain's low-income families – their circumstances, well-being and health, their access to the labour market and social-security policy. His recent publications include A Marsh and S McKay (1993) *Families, Work and Benefits*, PSI; A Marsh and S McKay (1994) *Poor Smokers*, PSI; and A Marsh, R Ford and L Finlayson (1997) *Lone Parents, Work and Benefits*, The Stationery Office.

SUE MIDDLETON is director of the Lifestyles and Living Standards Programme and senior research fellow in the Centre for Research in Social Policy, Loughborough University. Among her research interests are the lifestyles and living standards of children and young people, in particular the transition from youth to adulthood. Relevant publications include S Middleton, K Ashworth and I Braithwaite (1997) *Small Fortunes: Spending on Children, Childhood Poverty and Parental Sacrifice*, York: Joseph Rowntree Foundation; and S Middleton, K Ashworth and R Walker (1994) *Family Fortunes: Pressures on Parents and Children in the 1990s*; London: Child Poverty Action Group Ltd.

JANE MILLAR is Professor of Social Policy and director of the Centre for the Analysis of Social Policy at the University of Bath. Research interests include gender and poverty, the policy implications of changing family and employment patterns. Recent publications include H Jones and J Millar (eds) (1996) *The Politics of the Family*, Aldershot: Avebury; and J

Millar, S Webb and M Kemp (1997) *Combining Work and Welfare,* York: Joseph Rowntree Foundation.

GILLIAN ROBINSON is a lecturer in social administration and policy at the University of Ulster. She teaches research methods and is closely involved in the university's centre for the study of conflict resolution (INCORE). Recent publications include G Robinson and N Heaton (1996) 'Work, Marriage and Family: A Time for Change?', in R Breen, P Devine and L Dowds (eds) *Social Attitudes in Northern Ireland: The Sixth Report,* Belfast: Appletree Press; V Morgan, M Smith, G Robinson and G Fraser (1996) *Mixed Marriages in Northern Ireland: Institutional Responses,* Centre for the Study of Conflict, University of Ulster, Coleraine.

KAREN ROWLINGSON is a senior lecturer in sociology at the University of Derby. She has carried out research into issues relating to families, work and welfare. Recent publications include *Disability Benefits and Employment,* London: The Stationery Office (1996) and *Social Security Fraud: The Role of Penalties,* London: The Stationery Office (1997).

KATE THOMPSON is a research officer in the School of Health Sciences at the University of Ulster. Recent publications include H McRea and K Thompson (1995) 'Role of Midwives in a Teaching Hospital in the Republic or Ireland', *British Journal of Midwifery,* vol 3, no 9; and D Whittington and K Thompson (1994) *Health and Lifestyles in the Western Board Area,* Blue Moon Publishing Company.

Chapter 1

Lone Parenthood in the UK: Policy Dilemmas and Solutions

Reuben Ford and Jane Millar

Living as, or with, a lone parent is an increasingly common experience for people in the UK today. Many lone parents rely on state provisions, particularly for income and housing, and the costs of providing such support increase annually. Nevertheless, lone parents are one of the poorest groups in the UK and lone parenthood is strongly associated with child poverty.

For a long time there was little change in the nature and aims of policy towards this group. Writing in 1975, in a comment on the Finer Committee proposals, George (1975: 6) noted that 'social security provision for one-parent families is the most striking example of how little progress has been made in the past 50 years'. At the end of the 1980s, commentators such as Brown (1988) and Bradshaw (1989) were pointing to rising rates of poverty among lone parents and a lack of coherence and consistency in policy goals. However, since the implementation of the Fowler reviews in 1988, there have been a number of policy initiatives (for example, the replacement of supplementary benefit with income support, the introduction of family credit, the child support legislation, and the introduction and abolition of extra needs premium on income support) which have started to change the nature of the support offered to lone parents, placing a greater emphasis on self-support through employment and on the obligations of the separated parent.

Nevertheless, support for lone parents and their children remains an area of considerable and continuing controversy. For some, state support for lone parents is tantamount to destroying the traditional family and with it the moral basis of society as a whole. For others, it is unacceptable that the costs of these private choices should fall so much upon the public purse. For others still, the concern is not that there is too much support for these families, but rather that there is too little or that it is of the wrong sort.

Many argue that it is unacceptable for over two and a half million children to be brought up in such difficult financial circumstances and point to the lack of state provision in certain areas, such as the level of income replacement benefits and childcare services, that restrict the opportunities for employment among lone parents. The 'problem' of lone parenthood is defined in many different ways and each definition of the problem prompts a particular solution – solutions that are often contradictory and incompatible with each other.

This volume represents the principal output of a policy seminar held at the University of Bath in June 1997. The purpose of the seminar was to debate the principles, goals and nature of state provision for lone parents in the light of empirical evidence on their comparative circumstances and needs. Papers presented at the seminar form the chapters that follow. The seminar was structured around five main areas (lone parenthood and family formation, the quality of life of lone-parent families, historical and cross-national definitions of policy goals, employment opportunities and barriers, and supporting children in lone-parent families) and, while each of these raises their own particular issues and dilemmas, each chapter also in some way addresses these underlying themes and questions.

In this introductory chapter, we set out the contours of the debate, describe recent policy measures and outline questions and issues discussed at the seminar. In Chapter 2, John Haskey draws on the most recent national data to offer new estimates of the numbers of lone parents in the UK. He expands on the demographic picture from a number of perspectives: family size, marital status and age. He considers how likely children of different birth cohorts are to experience lone parenthood, and plots the marital and cohabitation histories of lone mothers.

These routes of entry into lone parenthood are the subject of more detailed exploration in the following chapter by Stephen McKay and Karen Rowlingson. Using both quantitative modelling and depth interviews with lone mothers, they explore the intricate processes involved in becoming, remaining and leaving lone parenthood. Their work suggests a dichotomy between 'solo' and 'separated' lone motherhood both in terms of the factors influencing family formation and the extent to which lone mothers consider their situation a 'problem'.

This analytical perspective – how lone parenthood *affects* lone-parent families – is pursued in the four chapters that follow. To varying degrees, these consider lone parents' income sources, living standards and quality of life. In Chapter 4, Eileen Evason, Gillian Robinson and Kate Thompson look more closely at the circumstances of lone mothers using recent survey data from Northern Ireland. The authors quantify many of the everyday realities of life as a lone mother, including financial insecurity – managing bills and debts, Social Fund loans, material deprivation – and psychological distress.

The policy focus of the seminar meant that discussion tended to concentrate on the problems of lone parenthood. Nonetheless, to place the dilemmas posed for policy in perspective, it is necessary also to identify the positive aspects of lone parenthood. These emerged in lone mothers' own accounts in Chapter 3, and are quantified more clearly in Chapter 5. Here, John McKendrick also mixes quantitative and qualitative methods to focus on the quality of life of lone parents. Lone parents identify many positive aspects of their situation, not only in terms of the independence and autonomy available to those who bring up their children alone, but in terms of their own pride in and love for their children.

In Chapter 6, Sarah Jarvis and Stephen Jenkins use panel data to focus on the economic resources available to family members before and after family separation. Mothers and children tend to fare less well than fathers, receiving a disproportionately small share of their previous family income. The finding is robust to different assumptions about the income requirements of different family members.

Sue Middleton and Karl Ashworth compare the patterns of spending on children by lone parents and couples in Chapter 7. They use data from their extensive study of family spending to identify the sources and destinations of spending and the factors that best explain the amounts spent. Their findings suggest that lone parenthood itself is a less powerful marker of the resources available for children than employment status and the receipt of benefits.

The next two chapters place current British policy towards lone parents in broader perspective. Hilary Land and Jane Lewis in Chapter 8 review the changing policy orientation towards lone parents in Britain and the expectations placed upon them. In Chapter 9, Jonathan Bradshaw compares the demographic and economic characteristics of lone parents in different Western countries. He uses this international comparison to identify distinctive factors that might explain the low rates of labour market participation among lone parents in Britain.

The following chapters review the employment position of lone mothers in Britain in more detail, and consider how policy is intended to influence lone parents' behaviour. Alex Bryson, in Chapter 10, uses longitudinal data to examine the principal influences upon lone mothers' employment participation and earnings. He attributes positive effects on employment rates but negative effects on earnings in the medium term to the most long-standing policy lever in this area: family credit. In Chapter 11, Louise Finlayson and Alan Marsh also assess the gains and losses associated with lone parents' moves into work while claiming family credit. They find a high proportion of families gain financially in work – even when still in receipt of income tested benefits – compared with their income position out of work.

How lone mothers assess these potential financial gains and losses against less tangible advantages and disadvantages of employment is explored in Chapter 12 by Reuben Ford. He proposes that policy decisions take account of the delicate balancing act lone mothers must undertake before work becomes a viable and attractive option to them. His particular focus is on how childcare considerations are placed in this decision-making process.

The next two chapters examine child support. In Chapter 13, Mavis Maclean places the forces that determined the demand for and shape of the new agency in historical perspective. She is supportive of the explicit and implicit role an effective agency would play in meeting social policy objectives for lone mothers. Karen Clarke, Caroline Glendinning and Gary Craig in Chapter 14 draw on in-depth discussions with lone mothers to offer a critique of the agency in practice, and suggest ways in which objectives could be better met with reforms that took the needs of lone mothers into account.

The chapters taken together – using different data sources and methods – offer a surprisingly coherent account of the tasks facing policy makers who attempt to tackle the diverse problems lone parents face. Perhaps less surprisingly, policy response appears more piecemeal and ambiguous. In the final chapter, Jane Millar and Reuben Ford draw on this common core of research findings to propose key areas for future policy focus, and to list ten areas where immediate policy action may be needed.

THE PROBLEM OF LONE PARENTHOOD

Why is lone parenthood a problem? There is no one answer to this, as the perception of the nature of the problem posed by lone parenthood has varied over time (Lewis, 1989; Land and Lewis, 1997), across countries (Millar, 1989), and among those of different political, religious and moral views (Silva, 1996). In contemporary British debate, there are a number of different ways in which the problem of lone parenthood has been defined.

1. Lone parenthood presents a problem of *poverty*. Lone parenthood is almost synonymous with poverty and increasing numbers of such families mean – all else being equal – increased national poverty. Poverty has both immediate and more long-term negative consequences and is a problem that requires government action.
2. A commonly aired *fiscal* perspective views lone parenthood as a problem because of the propensity for such families to depend on state

benefits for a substantial proportion (at present around two-thirds) of their income. The growth of lone parenthood is thus synonymous with growth in public expenditure and many recent policy initiatives have had the explicit or implicit aim of curbing public expenditure on lone-parent families.

3. A related, but less commonly-aired, perspective views lone parenthood as a problem because of the potential *long-term impact of changing patterns of fertility*. Lone parents have fewer children than women in couples and have smaller completed family sizes. The growth in lone parenthood may lead to long-term disadvantageous changes in dependency ratios. At the micro scale, lone parents may have fewer children to care for them in old age.

4. Lone parenthood is seen as a problem because of the *effects upon children*. Some evaluations of the impact of changing family forms suggest that children from lone-parent households are more prone than others to behavioural and educational difficulties (Burghes, 1994). It is necessary for such studies to be methodologically complex; conclusions are often disputed and the mechanisms that produce negative outcomes are not clearly understood. For example, it may be that living on a low income is the instrumental factor rather than lone parenthood itself; or it may be that it is the family disruption and change that causes problems. The effect of alternative outcomes, for example 'stressed' families staying together or lone parents remarrying, must also be considered. The controversial Exeter family study (Cockett and Tripp, 1994) suggests that it is better for children if parents stay together but conversely that repartnering tends to increase the risk of negative developmental outcomes.

5. The problem of lone parenthood is a problem of *gender inequality*, because it differentially affects women. Spending time as a lone mother is detrimental to women's potential lifetime income (Evandrou and Falkingham, 1995) and increasing numbers of poor lone mothers have contributed to a 'feminisation' of poverty. More fundamentally, it has also been argued that the 'lone mother' classification simply exposes the high poverty risk of all women in terms of access to resources and their own independent income, previously hidden within male-headed households (Millar, 1989; Glendinning and Millar, 1987/1992; Joshi, 1996). The problem of lone parenthood from a feminist perspective is thus not so much a concern about this type of family structure (which may be seen as providing women with greater autonomy than marriage) but the poverty of lone mothers is seen as symptomatic of wider gendered divisions of resources in society.

6. Lone parenthood is seen as a *moral* problem because some consider that such families transgress certain religious and moral values about the functions of marriage, family formation and divorce. Widely differ-

ing beliefs hold in Britain. At one extreme, some prefer to see family formation as a very tightly regulated activity, with reproduction formed within a prescribed sequence of ceremonies and within sanctioned social structures. At the other extreme, the reproductive and family formation decisions of individuals are seen by many people as personal issues, and not answerable to public scrutiny. Lone parenthood is also viewed as a moral problem in the sense that those involved in forming such families are seen as behaving in particularly immoral and irresponsible ways: unmarried mothers who are at best careless about contraception and at worse deliberately choosing single motherhood; feckless fathers who have no intention of supporting their children.

7. Lone parenthood is seen as a *social* problem because it is one of the chief factors leading to the breakdown of the family, the creation of an underclass and the alienation of young men from family and so from society. Families without fatherhood (Dennis and Erdos, 1992) are families without male role models and create communities without authority and without accepted and recognised limits to behaviour.

From whichever standpoint lone parenthood is viewed, problems can be identified. How can/should policy respond? Two main types of answer have been given to this question: discourage lone parenthood (by making it more difficult to become and remain a lone parent and more attractive to marry and remarry); and/or alleviate the problems associated with lone parenthood (by identifying and responding to their needs). Here we examine each of these broad approaches in turn.

DISCOURAGE LONE PARENTHOOD

Trends in the numbers of lone parents

Estimating up-to-date numbers of lone parents and the rate of increase in numbers is not straightforward. In 1995, a total of 1.3 million lone parents claimed income-tested benefits (income support and family credit). As around one-sixth of lone-parent families claim neither benefit, an estimate of the number of lone-parent families in Britain can be placed at 1.5 to 1.6 million, or 20–24 per cent of families with dependent children. In the next chapter, John Haskey places a provisional estimate for 1995 at 1.7 million. Around one in ten lone parents (2 per cent of all families with dependent children) are lone fathers.

Historic trends such as those in Table 1.1 are clearer. Growth has been continuous over the past 25 years, but has accelerated during the 1990s. The majority of the increase between 1971 and 1991 can be attributed to the breakdown of marriages, although the total has been added to increasingly in recent years by never-married mothers who have separated from a cohabitation with their child's father, or who have never lived with him. Parents separated from a cohabitation accounted for 24 per cent of lone-parent families in 1994, while the never-partnered accounted for another 21 per cent (Marsh et al, 1997). Lone fathers were 2 per cent of all families in both 1976 and 1995, suggesting most of the recent growth in lone parenthood has been in lone motherhood. While the number of widowed parents has declined slowly but steadily since the war, the *proportion* of widows among lone parents has dropped rapidly in the past 25 years, from nearly a quarter to around one in 20 by 1994 (Haskey, 1991; Marsh et al, 1997).

Table 1.1: *UK lone parents over 25 years*

	1971	1995/6
Number of lone parents	570 000	1 690 000
% of all families with children	8	24
% lone mothers employed	52	41
% married mothers employed	39	71
% lone mothers receiving SB/IS	37	59
% lone mothers with a youngest child aged 0–4 years	29	36
% lone mothers who are		
widows	21	5
divorced	21	34
separated from marriage	30	23
never-married	16	38

Sources: General Household Surveys; Social Security Statistics; Social Focus on Families.

There is also evidence that another factor is influencing the growth in the number of lone-parent families, besides changes in the rate of entry by different routes. Ford et al (1995) suggest that the rate of outflow is slowing, such that the average duration of lone parenthood is increasing. Such an explanation accounts for why the average age of lone parents, and their families, is remaining stable, or even increasing, despite larger numbers of young, never-married parents flowing into lone parenthood.

Projecting from recent trends, around a quarter of all families are likely to be headed by a lone parent by the turn of the century. At any one point in time, therefore, nearly a quarter of children will live with just one of their parents. The evidence of birth registrations made by the mother alone, together with estimates of the likelihood of children experiencing their parents' divorce (Haskey, 1990) suggests that the proportion of children likely to experience lone parenthood before they leave dependency is much higher, at least a third and possibly approaching a half (Ford et al, 1995; Clarke, 1996). So lone parenthood affects not just one-fifth of families with children, as cross-section surveys suggest, but over time probably twice that proportion. At least one-third and perhaps up to one half of the next generation will experience lone parenthood as a child, and yet others will become lone parents themselves.

Family policy

The UK does not have a family policy, if 'family policy' is taken to mean a defined set of goals, pursued by a coherent set of policies and implemented through an institutional framework of a designated government department. There is no national or constitutional set of objectives for government activity in relation to the family; existing policies are sometimes contradictory and certainly uncoordinated; and there is no 'Department of the Family', and policy in respect of families and children is spread across a number of government departments (Bradshaw, 1996; Hodgkin and Newell, 1996; Millar, 1997). The role of 'Minister for the Family' has been attached to the duties of the Secretary of State for Health but has not been given any great priority. During the International Year of the Family, the then minister, Virginia Bottomley, argued that governments should acknowledge the privacy of the family and recognise the importance of keeping the state out of private family matters (Jones and Millar, 1996). The 1995 *Social Security Departmental Report* (DSS, 1995a) carried one paragraph under the heading 'Family Policy', which started: 'The Government believe the best way to help parents with children improve their standard of living, is through measures which *assist their attempts to help themselves* through taking full or part-time work [emphasis added].'

An even more 'hands-off' approach has applied to family formation and structure (notwithstanding some strong rhetoric from various politicians on this topic). Bradshaw et al (1996a) argue that British government policy in this area has generally been neutral – not pro-natalist, not concerned with encouraging or discouraging particular family structures or forms. Of course, policy cannot be wholly neutral as to form. Some family types have a more protected status in law than others. Tax rates and benefit rates vary between families; housing and childcare are differentially allocated. Every social security change involving children will favour some children over others. Some of these differences can be rationalised against equivalence scales based on empirical assessments of need. Other differences simply reflect political priorities and ideologies.

Some commentators and politicians have argued that many recent policy measures, particularly in respect of tax and social security, have disadvantaged traditional families (namely co-resident married couples with one breadwinner) and that policy should not aim to be neutral as regards family form. On the contrary, policy measures should seek to influence family formation decisions and should actively support one family form – co-resident married couples – over others (Parker, 1995; Morgan, 1995; Murray, 1994). They advocate moving beyond a 'neutral' stance to a 'pro-marriage' stance, in particular by changes to the tax and benefit system to make marriage more financially attractive. Until recently, these proposals have not made much direct policy impact. The 1992 Cabinet briefing paper on lone parents floated some ideas for policies directed towards discouraging lone parenthood and other ways of reducing public expenditure that do not harm the interests of the children of lone parents, but even the existence of the document raising these ideas proved controversial. However, the recently announced abolition of one-parent benefit and the lone-parent premium on income support have been justified as redressing the balance between lone parents and couples by removing 'additional' support for lone parents.

Looking beyond the tax and benefit system, there are other areas where policy intervention to change family formation and dissolution behaviour might be possible. Implementing such policies would however raise many difficulties and dilemmas depending on the aspect of growth targeted for curtailment: reducing inflow to lone parenthood or increasing outflow.

Reducing inflow

The number of lone parents at any one time is related to the number of families, so measures that discourage family formation, or family formation among those prone to lone parenthood, could reduce future numbers of lone parents. Ethical dilemmas would surround this selection process (also open to charges of eugenics). Less contentious would be measures to reduce the incidence of teenage pregnancy through sex education and through promoting education and employment opportunities for teenagers. Although UK teenagers have low birth rates now compared with the 1960s and early 1970s, the rates are still much higher than in most neighbouring European countries. About half of all teenage conceptions resulted in births in 1994, and about 35 per cent in legal abortions. Promotion of abortion is again, more contentious.

A tightening of divorce law might reduce the number of divorcees but would not prevent the separation of couples, which is the *de facto* route of entry into lone parenthood for the majority of lone parents. Alternatively, divorce or marriage law restrictions might work to discourage marriage in the first place. With fewer marriages there would be fewer marital breakdowns and thus fewer lone parent families *separated from marriage*.

Conversely, rates of cohabitation may rise alongside births outside marriage. Already, one fifth of lone-parent families arise from a breakdown in a cohabitation, and more than one sixth of births take place to non-married, yet co-resident adults. This is due in part to the decline in the popularity of marriage, but also to a breakdown in the traditional ordering of first births and marriage. This gives rise to a phenomenon some have termed 'postdated marriages' (Marsh et al, 1997).

Increasing outflows

Substantial ethical concerns would surround measures that seek to increase outflow from lone parenthood through increased adoption and placing of children in care. While the fiscal implications of the former option would be low compared with the latter and compared with supporting an out-of-work lone parent, the emotional costs to parent and child are likely to be very high.

The other route out of lone parenthood is through repartnering. Lone parents have a relatively low rate of repartnering (one in ten over an 18-month period surveyed by Ford et al, 1995), although half state they would be happy with such an outcome (Marsh et al, 1997). The proportion who oppose the idea of repartnering rises with age and with the duration of lone parenthood. Only about one in six lone parents in 1994 said they had had the opportunity seriously to consider living as a couple with anyone during their current spell of lone parenthood. To increase repartnering rates, policy would need to encourage this process. Venturing into such a delicate area of private lives would seem a daring move for public policy, not attempted elsewhere and with no proven methods to apply.

To encourage repartnering is also a potentially risky exercise if the objective is to minimise the number of children dependent on benefit. Policies aimed at encouraging repartnering would need to embrace many of the same measures that encourage partnering and new parenthood. Thus, it would be difficult for policy to encourage moves to repartner without also encouraging the never-partnered into partnerships and potential parenthood.

It is this final process – having new children – that lengthens lone parenthood, and particularly the duration of dependent lone parenthood – notably when it takes place outside the context of partnerships and marriage. About a fifth of lone parents look forward to having more children (Marsh et al, 1997). One in nine lone parents first interviewed in 1991 had had a new baby or was pregnant 18 months later (Ford et al, 1995). Although the majority of such births are anticipated in the context of new partnerships, at least one in twelve lone parents has more children in circumstances that are likely to prolong their lone parenthood.

Discouragement of new births is also controversial, given parental preferences to provide siblings for their existing children. There has been a policy response to this issue in a number of US states. 'Family caps' or 'child exclusions' remove or reduce social assistance to additional children born to families already in receipt of aid to families with dependent children (AFDC), or to certain types of lone mother. Such a system has been in place since 1993 in New Jersey. Another policy proposal voiced in some US states is to make social assistance receipt among lone mothers dependent upon acceptance of semi-permanent contraceptive implants. The scheme has many controversial elements – not least concerning the safety of the contraceptive implant (Eilers and Swanson, 1994). As yet, British policy shows few signs of moving in this direction. Even if policy does move to favour influencing future family form, lessons from abroad are not encouraging. It will prove difficult to implement programmes that hold any expectation of making real progress towards their supposed aims.

Developing a new approach to family policy?

Policy might look beyond the legislative framework in which partnerships are formed and dissolved to wider factors that influence the decisions people make to enter relationships and parenthood or that precipitate family breakdown. Changes in the role of family relationships have accompanied changes in the social and economic structure of society. The differing potential roles of couple relationships – marriage and cohabitation – and the implications for parenting have been the subject of considerable academic and public debate. Some argue that marriage has shifted from the 'traditional' institutional form with differentiated roles for each partner to a more symmetrical, companionate relationship in which partners share tasks (Young and Willmott, 1973; Utting, 1995). Accordingly, the system of social support for individuals in relationships is changing. Whereas partners in a differentiated relationship could call on other societal relationships with work colleagues, neighbours and extended family, the symmetrical relationship is less outward looking.

The increasingly prevalent experience of non-monogamous premarital relationships invests modern marriage with high expectations of an exclusive relationship, one where partners principally look to each other for both material and emotional support. The argument continues that it is thus partners' inability to live up to the increasing demands placed on the marital (or consensual union) bond that precipitates separation and divorce. The intrusion of children into relationships based on mutual respect and shared activities may be particularly destabilising. Growth in divorce rates in recent decades is thus seen as a product of higher rather than lower expectations of marriage.

In reality, couples may not follow either the new or traditional family models, but take up some division of responsibilities in between. Whether or not the role of economic provider falls to one or both partners, changes in external economic circumstances can make the fulfilment of marital roles more difficult. New employment patterns may make the breadwinner role less stable or certain. Where opportunities for remunerative employment become less accessible, this may be expected to destabilise the relationships based on the provider role. Likewise, changes in educational, childcare and health services may alter the demands placed on parents with the responsibility for caring for children, making them less able to fulfill their marital role and increasing the chances of marital break-up.

The role of government could therefore be seen as creating the right social and economic conditions under which stable partnerships can be formed and supported. The problem here, though, is what we understand by 'stable partnerships'. For some this must mean marriage. For others, marriage is no longer central to this. Land and Lewis (1997) argue that there have been two major changes in family formation behaviour in the postwar period: the separation of sex from marriage (with the advent of efficient and widely available contraception) and the separation of marriage from parenthood (with the growing acceptance of unmarried motherhood and divorce). To this, we might add that the demographic trends (outlined above) suggest that now lone parenthood is maturing as a family form, affecting a significant proportion of people and representing a stage in the life cycle that many will experience, albeit in different ways. For women, there is an increasing likelihood that they will spend some time living alone with their children, for men there is an increasing likelihood that they will spend some time living apart from their children.

One issue that is receiving increasing attention is the institutional basis for family policy, and in particular the place of children in administrative and political structures. There are moves to establish a House of Lords Select Committee on Children. In a recent report from the Gulbenkian Foundation, Hodgkin and Newell (1996) argue that there is a case for substantial reform at both central and local government level in order for the needs of children to be properly recognised and addressed. The increasing commitment from the European Commission on the need for measures to reconcile work and family life may also push in the direction of institutional reform, as also might party political commitments to support and strengthen families.

A more integrated approach to policy could act to the benefit of lone parents and their children. For example, family issues could be brought into the remit of one designated government department; alternatively, integration of a family policy within existing structures could include an obligation to consider the implications of every policy for families or children. On the other hand, it is not necessarily correct to assume that a more clearly defined 'family policy' would always be to the advantage of families, including lone-parent families. Perhaps the lack of consensus over goals means that it is preferable to steer clear of such an approach.

ALLEVIATE THE PROBLEMS OF LONE PARENTS

Lone parent families are one of the most disadvantaged groups in society. Two-thirds rely on income support equivalent to half the amount estimated as necessary to achieve a modest but adequate living standard (Whiteford and Hicks, 1992). Lone parents on income support report high levels of material hardship (Marsh and McKay, 1993b). An erosion in the real level of such benefits relative to earnings has occurred, potentially placing lone parents at even greater risk. This has accompanied a gradual shift in policy emphasis: from the state's role in meeting the needs of the child, to encouraging a lone mother to seek work (and maintenance from her former partner) to meet her family's needs (Lewis, 1995). However, at each step of the way towards securing such an income independent of the state, lone mothers can face considerable barriers relative to other families.

To move off income support and enter full-time employment, lone mothers must compete in the labour market with women in two-parent families, who have the option of sharing childcare tasks with their partners, or pooling the cost of childcare charges. In the absence of such childcare support, lone mothers may find themselves less flexible and restricted in the range of vacancies they can consider.

Once in work, lone parents can secure no more than one earned income to support their families, while for the majority of couples with children, both partners are earners. This means that even when earning, and when supplementing those earnings with in-work benefits, lone parents have lower incomes than couples.

Thus, in and out of work, lone mothers are much more likely than other mothers to have low incomes. Five in every six lone mothers claim a means-tested benefit. Consequently, the policy focus for discussions of the problems of lone parenthood is frequently in terms of the potentially conflicting roles of social security: providing adequate levels of income replacement to those out of work, while maintaining an incentive for parents to enter full-time paid work. However, the problems of lone parents are not only manifested in terms of income and welfare. Lone parents report high levels of long-term and limiting illness among themselves and their children. They also tend to live in social housing.

Lone parenthood has a substantial ethnic minority dimension, although this is largely overlooked by policy. The small proportion of non-white lone parents (7 to 8 per cent) masks the high proportion of particular ethnic minority families being brought up by one parent alone. The PSI fourth national survey of ethnic minorities found 36 per cent of Caribbean families to be lone-parent families (Berthoud and Beishon, 1997). These mothers face problems additional to those of their white counterparts of discrimination and racial stereotyping (Song and Edwards, 1997). They may also align with different social norms concerning childrearing and paid employment (Duncan and Edwards, 1997).

As a population, therefore, lone parents are likely to be more sensitive than other families to changes in employment, social security, health and housing policy. In recent years, in each of these areas (other than in health), lone parents have been the explicit or implicit target of specific policy initiatives.

Social security policy: welfare to work

Box 1.1 is a summary of the key changes in social security policy over the past ten or so years. The most important point to note is the shift in policy as regards employment. This has moved from an assumption that mothers should stay at home and care for their children through a 'neutral' position that mothers should themselves decide whether they wish to seek paid work, to the current position that policy should encourage, but not compel, mothers into employment where possible. Employment is seen as providing the best route to achieving an adequate income and also fits with the stated aspirations of many lone mothers themselves. Policies to encourage employment have so far mainly involved the manipulation of financial incentives (in-work benefits, the disregarding of certain incomes and costs) but more recently the 'New Deal' for Lone Parents scheme will use a caseworker approach, which aims to tailor help to individuals on the basis of an assessment of their particular needs. But the employment route may also contain dangers. Some argue that it devalues the mothering role and that those providing care for others (in this case mothers for their children) should be entitled to receive public support. There is concern that 'encouragement' may turn into 'compulsion'. The jobs that lone mothers find are often relatively low paid and even with in-work benefits such as family credit, incomes are low and levels of hardship are high (Marsh and McKay, 1993a; 1993b). Achieving an income that is both adequate and secure seems to be difficult for many of these families. Trapping lone parents into low wages and long-term dependency on family credit may seem little improvement over the current position of lone parents trapped in income support – with the added disadvantage that their time for parenting is reduced.

Box 1.1: *Social security policy initiatives since 1988 relevant to lone-parent families*

1988
- implementation of the Fowler social security review;
- replacement of special needs payments with the Social Fund;
- replacement of supplementary benefit with income support;
- loss of additional payment for extended spells of lone parenthood;
- replacement of family income supplement with family credit – subsidy for low-waged working families where at least one partner works 24 hours or more each week and where income falls below a family-specific threshold. Payments normally made to the mother.

1992
- maintenance disregard in family credit;
- minimum number of hours work each week to claim family credit reduced to 16.

1993
- implementation of the Child Support Act.

1994
- introduction of the childcare allowance – up to £40 of income spent on formal childcare disregarded in the calculation of means-tested benefits.

1995
- a bonus is introduced in family credit for work of 30 hours or more each week;
- pilot of caseworkers – support for lone parents seeking paid employment of 16 hours or more each week.

1996
- childcare allowance increased to £60;
- introduction of back to work bonus payments on movement from part-time to full-time work.

1997
- introduction of maintenance bonus payments on movement into full-time work;
- launch of 'new deal' for lone parents: individual caseworkers to aid transition to employment.

1998
- lone parent premium in income support and one parent benefit to be abolished for new lone parents;
- childcare allowance to be increased to £100 where two or more children are eligible;
- 'new deal' to be implemented nationally.

lone parents trapped in income support – with the added disadvantage that their time for parenting is reduced.

There are likely to be demand-side constraints on the employment model too. Though labour market expansion in recent years has been primarily in jobs traditionally held by women, jobs are not necessarily available for lone mothers. Very few studies have examined employers' attitudes towards employing lone mothers – either continuing employment of mothers after they have entered lone parenthood or differences in recruitment practice. The evidence that exists is largely anecdotal and from the lone parents' perspective. Lone mothers interviewed in Ford (1996) spoke of discrimination on grounds of childcare, and for intending to combine earnings with benefit. Some lone mothers also favoured particular employers they considered to be more sympathetic. In this way, employers' attitudes further restricted these lone parents' labour market options.

Housing

Fewer than a third of lone parents live in owner-occupied accommodation, compared with over three-quarters of couples. Part of the difference is accounted for by tenure differences before entry into lone parenthood, but moving into lone parenthood is also associated with downward mobility in the housing market (Bradshaw and Millar, 1991). Housing is also an area lone parents consider very important themselves. They are disproportionately likely to live in housing of poor quality or lacking amenities (McKendrick, 1995).

The majority of lone parents live in local authority rented housing. Routes into such accommodation until 1996 were increasingly dominated by allocation under Part III of the 1985 Housing Act, which requires local authorities to house priority-need homeless households including pregnant women and people with dependent children. Steadily fewer dwellings were allocated to those on housing waiting lists. There have been accusations that such provisions encourage the formation of lone parent households, although the number of parents has no bearing on local authorities' responsibilities under the Act (Wilson, 1994). Fewer than one in seven homeless households allocated dwellings in 1993 were for reasons of pregnancy. The 1996 Housing Act, implemented in 1997, is intended to reduce access to permanent housing for homeless households. Such households should have their needs met by temporary housing while permanent housing is allocated solely via the housing register.

The new legislation may result in increasing mobility between sites of temporary accommodation among newly-formed lone parent households, with implications for employment and children's education. If access to social housing is reduced, more lone parents may seek housing in private-rented or owner-occupied accommodation. These tenures produce higher in-work housing costs and may reduce the level of work incentives.

Maintenance/child support

At least nine in ten lone parents have at least one non-resident parent who is alive and available, at least in principle, to provide maintenance income for their children. Yet fewer than a third of lone parents receive maintenance from a former partner. The 1990 Child Support Act was intended to increase the proportion of non-resident parents paying regular maintenance, and to raise the size of awards. The CSA began these tasks – focusing first on new income support and family credit claimants – in April 1993.

Four recent surveys (in 1989, 1991, 1993 and 1994) have each placed the proportion of lone parents in receipt of regular maintenance payments at three in ten. It is notable that the introduction of the CSA in 1993 produced no immediate change in the proportion in receipt. Of course, at the time of the last of these surveys, the agency's activities had yet to reach the majority of lone parents. The average payment received in 1994 was higher than in 1993 (£39 versus £32) – partly due to the higher level of CSA assessments than court and voluntary agreements. High CSA assessments were, however, less likely to be paid (Marsh et al, 1997).

The receipt of maintenance has been found to be independently and positively associated with participation in full-time work (Bradshaw and Millar, 1991; McKay and Marsh, 1994; Ford et al, 1995). Accordingly, a disregard of the first £15 received each week in maintenance from income assessable for in-work benefits (available since 1992) is intended to enhance work incentives. For each additional pound of maintenance after the first £15, a new family credit award is reduced by 70p.

However, as Gibson (1991) has pointed out, the majority of lone parents are unlikely to see immediate improvements in their standard of living from new or increased maintenance payments. Two-thirds claim income support against which entitlement is reduced by one pound for every pound received in maintenance. Increased income from maintenance may lift families off income support and remove entitlement to 'passported' benefits such as free school meals and free prescriptions. The more dependent parents become on maintenance, the greater the potential for irregularities or delays in payment to affect income security (National Association of Citizens Advice Bureaux, 1994). Those in receipt of family credit and maintenance are especially vulnerable to maintenance shortfalls or cessation, since they cannot adjust the size of their family credit awards for up to six months.

CHILDCARE

A considerable body of evidence suggests that a lack of affordable child-care holds lone parents back from entry into the labour market. Four recent analyses of lone parents' labour market participation have each assigned a strong role to the age of the youngest child in the household (Marsh et al, 1997; Bryson et al, 1997; McKay and Marsh, 1994; Bradshaw and Millar, 1991). Between a third and a half of out-of-work lone parents say that the cost or availability of childcare keeps them out of work. Others give reasons that may indirectly be associated with the affordability or accep-tability of childcare. They feel their children are too young (41 per cent) or that they are better off not working (26 per cent) (Ford, 1996).

Answers to such questions are often taken together to imply that as many as seven in ten lone parents would be employed if they could combine suitable work and childcare (Bradshaw and Millar, 1991). Comparisons with countries offering greater institutionalised provision of childcare suggest similar results (Bradshaw et al, 1996a; 1996b). Recent research suggests these estimates may be over optimistic, once the multiple other reasons for not working that parents give alongside childcare are taken into account (Ford, 1996). Even without the childcare barrier, other factors would hold the majority of lone parents back: ill health, the need for readjustment following separation, resistance to formal childcare provision, low wages or poor employment prospects. Out of work parents are also reluctant to place their children with formal childcare providers – more than one-third would only be happy leaving their children with relatives or friends.

Since 1994, up to £40 worth of earnings spent each week on formal childcare could be disregarded from income assessable for in-work bene-fits. In 1996, the value of the disregard was increased to £60, which meets the anticipated cost of childcare in work of up to 90 per cent of those out of work who anticipated any cost (Ford, 1996). But two years on from its introduction, just 23,000 family credit claimants were making use of the childcare disregard. Possible reasons for low take-up include parents' preferences for informal care, the need to cover shift work and irregular hours, the restriction to children under 11 years and poor awareness of the mechanics of the scheme. Other policy initiatives, like the out-of-school childcare grant initiative, while not aimed directly at lone parents, have offered additional childcare support for lone parents in work (Sanderson et al, 1995, O'Brien and Dench, 1996).

Many out of work lone parents will also value the educational and developmental benefits for their children arising from access to childcare (Edwards, 1993). Most will find it difficult to meet charges for such care from their income support. However, subsidised access to a nursery school or playgroup place may be available. This access may be conditional on income support receipt which may reduce work incentives. Nonetheless, nursery education is soon likely to be available to nearly all four-year-olds. Should the parents wish to take up work, such care is unlikely in itself to extend sufficiently to cover working hours.

ISSUES AND QUESTIONS

Each area of policy – and there are many we have not touched on here, such as health care and education – raises particular dilemmas and diffi-culties. The solutions to these problems depend in part on how the problems of lone parenthood are perceived. In the following chapters, authors have had to address how their own perspective shapes their pro-posals for policy change. Here we finish with some broad questions that underpin policy towards lone parents in general terms.

1. To what extent is the category 'lone parent' useful?

An important consideration is the extent to which 'lone parenthood' itself is seen as a problem distinct from concerns over low-income families and the welfare of children more generally. Given the demographic trends outlined above, it may be that it is more appropriate to view lone parent-hood as simply a life-cycle stage. It can also be argued that the problem of lone parenthood is symptomatic of more pervasive structural problems in society: poor educational and employment prospects for young men and women (Land, 1996; Selman and Glendinning, 1996); gender-specific low earnings potentials and vacancies (Millar, 1987); differentials in preschool, primary and secondary education; low levels of material and practical support for families (Kempson, 1996; Smart, 1991). Such shortfalls may affect a broad range of family types without the protection of substantial financial resources. But their effects will fall disproportionately on those families with fewest material resources: hence they show up more frequently among lone parents.

Even if 'lone parenthood' itself is not the problem, lone parents are more likely to experience problems. The reasons are complex, and rooted in the circumstances in which people bring up families. A continuation of this line of argument might suggest that many of the problems lone parents and their children face would arise even if the families had remained as couples. Lone parenthood could be viewed as much a *product* of these families' circumstances as a *cause*. Targeting lone parents alone will only partially solve the problems, and potentially create others, since children in couple families would continue to experience similar disadvantages.

The lone-parent classification may therefore be both helpful and unhelpful in formulating policy. It can be helpful in focusing attention on a particularly disadvantaged population, and it can be unhelpful in directing attention away from some of the underlying causes of their problems. There may be situations where the 'lone parent' label is useful to identify people in need of additional help, and others where it would be more helpful to identify them not by their family structure but by other characteristics.

2. Would a more explicit family policy help or hurt lone parents?

One way to help lone parents would be to help all families and one way to help all families would be to offer more integrated support, perhaps through the establishment of a single government department. But would such an approach stigmatise lone parents rather than support them? An alternative might be to direct attention much more clearly into children, with the establishment of a Department for Children, or (more modestly) reforms to bring responsibility for child-care provisions within the remit of one government department.

3. To what extent would policies to promote gender equality help lone parents?

Some have argued that the underlying cause of the high rates of poverty among lone parents is the fact that they are women and women are discriminated against in employment and in state policy. Policies to break down gender segregation in employment and to promote equal pay and equal opportunities may be effective ways to help lone mothers achieve greater independence. Without such policies, moves to encourage more employment among lone mothers may simply be condemning them to long-term working poverty.

4. How to achieve income security for lone parents?

The fiscal implications of the growth of lone parenthood need to be addressed through the encouragement of private income generation, independent of the state. But the encouragement of private income generation must necessarily lead to a strengthening of lone parenthood since the logic of this approach is that lone parenthood must become a financially secure option. What role might child support play in this? Can security, adequacy and equity all be achieved?

5. Mass schemes or targeted help?

The weight of numbers of people seeking divorce and in need of financial help have perhaps inevitably led to a focus on developing provisions that can deal with large numbers of people in relatively standardised ways. This was part of the impetus behind divorce law reform and behind the child support legislation – standardised, rule-bound systems that treat people as far as possible in the same way. Similarly, the income support scheme represents a more standardised approach even than supplementary benefit (itself designed for larger numbers than national assistance). Now, however, the pendulum seems to have swung back in favour of more individualised and tailor-made measures. The child support legislation allows 'variations' from the basic formula. 'Caseworking' has become more popular as a way of identifying the individual needs of unemployed job seekers and lone parents. What are the advantages and disadvantages of this individualised approach?

Chapter 2

One-Parent Families and their Dependent Children in Great Britain[1]
John Haskey

One-parent families and the children living in them have long been of interest to policy-makers, legislators and those concerned with social welfare. Furthermore, because of the rising prevalence of lone parenthood – and hence the increased significance of one-parent families to the changing patterns of family formation and dissolution – they have also been of growing interest to demographers, sociologists and population scientists.

DEFINITION OF A ONE-PARENT FAMILY

The definition of a one-parent family is the one used by the Department of Social Security – and before that by the Department of Health and Social Security – and has been used for official purposes since 1971. It is the definition adopted in the Finer Report (DHSS, 1974, Cmnd 5629) on one-parent families commissioned by the former Department of Health and Social Security in 1969: 'a mother or a father living without a spouse (and not cohabiting) with his or her never-married dependent child or children aged either under 16 or from 16 to (under) 19 and undertaking full-time education'.

ESTIMATING NUMBERS

The difficulties involved in deriving accurate estimates of the number of one-parent families have been described in earlier articles (Haskey, 1991 and 1994) in which a series of 'best estimates' were made. The process of deciding those 'best estimates' has consisted of evaluating different

---

1. A slightly different version of this text also appears in *Population Trends*, vol 91 (1998).

Table 2.1: *Alternative estimates and 'best estimate' of number of one-parent families (OPFs), Great Britain, 1990–6*

Method of estimation/data sources	Thousands							
	1990	1991	1992	1993	1994	1995	1996	1997
Proportion of all OPFs with dependent children (from GHS) applied to total number of families with dependent children (from Child Benefit statistics)	1240	1340	1400	1490	1530	1530	1500*	
Proportion of all OPFs with dependent children (from FES) applied to total number of families with dependent children (from Child Benefit statistics)	1180	1260	1370	1480	1540	1550*	1570*	
Proportion of all OPFs with dependent children (from FRS) applied to total number of families with dependent children (from Child Benefit statistics)				1570*	1630	1660*		
Proportion of all OPFs with dependent children (from BHPS) applied to total number of families with dependent children (from Child Benefit statistics) (all estimates based on a single year's data)		1230	1340	1450	1440	1450		
Adjusted number of OPFs from LFS (subject to possible revision) (estimates derived from spring quarter data for year concerned)			1280	1380	1520	1660	1760	1710
OPFs receiving one or more benefits (from Social Security statistics)	1280	1390	1500	1600	1680			
'Best estimates' (thousands) (provisional for 1995 onwards)	1230	1300	1370	1440	1510	1560	1600	

Notes: All estimates are based on three-year average data unless otherwise stated; *estimates based on survey data for a single year. For an indication of the size of the confidence intervals for the estimates from the different surveys (see Haskey, 1994). The estimates derived from Social Security statistics are included for comparative purposes only; they have *not* been taken into account in deciding the 'best estimates'.

estimates derived from a variety of data sources and using different methods, with an assessment of the reliability of each data source and method. Inevitably, there is some uncertainty about the accuracy, and possible presence of bias, involved in the estimate from each data source and inevitably, too, concluding the resulting 'best estimate' involves a degree of subjective judgement.

Wherever possible, the 'best estimate' is chosen such that it is either consistent with a linear trend in the immediately preceding 'best estimates', or else is consistent with a smoothly changing rate of increase. The reason for adopting this rule is not due to a fundamental belief that the yearly numbers in fact change in this way; rather, it is more a recognition that the data sources cannot collectively discern more complex movements in numbers because they are not sensitive enough. Consequently, the 'best estimates' are inappropriate for estimating annual rates of increase, from one year to the next, in the number of one-parent families.

Table 2.1 presents various estimates, including the 'best estimate', for the number of one-parent families for each year from 1990. The General Household Survey (GHS), the Family Expenditure Survey (FES), and the Labour Force Survey (LFS) have all been used to derive estimates, as also, for the first time, have the Family Resources Survey (FRS) and the British Household Panel Survey (BHPS). Most of these survey data have been used in conjunction with the number of families with dependent children – which has been estimated using child benefit statistics.

Estimates based on LFS data were not used in the previous estimation exercise because of three separate problems – described elsewhere (Tate, 1997) – each of which would have exaggerated the number of one-parent families. These factors have been corrected in the LFS estimates that appear in Table 2.1, though the resulting estimates – which may yet be revised in the future – are believed to be very slightly over-deflated (Hastings, 1997).

A previous article published on one-parent families gave a final 'best estimate' for 1991 and a provisional 'best estimate' for 1992 (Haskey, 1994). Table 2.1 updates these results, providing final 'best estimates' of the numbers of one-parent families in 1992, 1993 and 1994, and provisional 'best estimates' of their numbers in 1995 and 1996.

In normal circumstances, a final 'best estimate' would probably also have been made of the number of one-parent families in 1995, given that for two of the series – those derived from the GHS and FES – a centred three-year average estimate is available, as well as estimates – albeit based only on a single year's data, 1995 – from the FRS and BHPS. However, although the estimates from the different surveys agree quite well in 1992, 1993 and 1994, they diverge in 1995 and 1996.

More particularly, the GHS, the survey with a section specially devoted to collecting accurate demographic information on the family – and consequently one whose estimates are given extra weight – suggests a levelling-off in numbers between 1994 and 1995 (and even a tentative fall in 1996, based on a single year's data, although this fall is not statistically significant). This flattening from 1994 to 1995 occurs not only in the GHS-based estimates, but also in those using the FES and BHPS. In contrast, the LFS and FRS-based estimates point to an increase continuing between 1994 and 1995 at the same rate as before. Consequently, it is advisable to await further evidence before concluding a final 'best estimate' for 1995. However, a provisional estimate is provided which incorporates an assumption of some slackening in the rate of increase.

Table 2.2: *'Best estimates'* of numbers of one-parent families (OPFs) and their dependent children, Great Britain, 1971–96*

	OPFs (millions)	Dependent children in OPFs (millions
1971	0.57	1.0
1976	0.75	1.3
1981	0.90	1.5
1984	0.94	1.5
1986	1.01	1.6
1988	1.09	1.8
1990	1.23	2.0
1991	1.30	2.2
1992	1.37	2.3
1993	1.44	2.4
1994	1.51	2.6
1995	1.56	2.7
1996	1.60	2.8

Note: *estimates for 1995 onwards are provisional.

In general, the set of alternative estimates do seem to suggest that the number of one-parent families continued to rise at much the same pace from 1992 to 1994 as they had between 1988 and 1991. However, after 1994, there is some tentative evidence that the rate of increase may have moderated slightly. These general trends have been reflected in the set of 'best estimates' which have been made, although the changes in these estimates from one year to the next have been made as smooth as possible because of the data sources' limited scope for reliably detecting such changes. Overall, the provisional 'best estimate' of the number of one-parent families in Great Britain in 1995 is 1.56 million, 27 per cent higher than the corresponding estimate five years previously of 1.23 million in 1990. It is estimated that, in 1995, one-parent families represented 22 per cent, one in five, of all families with dependent children.

The 'best estimates' of the numbers of one-parent families since 1971 are summarised in Table 2.2, which also gives the corresponding numbers of dependent children living in these one-parent families. These latter estimates have been derived by multiplying the 'best estimate' of the number of one-parent families with the corresponding average number of dependent children per one-parent family derived from the General Household Survey (GHS).

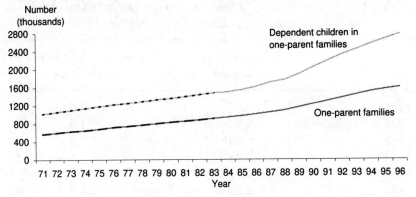

Figure 2.1: *'Best estimates' of numbers of one-parent families and of dependent children living in them, Great Britain, 1971–96*

The number of dependent children living in one-parent families is provisionally estimated to have been 2.7 million in 1995, about one-third more than in 1990. On this basis, it is estimated that one in five, 20 per cent, of dependent children in Great Britain in 1995 were living in one-parent families. The growth in the numbers of one-parent families and dependent children living in them are depicted in Figure 2.1 from which it can be seen that the growth in the number of dependent children living in one-parent families has been faster than that of the number of one-parent families. The basic reason for this phenomenon is a divergence in the trends in the average family size between lone parents and couple families – a topic explored later in this chapter.

THE MARITAL STATUSES OF LONE MOTHERS AND LONE FATHERS

One-parent families have very diverse characteristics and circumstances; probably the two best predictors of the features and situation of a one-parent family are the sex and marital status of the lone parent concerned. In so far as the profile of lone parents by their marital status has changed over the years, so too has the mix of circumstances of one-parent families.

Figure 2.2 shows the trend in the proportion of all families with dependent children that have been headed by a lone parent, distinguishing the proportions headed by lone mothers and lone fathers, and also by the lone mothers' marital status.

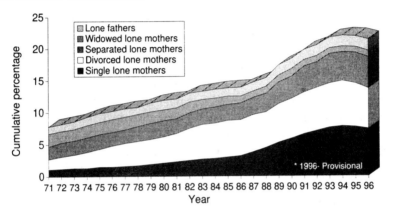

Figure 2.2: *Percentage of all families with dependent children headed by lone mothers (by their marital status) and by lone fathers, Great Britain, 1971–96*

It should be noted that information on marital status is collected in the GHS in two separate ways: from an initial question in which the alternatives are read out (the question being to establish the family groupings of household members); and from a more detailed set of questions in the Family Information Section in which various additional checks are made. In general, answers derived from the latter questions are to be preferred as they should be more accurate, although discrepancies are comparatively few. However, the Family Information questions are asked only of respondents who are aged under 60 (under 50 in earlier GHS years). Conversely, there is no age restriction imposed on those asked the initial marital status question and it is therefore used in this and the following section.

In 1971, approximately one in thirteen (8 per cent) of all families with dependent children was headed by a lone parent, but this proportion steadily rose to 22 per cent – more than one in five – in 1995. Virtually all this increase has been due to the growth in the proportion of lone mothers, although, since 1971, lone fathers have accounted for a gradually increasing proportion, rising from 1.1 to 1.8 per cent of all families with dependent children. Couple families (CFs) consisting predominantly of married couple families, formed just over three-quarters of all families with dependent children in 1995.

Figure 2.2 also shows the trends in the composition of lone mother families, according to the lone mother's marital status. These trends are also depicted in Figure 2.3, which allows a direct comparison with the corresponding trends for lone fathers. Single (never-married) and divorced lone mothers have both formed growing proportions of all lone mothers; they together accounted for 42 per cent in 1971 but 72 per cent in 1995. However, although divorced lone mothers were the most numerous of all the marital statuses throughout most of the 1970s and 1980s, single lone mothers eclipsed divorced lone mothers in relative numbers from the beginning of the 1990s. In fact, the proportion of all lone mothers who were single started to increase quite sharply around about 1986, when the incidence of births outside marriage began to rise at a faster rate.

In contrast to the growth in the proportions of divorced and single lone mothers, the proportions of separated and widowed lone mothers have both declined, the combined proportion falling from 58 per cent in 1971 to 28 per cent in 1995, less than half the 1971 proportion. However, the largest relative fall has been in widowed lone mothers; they accounted for one in four lone mothers in 1971, but only one in 25 in 1995. Of course, most of this decline is due to the considerable growth in the total number of lone mothers, though it is estimated that there has also been a slight fall in the absolute number of widowed lone mothers, the result of a decline in mortality among married men and women.

To some extent, the same trends also apply to lone fathers: divorced lone fathers predominating in relative numbers since the late 1970s but declining slightly in more recent years; and separated lone fathers accounting for a slowly diminishing proportion, but yet still forming around one-quarter of all lone fathers in recent years. Perhaps the most intriguing feature of Figure 2.3 is the steady growth in the proportion of all lone fathers who are single lone fathers. Although the sample numbers upon which the proportions of lone fathers are based are considerably smaller than those of lone mothers, it is entirely possible that this is a genuine trend, representing a small but growing phenomenon of never-married fathers bringing up dependent children as part of a one-parent family as a result, presumably, of the end of a cohabiting union in which there were children.

By the same token, of those men and women who answered that they

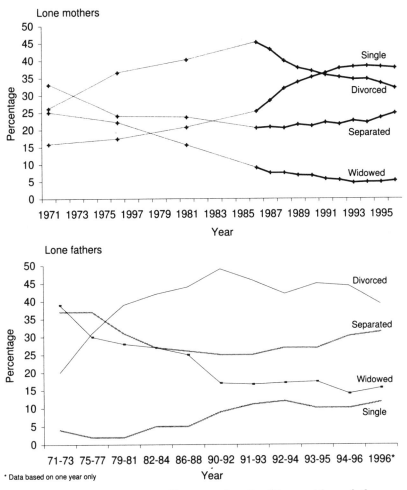

Figure 2.3: *Composition of lone mother families and lone father families with dependent children by marital status of the lone parent, Great Britain, 1971–96*

were separated in response to the initial marital status question, a small but growing proportion are likely to mean that they had separated from a partner in an informal union. In such cases, their legal marital status would probably not be married, unlike those who had separated from a spouse. Nevertheless, irrespective of this legal marital status distinction, both groups of 'separated' would previously have been living with partners as couples.

FAMILY SIZES OF ONE-PARENT FAMILIES

The pattern of family sizes – as measured by the number of dependent children – varies according to the type of family and, more especially, according to the kind of one-parent family. Table 2.3(d) provides estimates of the average number of dependent children per family for all one-parent families (OPFs), all couple families (CFs), and the three most important kinds of one-parent family: single, separated and divorced lone mother families. The average number of dependent children per one-parent family has increased steadily – by about 7 per cent between 1981 and 1995. This growth in the average family size of one-parent families explains why the number of dependent children living in one-parent families has risen at a faster rate than the number of one-parent families.

Sections (a) and (b) of Table 2.3 explore other aspects of the family sizes of both one-parent families and couple families over the period from 1971. Since 1981, one-child families among one-parent families have fallen in relative numbers, while those with three or four children have grown. The corresponding picture for couple families is the complete reverse; one-child families have become relatively more common since 1981, and three- and four-child families relatively less frequent. These results are confirmed directly by the ratios of the corresponding proportions in Table 2.3 sections (a) and (b) (given in section c); compared with couple families, one-parent families with one dependent child have declined in relative terms since 1981, while one-parent families with two, three, four and five or more dependent children have all grown in relative numbers.

On average, couples still have more dependent children than their lone-parent counterparts, although the differential in family size has been narrowing (Table 2.3 section d). It may be seen that the average family size of single lone mothers has grown the most (by 30 per cent since 1981) followed by that of separated lone mothers (by 13 per cent since 1981) while the average family size of divorced lone mothers has scarcely changed. Possibly there has been an increasing trend towards single lone mothers remaining never-married throughout their entire child-bearing years, so that this group of mothers has been having more children while still single than other single lone mothers who subsequently married or started cohabiting well before the end of their child-bearing years.

AGES OF HEADS OF ONE-PARENT FAMILIES

Lone mothers tend to be younger than lone fathers, as judged by their age profiles, which are portrayed in Figure 2.4(a). The peak age group for lone mothers is the early thirties, whereas for lone fathers it is the early forties.

Table 2.3: *Profile of one-parent families (OPFs) and couple families (CFs) by number of dependent children, Great Britain, 1991–6*

Number of dependent children	1971	1981	1986	1991	Year* 1992	1993	1994	1995	1996
(a) OPFs									
1	53	57	56	52	51	53	52	51	50
2	28	31	31	32	33	33	32	32	33
3	11	9	9	12	11	11	11	12	13
4	5	2	2	3	3	3	3	3	3
5 or more	3	1	1	1	1	1	1	1	1
(b) CFs									
1	36	30	39	39	37	37	37	38	39
2	39	44	44	43	44	44	44	44	43
3	17	18	13	14	14	14	14	4	13
4	6	5	3	3	3	4	4	4	4
5 or more	3	3	1	1	1	1	1	1	1
(c) Ratio[+] of %s *(a):(b)*									
1	1.47	1.88	1.43	1.35	1.37	1.41	1.42	1.36	1.29
2	0.73	0.71	0.71	0.74	0.76	0.74	0.72	0.75	0.75
3	0.69	0.48	0.73	0.86	0.81	0.76	0.80	0.85	1.00
4	0.79	0.46	0.77	0.85	0.91	0.83	0.93	0.91	0.89
5 or more	1.01	0.41	0.77	0.85	0.81	0.98	0.99	1.14	0.92
(d) Average no. of dependent children per family									
One-parent families	1.79	1.60	1.60	1.68	1.69	1.67	1.69	1.71	1.73
Couple families	2.03	2.07	1.83	1.86	1.88	1.88	1.89	1.87	1.85
Single lone mothers	1.25	1.19	1.33	1.40	1.47	1.48	1.48	1.55	1.56
Separated lone mothers	2.03	1.81	1.78	1.97	1.97	1.94	2.00	2.04	2.08
Divorced lone mothers	1.93	1.75	1.76	1.84	1.79	1.75	1.70	1.73	1.75

Notes: *Three-year averages (apart from 1996); [+]calculated directly from the sample numbers.

Source: General Household Survey.

More than two in every ten lone mothers are in their early thirties, while three in every ten lone fathers are in their early forties. Of course, part of the explanation for this large difference lies in the different marital status compositions of lone mothers and lone fathers which were investigated in Figure 2.3.

The contrasting age profiles of lone mothers by their marital status are portrayed in Figure 2.4(b).[2] Single lone mothers tend to be the youngest, followed by separated lone mothers, divorced lone mothers and widowed lone mothers. This sequence is to be expected since the events of separation, divorce and widowhood tend to occur at increasingly older ages, with the state of being single applying at the youngest ages. Three in ten single lone mothers are in their early twenties, with over one-third being aged under 25. In contrast, the peak age groups for both separated and divorced lone mothers are the early and late thirties; about one-quarter of both groups falling in these two age groups. Just over one-quarter of widowed lone mothers are in their early forties, the peak age group for this group of lone mothers.

Figures 2.4(c) and 2.4(d) contrast the age profiles of separated lone mothers and separated lone fathers, and the corresponding age profiles for divorced lone mothers and fathers, respectively. In both instances, the lone fathers tend to be older than their lone mother counterparts; in addition, in both cases there is slightly less variation in the ages of the lone fathers about the peak age than for lone mothers. This finding may be partly due to lone fathers being less likely than lone mothers to remain being lone parents for a given period of time after becoming lone parents.

Of course, almost all lone mothers and lone fathers were formerly married, or living in a cohabiting union, before they became lone parents. (About one in seven, though, had not previously lived in *any* partnership.) It is therefore appropriate to consider the age distributions of the men and women from which the vast majority of lone fathers and mothers are drawn. The pairs of age profiles of married men and women and also of cohabiting men and women with dependent children in their family are depicted in Figure 2.4(e). Those who are cohabiting tend to be younger than their married counterparts and, in general, men in partnerships – whether these are marriages or cohabiting unions – tend to be older than women in the same kind of partnership. However, the age profile of cohabiting men is not much older than that of cohabiting women, while the age profile of married men is distinctly older than that of married women.

For completeness, the age distributions of lone mothers and lone fathers with only non-dependent children in their family are graphed in Figure 2.4(f). The same general pattern of lone fathers tending to be older than

---

3. In this section, the legal marital status of the lone parents has been derived from the Family Information Section questions of the GHS.

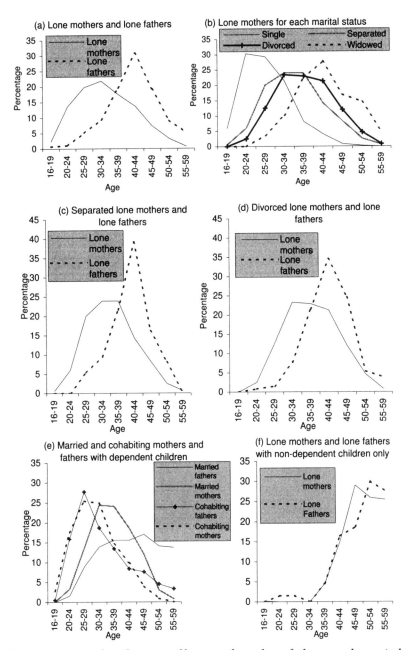

Figure 2.4: *Age distributions of lone mothers, lone fathers, and married and cohabiting mothers and fathers with dependent children, Great Britain, 1992–5 (1990–5 for lone fathers and widowed lone mothers)*

their lone mother counterparts may be observed as in Figure 2.4(a) except, understandably, that those with non-dependent children only are likely to be older than those with dependent children.

MARITAL AND COHABITATIONAL HISTORIES OF LONE MOTHERS

A lone mother's current marital status provides important clues to her age, number of children, length of time as a lone mother and, indeed, her general demographic characteristics and financial circumstances, if such information is not readily available. However, while current marital status undoubtedly does distinguish different demographic patterns among the different groups of lone parents, an ideal basis from which to gain a fuller understanding of, say, lone mothers' past childbearing, is to have the combined marital and cohabitational histories of the lone mothers.

Some findings from a special module of questions asked in the Omnibus Survey are presented in Table 2.4, which allow the marital and cohabitational histories of lone mothers to be compared with those of married mothers and cohabiting mothers.[3] Results are shown in Table 2.4 for the three sets of mothers (each aged under 60); their age profiles will have differed slightly. However, each set of mothers had to have one or more dependent children, which would have tended to reduce such differences. Indeed, Figures 2.4a and 2.4e showed that the age profiles are broadly comparable, although cohabiting mothers tend to be younger than lone mothers who, in turn, tend to be younger than married mothers with dependent children.

Overall, just under half (48 per cent) of lone mothers had never cohabited, and had only married once (their marriage being their first and only partnership). A further one in ten had also never cohabited, but had been married twice. One in seven (14 per cent) had lived in one cohabiting union only, which had ended, without the lone mother ever having married. Relatively small proportions had lived in other sequences of two unions in total — and this is perhaps the most important finding: that the vast majority of lone mothers have either married only once, or lived in only one cohabiting union, or else been married once and cohabited once. One in seven (15 per cent) of lone mothers said that they had never married nor lived in a partnership outside marriage. These lone mothers must have been single lone mothers.

A much higher proportion of married mothers than lone mothers had been married only once, roughly nine in every 10 and five in every 10

---

4. In Table 2.4, *premarital* cohabitation — namely where the marriage partners lived together before marrying — has *not* been counted as a separate cohabitation, but considered part of the marriage.

Table 2.4: *Lone, married and cohabiting mothers* and fathers* with dependent children – profiles of the parents' marital and cohabitational histories, Great Britain, 1994–5*

Marital/cohabitational history (in chronological order)	Previous C?	Ms?	CC?	Mothers with dependent children LM	MM	CM	All mothers	Fathers with dependent children LF	MF	CF	All fathers
Married once only; marriage continuing	none	none	no	48	86		64	(56)	84		74
Married once only; marriage ended	none	yes	no				8				1
Married once only; marriage ended, cohabiting	none	yes	yes			40	3			28	3
Married once only; cohabited, cohabitation ended	yes	yes	no	4			0.7	(11)			0.2
Married twice; second marriage continuing	none	yes	no		10		7		10		9
Married twice; second marriage ended	none	yes	no	10			2	(11)			0.2
Married twice; second marriage ended, cohabiting	none	yes	yes			5	0.4				–
Cohabited once only; cohabitation continuing	none	none	yes	–		42	4			57	6
Cohabited once only; cohabitation ended	yes	none	no	14			2	(11)			0.2
Cohabited once only; married once, marriage continuing	yes	none	no		3		2		4		4
Cohabited once only; married once, marriage ended	yes	yes	no	1			0.2	(6)			0.1
Cohabited twice, second cohabitation continuing	yes	none	yes			5	0.4			6	0.6
Cohabited twice, second cohabitation ended	yes	none	no	3			0.5				–
Cohabited three times, third cohabitation continuing	yes	none	yes			3	0.2			3	0.3
Other histories involving marriages and/or cohabitations				4	0.6	6	2	(6)	1	6	2
No relationships whatsoever	none	none	no	15			3				–
All marital/cohabitational histories+ – percentages				100	100	100	100	100	100	100	100
All marital/cohabitational histories+ – sample numbers				229	970	111	1310	18	863	98	979

Note: C = cohabitations; M = marriages; CC = currently cohabiting; LM = lone mothers; MM = married mothers; CM = cohabiting mothers; LF = lone fathers; MF = married fathers; CF = cohabiting fathers; *aged 16–59 and either head of household or spouse/partner of head of household, + including none; premarital cohabitation with future spouse has *not* been counted as a separate cohabitation.

Source: Omnibus Survey.

respectively, although one in ten of both groups of mothers had been married twice. Four in 10 cohabiting mothers had been married only once, compared with five in 10 lone mothers. However, the proportion of lone mothers who had been married twice was double that for cohabiting mothers – 10 and 5 per cent, respectively. Table 2.4 also gives corresponding results for fathers, although, unfortunately, the sample number of lone fathers is very small. In general, the pattern of marital/cohabitational histories of married fathers and married mothers is very similar, as is also that of cohabiting fathers and cohabiting mothers.

OTHER MEMBERS OF ONE-PARENT HOUSEHOLDS

It will be recalled that the definition of a one-parent family is essentially that of a *nuclear* family, in so far as any relatives who are other than the lone parent or their never-married children are not included as members of the (nuclear) one-parent family. This definition is a particularly practical one in that it easily allows relatives and non-relatives to be distinguished in lone parent households.

An earlier analysis (Haskey, 1991) showed that there has been an increasing trend for both lone mother and lone father families to live in their own separate accommodation, that is as a one-(nuclear) family household, rather than sharing a home with one or more other families as a multi-family household. Furthermore, this trend has been observed among both divorced and single lone mother families, particularly the latter; about one-third of single lone mother families lived in one-family households in 1974, but by about 1990 this proportion had more than doubled to almost three-quarters. Overall, around eight in ten lone mother and lone father families were living in one-family households around 1990.

Since 1993, the General Household Survey (GHS) has collected information on relationships between all possible pairs of household members, and it is therefore possible to examine these data to see whether there are other members present in lone parent households and, if so, their relationship to the lone parent. Furthermore, the profile of these relationships can be examined separately for cases where the lone parent is the head of household – which will usually indicate that the household is a single-family lone parent one – and also for cases in which the lone parent is not the head of household. These two sets of relationship profiles are given in Table 2.5 – separately according to the different type of lone parent.

Table 2.5 – left hand side – gives an analysis for households headed by lone mothers – separately by each marital status – and also for lone fathers. Not surprisingly, the vast majority of household members other

Table 2.5: *Households containing a lone parent: profile of relationships of other household members to the lone parent, Great Britain, 1993–5*

Relationship to lone parent	Lone parent head of household						Lone parent not head of household					
	Lone mothers				Lone fathers	Lone parents	Lone mothers				Lone fathers	Lone parents
	Single	Separated	Divorced	Widowed			Single	Separated	Divorced	Widowed		
Son or daughter*	97.7	97.6	97.5	96.9	91.9	97.1	33	52	38	(50)	(20)	36
Step, foster or in-law son or daughter	0.1	0.8	0.3	0.5	1.8	0.5	0.3	—	—	—	—	0.2
Brother, sister**	0.8	—	0.2	0.5	0.7	0.3	16	5	12	—	(24)	15
Parent	0.1	0.6	0.7	2.0	0.4	0.4	43	16	28	(50)	(36)	38
Grandchild	0.1	0.6	0.7	—	0.7	0.6	0.6	2	—	—	—	0.6
Grandparent	—	—	—	—	—	—	—	—	—	—	(4)	0.2
Other relative	0.3	0.1	0.1	—	2.2	0.3	4	5	7	—	(4)	4
Other non-relative	1.0	0.4	0.6	—	2.2	0.7	3	20	15	—	(12)	7
All relationships to LP(%)	100	100	100	100	100	100	100	100	100	100	100	100
All relationships to LP (sample no)	1036	864	1222	196	272	3590	347	56	68	2	25	498
Average number of relationships to LP per household	1.66	2.14	1.91	2.11	1.79	1.88	3.34	3.50	3.24	2.00	3.57	3.34
Average household size	2.66	3.14	2.91	3.11	2.79	2.88	4.34	4.50	4.24	3.00	4.57	4.34

Notes: *including adopted; **including adopted, step, half, foster and in-law brothers and sisters (counts for the last 4 categories were zero everywhere); LP = lone parent.

Source: General Household Survey.

than the lone parent are the natural children of the lone parent; the proportion varies from 92 per cent for lone father households to 98 per cent for single lone mother households. The proportion of children other than natural children of the lone parent is largest among lone father households and separated lone mother households, and smallest among single lone mother households. Most of the children concerned are stepchildren. Possibly in these situations, the natural parent has left the child living with the stepparent, while she or he has gone elsewhere to live – either alone or with a new partner.

The other main feature of lone parent headed households is a tendency for both single lone mothers and lone fathers to have either a brother or sister, or a more distant relative, or else someone other than a relative, living with them. Such a situation might be understood in terms of these lone parents having a greater need than others for more financial or practical support in their homes – for example, by having paying guests, or relatives to stay and help bring up the lone parent's children. It is understandable, too, that widowed lone mothers who head households should be more likely than others to have grandchildren living with them.

Inevitably, a very different picture is obtained on considering the situation where the lone parent does not head the household (right-hand side of Table 2.5). For the most part, sons and daughters are still the most likely relative to be present in the household, though the proportions are much smaller than in households headed by lone parents. Parents are comparatively numerous; the most likely explanation being that the lone parent has returned to live in their own parental home – or indeed, possibly had never left. The fact that the proportion is largest for single lone mothers adds weight to this hypothesis. In addition, one in five, and one in seven separated and divorced lone mothers respectively, live with non-relatives. It is possible that some of these mothers have left their former family home to set up a new home with friends or are living in someone else's home.

The results described above do not take into account the fact that different kinds of lone parent households will have different numbers of household members – and therefore different numbers of possible relationships to the lone parent. For example, if a given lone parent household contains three household members in all, there are two possible relationships to the lone parent, whereas if another household contains six members, there are five possible relationships to the lone parent. The average number of relationships to the lone parent per household is given at the foot of Table 2.5, separately for each kind of lone parent.

It may be seen that the averages vary considerably; and, in particular, are distinctly larger for households in which the lone parent is not the head.

Strictly speaking, therefore, to make a valid comparison between, say, single lone mother headed households and separated lone mother households in the proportions having children living with them, this factor should be taken into account. That is, the percentages shown in Table 2.5 should be weighted by the inverse of the average number of relationships given in penultimate line of Table 2.5. An alternative way of viewing the matter is to consider average household size – average number of members per household – which will vary according to the type of household; these are shown at the foot of Table 2.5.

WORKING PATTERNS OF LONE MOTHERS AND MARRIED MOTHERS WITH DEPENDENT CHILDREN

The financial position of lone parents in general, and of lone mothers with dependent children in particular, either depends critically upon state benefits, or alternatively upon the availability of suitable employment and the provision of child care. Figure 2.5 (left hand side) presents trends in the proportions of lone mothers and married mothers who were working, both full time and part time, and also for two important groups of lone mothers – the single and the divorced. All graphs refer to mothers with dependent children.

Overall, the proportion of lone mothers who were working has declined from about five in every ten in 1980, to about four in every ten in 1994 (Figure 2.5(a)). Despite this fall, the proportion who were working part time has remained virtually constant at about one in four, while the proportion who were working full time has declined from about one in four to one in six. It is notable that there was a decided fall in the overall proportion working between 1980 and 1984, the undoubted result of the recession at that time. In contrast, the proportion of married mothers who were working has increased, from about one half in the late 1970s, to two-thirds in 1994 (Figure 2.5(c)). There was a small drop in the proportion working between 1980 and 1982, but it was not as large as that observed among lone mothers. In contrast to the situation for lone mothers, the proportion of married mothers who were working part time has been approximately double that of those working full time, although there has been a slowly widening gap between the proportions of lone mothers who have been working part time and full time.

The picture for single lone mothers (Figure 2.5(e)) contrasts with that for all lone mothers and, particularly, with that for married mothers. Not only did single lone mothers decreasingly work full time during the 1980s – the proportion fell substantially – but for the past decade roughly equal proportions of single lone mothers – about one in six – have been

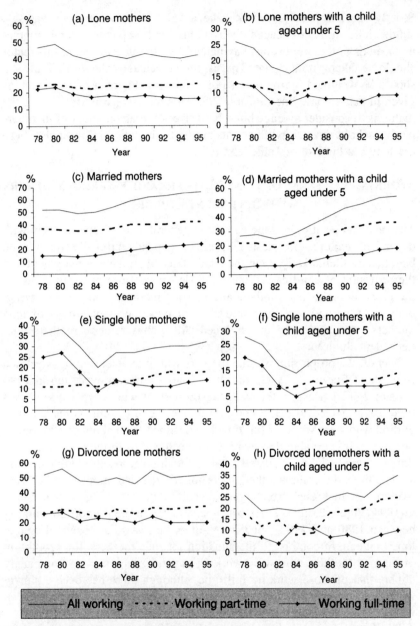

Note: *Estimated – based on three-year averages.
Source: General Household Survey, Office for National Statistics.

Figure 2.5: *Proportions of lone and married mothers with dependent children who were working, full and part time, Great Britain, 1978–96*

working full time and part time. The mid-1980s witnessed an important change in the pattern of working of single lone mothers; before that time more worked full time than part time, while the reverse was true subsequently.

Apart from the late 1970s and early 1980s, when smaller proportions of divorced than single lone mothers were working full time, relatively more divorced lone mothers have worked both full time and part time than single lone mothers (Figure 2.5(g)). Overall, in 1994, about one in two lone divorced mothers were working, compared with fewer than one in three single lone mothers.

The right hand side of Figure 2.5 shows the corresponding trends for a subset of each of the same groups of mothers with dependent children – those whose youngest child was aged under five. Understandably, the proportions of these latter mothers who were working were lower than those with dependent children of any age, and the proportions who were working full time were proportionately lower than those who were working part time. Perhaps the most notable feature is the relative lack of change in the proportions working – either full time or part time – among lone mothers (and single lone mothers in particular), compared with the growth in employment among married mothers with a child aged under five. Undoubtedly, these trends have led to a widening gap between the financial circumstances of lone parents and their married counterparts.

CONCLUSIONS

The prevalence of lone parenthood has increased further in recent years, although there is some tentative evidence that the pace of increase may have slackened in the very most recent period. In addition, and perhaps more importantly, the number of dependent children living in one-parent families has grown at a faster rate than that of the number of one-parent families. Given that the number of dependent children living in one-parent families is currently estimated to be some 2.7 million, or one in five of all dependent children in Great Britain, the policy issues concerning lone parenthood are important and of increasing relevance to a significant proportion of the child population. An additional conclusion is that analyses of the demographic and socio-economic characteristics of one-parent families and their children are increasingly needed to assess the circumstances of lone parenthood and to highlight those areas particularly requiring the application and implementation of appropriate social policy.

Chapter 3

Choosing Lone Parenthood? The Dynamics of Family Change

Stephen McKay and Karen Rowlingson

The growth of lone parenthood is well documented. In the early 1970s, there were fewer than 600,000 lone-parent families. This number had almost tripled to around 1.5 million in 1993. The incidence of lone-parent households is now higher than at any time in the last two centuries and is high in comparison with most other European countries. This phenomenon has raised a number of social, political and economic concerns, as discussed in Chapter 1 here. But any discussion about the 'problem' of lone parenthood and possible solutions to this problem should be informed by an understanding of why people become lone mothers, and why they may then form other types of family.[1]

In this chapter, we argue that people become lone mothers because it is seen by some women as a less problematic life course than the alternatives available to them at the time.[2] This, however, does not mean that it is unproblematic: the prisoner's dilemma[3] reminds us that action taken to improve an individual's situation may be collectively undesirable, and not yield the best outcome for that individual.

This chapter draws on recent quantitative and qualitative research, funded by the ESRC, into the causes of the growth of lone parenthood (Rowlingson and McKay, 1997).[4] It begins with details about the research

---

1. Although knowing the causes of the growth does not necessarily mean that the growth may be reversed – just as knowledge of why tides exist does not mean they may easily be prevented.
2. The same comment may also apply to fathers but the necessary evidence is lacking.
3. The prisoner's dilemma is a scenario used in game theory to explore the relationship between individual decision-making and the collective good. The best collective outcome will only be achieved if both consider the other's good, but this will depend on how much each person trusts the other.
4. The project was supported by the ESRC (Grant L315253002) and the authors acknowledge the support and comments of Richard Berthoud (Essex University) within this project.

methods used in the study. The main body of the chapter is divided into three parts, analysing:

- the process by which some women become single mothers;
- the process by which some women become separated mothers; and
- the length of time that women remain lone mothers.

In these sections, we consider why some women become lone mothers. We also analyse whether lone parenthood is perceived as a problem by women before and/or after they become lone mothers. We also discuss the feasibility (rather than the desirability) of reducing the incidence of lone parenthood, and mitigating some of the problems facing this group.

RESEARCH METHODOLOGY

Definitions and concepts

The typical definition of a 'lone mother' owes a great deal to policy interests, being a replica of the family conditions required to receive the lone parent premium in income support. In policy terms, lone parents have often been regarded as a specific group with particular needs and problems. But it is crucial to understand that lone parenthood is a diverse and not a uniform family type.

Among the key differences are those of marital status. Put in more dynamic terms, the route of entry to lone parenthood may constitute a key difference within the group, affecting living standards and likely duration. The two principal routes into lone parenthood are having a child while single, and separating from a couple in which there are dependent children. The similarities between a widowed mother with a 14-year-old son, and a single, never-married mother with a baby may be few: certainly, our research finds little apparent solidarity among all lone mothers. In explaining the growth of lone parenthood, we are actually trying to explain several different types of phenomenon, not a single process because these different routes into lone parenthood may have quite different causal antecedents. Divorce has been alleged to be associated with higher rates of women working (Ermisch, 1996): but the growth of never-married lone mothers may have more to do with the employment prospects of young men (Garfinkel and McLanahan, 1986).

It is also important to realise that lone parenthood as a family status may be of quite varying duration. An episode may be quite short term, or last 20 or more years. Any change in the number of lone mothers may be the result of either more people becoming lone mothers, or people staying as lone mothers for longer (or both). The policy implications of changes in family status may be quite different depending on which is the major engine of growth. If most lone mothers remain in that family status for decades, any negative consequences on children, and on their employment prospects, will be greater than if they remain lone mothers for only a year or two. However, as others have argued in relation to poverty, optimism that people may rapidly exit a state with low welfare should be tempered by pessimism at the knowledge that more people will go through such a condition (Walker with Ashworth, 1994).

Methodological and theoretical issues

In conducting research into the underlying causes of family change, there are a number of different epistemological perspectives. First, one might argue that decisions about families are the result of so many individual circumstances as to be not readily amenable to social scientific analysis. When qualitative researchers have investigated the reasons for (say) increased divorce, divorcees often mention very personal factors – such as the effects of alcohol, violence or extramarital affairs – rather than more general societal trends. However, the fact that the observed changes in family formation are common to so many countries makes this seem an overly simplistic view. For example, simple aggregate analysis suggests a strong correlation between rates of divorce and the proportion of women in employment, and between fertility rates and women's pay (Ermisch, 1996), which may be taken as at least initial evidence of some overarching structural forces at work.

Second, people may put forward a range of rather *ad hoc* theories. These suggest that behavioural changes result from changes in 'attitudes', or from changes in the legal framework governing family life. It is commonly argued that divorce, lone parenthood, premarital childbearing and so on were socially stigmatised in past decades, but that changing social attitudes have made them acceptable today. This explanation implies that if changes in social attitudes were to take place, this might halt or even reverse trends in family structures. This explanation may be partly helpful, but suffers from a number of flaws. It must first be explained why attitudes have moved in similar directions in many countries, although at different rates. Moreover, it is not only conceivable that changes in attitudes come *after* changes in behaviour, but this is indeed what American research tends to suggest. In the United States it seems that attitudes towards divorce only 'softened' some time after divorce rates had climbed (Cherlin, 1992: 45).

An alternative view attributes change in family formation to changes in the relevant legal framework. For example, divorce laws have been 'weakened', or the grounds for divorce extended. Of itself, this seems a rather weak 'theory'. Changes in the law may enable those who are separated to become divorced more easily, but of itself this is not a convincing explanation of why people separate in the first place. Instead, a more sophisticated theory would need to use the option of divorce – and perhaps particularly of remarriage – as the driving force behind a higher rate of separation. Even so, this view is subject to the same uncertainties as theories based on changes in attitudes. Is it not more likely that changes in the law followed rather than caused changes in family behaviour? This seems the case with the 1971 change in British divorce law, which now seems somewhat ahead of its time. Those who look towards the legal system for answers must also counter changes that might have been expected, in isolation, to stem the rise in the number of lone mothers – such as the more widespread availability of widespread contraception and the legalisation of abortion.

Within economics, there are more encompassing theoretically-based explanations of family change. The work of Nobel laureate Gary Becker (Becker, 1981) has inspired an 'economics of the family' approach, which applies micro-economic analysis to decisions about family formation and dissolution. It is hypothesised that people are rational, informed individuals who take steps to maximise their level of satisfaction. It is further assumed that marriage becomes more likely the greater the gains from it, which in Becker's particular formulation has much to do with the degree of complementarity between the two partners – men having a comparative advantage in production outside the home, women for production inside the home. The gains to being in a couple are reduced to the extent that men are unable to fulfil such a role, or women can be as well-off as in individual units. This type of model has been applied to British data on family formation (Ermisch, 1991a and 1991b). Of course, such a model has several critics (for example Leibenstein, 1974) and may seem to ignore the importance of social norms and instead impose somewhat stereotypical pictures. The same type of predictions could also be consistent with alternative models. For instance there is considerable overlap with the 'social exchange' theory of marital breakdown, which analyses the gains traded between marriage partners (Price and McKenry, 1988).

In the absence of a universally accepted theoretical framework, the UK analyst must therefore draw on a range of resources and hypotheses to inform statistical modelling.

Empirical research

The research reported on here uses both quantitative and qualitative methods. Full details of the research methods and findings from this study are contained in Rowlingson and McKay, 1997.

The quantitative data analysed in this study were from the Social Change

and Economic Life Initiative (SCELI). This data set consists
of around 1000 interviews carried out in each of six areas in 1986. As
well as information on family change, the questionnaire covered a
range of employment and other personal areas. Complete life and work
histories were collected – to the nearest month in most cases – for the
period from age 14 to the date of interview. The analysis applies event-
history methods to link movements into and out of lone parenthood with
several different characteristics of the individual, which may vary at each
point. In essence, some groups are at risk of entering or leaving lone
parenthood during particular time periods, and the modelling may identify
the characteristics associated with higher and lower risks of such
transitions taking place.

The qualitative research involved in-depth interviews with 44 women
who were, or had recently been, lone mothers. The interviewees were
categorised by two criteria. The first was whether a woman had become a
lone parent by having her first baby while *single* or by *separating* from a
partner with whom she already had children. The second criterion was
whether a woman had *recently* become a lone mother (within the previous
two years) or had been a lone mother for a *long time* (more than two years)
or had been a lone mother in the past but was now part of a couple (a
former lone mother).

The following sections look at two key routes into lone parenthood, and
at leaving lone parenthood. They look at the main apparent causes of
family change, whether lone parenthood is seen as being a problem, and
how policy reforms might affect the situation at the particular relevant
transitions between family types.

BECOMING A 'SINGLE' LONE PARENT

Single, or unmarried, lone mothers have become an increasingly important
component of lone parenthood. Between 1971 and 1992 there was a five-
fold increase in the number of single, never-married mothers from 90,000
to 490,000. About a third of all lone mothers in the early 1990s were
single, never-married mothers. But about half of these (according to
McKay and Marsh, 1994) would have separated from a cohabiting relationship and so may have more in common with separated lone mothers
than women who have their first babies while single (see also Ermisch,
1995). Because of this our quantitative and qualitative research has defined
'single mothers' in a slightly different way to official statistics. We have
defined them as women who had a first baby while not living with a
partner. Those who have separated from a cohabiting relationship are
defined as 'separated' lone mothers and considered in a later section,
alongside those who have separated from a husband.

While having a baby when single is the beginning of lone parenthood, it can also be seen as the end of a process that involves a number of stages: having sex while single; not using contraception or using it unsuccessfully; getting pregnant; not having an abortion; not getting together with the baby's father (or another partner); and not giving up the baby for adoption. At each of these stages, women face a series of choices and constraints that affect their decisions and therefore the eventual outcome. Over time, the nature of the outcome has changed as, according to our research evidence, lone parenthood has become seen by some women as less problematic than the available alternative outcomes.

From the 1970s to the 1990s, the number of conceptions outside marriage more than doubled from 161,000 in 1975 to 364,000 in 1993 (OPCS birth statistics). The proportion of these that resulted in legal abortion dropped over the same period (from 40 per cent to 33 per cent), as did the proportion that ended in births within a marriage (from 27 per cent to 8 per cent). There was thus a huge increase in both the number and proportion of extramarital conceptions that led to births outside marriage. Most of these in the 1980s were registered by both parents and while this does not necessarily imply that the mothers were cohabiting, more than two-thirds were (according to OPCS birth statistics). Sole-registered first births, probably equivalent to the formation of a single-mother family, actually became a less common outcome of extramarital conceptions (from 17 per cent to 13 per cent between 1975 and 1993). But the rise in the number of extramarital conceptions means that the number of sole-registered births actually increased from 27,000 in 1975 to 49,000 in 1993. The growth of single lone parenthood is therefore due as much to a general increase in pregnancy (and by implication in sexual activity) among single women as to an increase in the proportion of single pregnant women who 'choose' to become lone mothers. The increase in births to cohabiting couples also serves to exaggerate the growth of truly single lone motherhood.

The SCELI data set contains information on most major life events from the age of 14 onwards and this enables us to look at who had become single mothers, by given ages, and who had become part of a couple, or did not have children. Each woman was treated as being 'at risk' of becoming a single mother from the age of 14, until either the date of interview or joining a partnership. The probability of doing so was modelled as a function of various constraints and time-varying characteristics of both the woman and the local area. For example, the employment status of the woman is a time-varying characteristic and the model took into account how each woman's situation changed from month to month.

Multivariate survival analysis of the SCELI data found that single women who were black or from a poor socio-economic background were much more likely than others to become single lone mothers. Analysis also found that the local unemployment rate had a statistically significant impact on single parenthood. As the local rate of unemployment rose so too did the probability of becoming a single lone parent.

The qualitative research highlighted great diversity even within the category of single lone mother. For example, there was considerable variation in terms of the relationships these women were having at the time of conception. Some had got pregnant after fairly casual sex. Others had regular boyfriends with whom they were not cohabiting and others had been cohabiting in the past but had separated from their partners at some point before the baby was either conceived or born.

Only one woman had deliberately planned to become a single lone mother. In common with previous research (Renvoize, 1985), she was older and more middle class than the other single lone mothers. The question for the research was therefore why the remaining women had become pregnant and then why they had continued with the pregnancy and become single mothers.

Some single lone mothers had become pregnant because they did not use contraception even though they did not particularly want to conceive. This was mostly due to trusting a partner; taking risks; and an eagerness not to feel, and be seen as, promiscuous. Most women had felt that the risk of getting pregnant had been low and, though pregnancy was seen as an undesirable outcome, it was not seen as particularly disastrous. Other women had become pregnant because their contraception use was unsuccessful, for example they had missed one or more pills or had been taking antibiotics, which reduced the pill's effectiveness. Some women were using unreliable methods.

Becoming pregnant is only one step on the road to lone parenthood and, once pregnant, some women did consider having abortions. Some women disagreed on principle with abortion. Others had had previous experiences of abortion they did not wish to repeat. Others, however, after the initial shock had worn off, simply became accustomed to the idea of having a baby while single and did not see it as a 'problem' that needed a 'solution' such as abortion. This links to the quantitative results: women from poor economic backgrounds saw motherhood as an acceptable, and in some cases desirable, alternative to life in low-paid, low-status work.

Motherhood in general may have had its attractions, but this does not necessarily mean that *lone* motherhood would be attractive and these women might, in theory, have cohabited with the father of their child. However, some of the men involved would not consider living with the woman. And some of the women did not consider their boyfriends to be suitable for marriage or partnership, mostly because they were not seen as very industrious or trustworthy. This also links to the quantitative finding about the level of unemployment. Men without jobs or in poorly-paid jobs were not considered useful as breadwinners, partners or full-time fathers.

The final choice open to women wanting to avoid lone parenthood would be adoption. This was very rarely considered by single pregnant women. It was incompatible with their identities as women/carers and was regarded as more highly stigmatised than lone parenthood.

The reactions of lone mothers' mothers were very important in shaping the eventual outcome. Mothers were usually shocked on first hearing the news of their daughter's pregnancy. But most were then supportive and said they would respect whatever choice their daughter made. There were no signs of any shotgun weddings. There is thus some evidence that, compared with the past (see Marsden, 1969), single motherhood is considered to be less of a problem by mothers of potential lone mothers.

Most women expected to receive social security once they became lone mothers. They did not expect this to be generous but in some cases it was seen as preferable to the available alternatives, such as living on benefit as a couple. And it did not entail a drastic drop in living standards compared with their previous situation.

In the past, stigma against lone motherhood may have been enough to discourage single women from having or keeping babies. Our evidence suggests that stigma was still rife in communities but the women did not identify themselves as those who had deliberately got pregnant for social security and council housing – a group most of the lone mothers we interviewed confidently asserted did exist. They could therefore disassociate themselves from much of the general stigma that existed.

Do women perceive single lone motherhood to be a problem?

Many women perceive lone motherhood as a problem, which is why so few deliberately set out to become single lone mothers. As we have seen, our research supports previous work (Renvoize, 1985) that suggested that those who 'go solo' by choice are likely to be older and better educated than the more typical single mother. By and large, getting pregnant while single is viewed as a problem and about a third of those who do conceive while single terminate the pregnancy. Some of those who carry on with the pregnancy will live with, and in some cases marry, the father. Others carry on with the pregnancy and remain single, but even these have concerns about becoming a single mother. However, despite these concerns, the prospect of lone parenthood is not seen as so problematic that they take great pains to avoid pregnancy (by abstaining from sex or using contraception successfully). Nor is it seen as so problematic that they decide to have a termination or live with the father. Lone parenthood is therefore seen by some women as a reasonable (but not ideal) alternative life course. This is for two main reasons.

The first reason is that most of these women come from poor economic backgrounds and work in low-status, low-paid jobs. The prospect of becoming a mother therefore provides a potentially more rewarding role (emotionally if not financially) than carrying on in paid work. These women had expected to become mothers at some point in the future but had hoped to do so in a more conventional way – finding a partner, getting married and then having children. The sequence of events had not followed exactly according to plan but this was seen as just unfortunate rather than devastating.

The second reason why lone parenthood is seen as an acceptable life course is that the boyfriends of the lone mothers are generally not seen as acceptable husbands. This is because some of them are unemployed or in low-paid work and therefore cannot provide the kind of stable, good income that would be expected from a husband/breadwinner. But even where a boyfriend had a stable income, women were concerned that their access to this money would be problematic. Lone motherhood provided direct access to a stable, if very low, income (in the form of income support), which was paid directly to the mother. Once again, this was not an ideal way to live, but it was better than the alternative.

Ways of reducing single motherhood

So the prospect of becoming a single mother is not considered ideal by most women but nor is it considered to be a dreadful fate. Of course, expectations may not match reality. Given that single motherhood is not considered ideal by many women and that some other groups in society see it as highly problematic, we can use our research to consider the likely effectiveness of ways of reducing the incidence of single motherhood. We are not arguing that such measures should be taken, but discussing what our research can contribute to discussing the effectiveness of specific measures.

One way of reducing the incidence of single motherhood might be to reduce the amount of sexual activity occurring outside a marital or cohabiting relationship. Given that cohabiting relationships are more likely to end with the production of a lone parent family (Ermisch, 1995), then sexual activity might best be contained within marriage. It is difficult to see how this could be achieved except through general attitudinal change that more heavily stigmatised sex outside marriage, as Hilary Land and Jane Lewis point out in Chapter 8 here. It is difficult to see how such attitudinal change could be set in motion, but even if such attitudinal change could be engineered, it is likely to produce a climate in which knowledge about, and access to, contraception would be more limited to single women. The unintended consequence might therefore be to increase rather than decrease pregnancies outside marriage.

Another approach would be to increase knowledge about and the successful use of contraception. This should lead to some reduction in extramarital conception, but our research suggests that lack of knowledge about contraception was only one factor leading to unplanned pregnancies. Some women knew about contraception but failed to use it. Although they did not particularly want to get pregnant, they were nevertheless not particularly concerned about the possibility that it might happen. This was because the prospect of becoming a lone mother was not one of which they were particularly fearful. As argued above, this was because of their poor job prospects and those of the men around them. The incidence of lone parenthood (or its growth) might therefore be reduced if there were an improvement in the job prospects of young men and women. The other side of the coin, however, might be to reduce social security payments so that the prospect of lone parenthood becomes less attractive than remaining single and childfree, or in a couple with a man. Other research, however, suggests that social security reforms actually do little either to encourage or discourage the formation of lone-parent families (Whiteford and Bradshaw, 1994; Hoynes, 1996).

BECOMING A 'SEPARATED' LONE PARENT

Separating from a partner remains the most common route into lone parenthood. In 1971, there were 290,000 separated or divorced lone mothers and by 1995 this figure had risen to 970,000. Once again, it is important to define our terms and, for the purpose of this chapter, we define separated lone mothers as women with children who became lone mothers by separating from a husband or cohabiting partner.

Our quantitative research was based on couples, both married and cohabiting, who had children while living together. The modelling tracked them through successive months, relating any separation to their characteristics during each month. The modelling showed that various factors were associated with increasing the likelihood of separation and divorce. These included getting married at a young age; having children early in marriage or having a premarital conception; being a social tenant or private tenant; and the woman having qualifications at O-level or above. Surprisingly, neither the economic activity of the woman nor the local unemployment rate had any impact. All ethnic groups seemed alike.

So, in at least some respects, the factors associated with separated lone motherhood are different from those associated with single lone motherhood. Separation is linked to some markers of social disadvantage, but

fewer than for single lone motherhood. Those living in rented accommodation and those with an unemployed partner were much more likely to
become lone parents than those in owner-occupied housing and those with
a working partner.

The qualitative research found that the personal reasons for relationship
breakdown included conflict over gender roles and the control of money.
The arrival of children often produced or accentuated these difficulties
because there was less money to go round and, contrary to the wishes of
the women, there was a reversion to more traditional gender roles. Men
were sometimes considered to be irresponsible with money and neglectful
of their childcare responsibilities. Some women, especially those who had
married early (linking in to the quantitative findings), said their partners
felt they had 'missed out' on having a carefree youth. These men subsequently wished to 'escape their responsibilities' by ending the relationship
or having affairs, which contributed to the relationship breakdown.
Domestic violence was a key factor in a number of cases. Some women
had stayed in violent relationships for a long time, in some cases until their
partner left. Others left after some trigger incident, such as their child
being caught in the crossfire. Others simply reached the point where they
were no longer prepared to put up with the violence.

Although these relationships ended, there were signs that most couples
had tried hard to avoid separation. Couples often stayed together for a long
time after their problems began. In some cases, there were several
temporary separations before the relationship ended for good. So, marriage
or cohabitation was not being rejected lightly. There was still a fair amount
of commitment to the ideal of a lasting partnership.

Although women often stayed in unhappy relationships, they felt that
they were less likely to put up with unhappiness than their mothers would
have been. This was because they generally felt more confident and had
greater financial independence – in the form of potential access to
employment. Stigma against separation, divorce and lone parenthood did
encourage women to remain longer in unhappy relationships than they
would otherwise have done. But, they felt that there was less stigma than
in the past and they developed strategies to deal with that which remained.
For example, they got jobs, they blamed their partner for the relationship
breakdown and they distanced themselves from, and looked down on, the
stereotypical lone parent scapegoat – the teenage mum.

Do women perceive separated lone motherhood to be a problem?

Women in couples with children do not, ideally, want to become lone
mothers. In cases where their partner decides to leave them, they sometimes have little choice over the process. In other cases, there still seems to

be great reluctance to end a relationship. So, lone motherhood is viewed as a problem but, once again, it is seen as a viable alternative to life in an unhappy and sometimes violent relationship.

The prospect of being on a low income as a lone mother is seen as part of the problem, but some of these women were on low incomes with their partners and, regardless of the joint level of income, some women had very unequal access to money. For these women, the prospect of direct access to money (in the form of benefits) is appealing and some are also keen to go out to work to increase that income.

Ways of reducing separated lone motherhood

Changes in divorce law are sometimes advocated as a way of reducing separated lone parenthood, but such changes are unlikely to affect the number of couples who separate. Even if they did keep some couples together, this would only tackle the symptom, not the cause of the problem. Ways of improving the quality of relationships would address the more fundamental issues. Problems seem particularly likely to occur after the birth of children, when many women leave paid jobs or transfer from full-time to part-time work. This causes friction between couples as a degree of equality in the relationship (in terms of wage earning, access to money and completion of household chores) is reduced. Improved childcare facilities and flexible working patterns for men and women might maintain a greater degree of equality in the relationship. This, of course, presupposes that both men and women wish to do so. Women may want to stay at home with their children, even if it were made easier for them not to do so. Also, men may not want to spend more time with their children.

In the section on single mothers, we mentioned that research does not indicate that reducing benefit levels affects family formation and disso-lution. But one change in the benefit system might have some effect. One of the main problems among couples is conflict over access to money, particularly when on a low income: this might be reduced by moving away from the family basis of benefit entitlement, though this would not be without problems elsewhere (Esam and Berthoud, 1991).

LEAVING LONE MOTHERHOOD

Lone motherhood is a life-cycle stage rather than a permanent status. Our models looked at the rate of monthly exits from lone motherhood, with the end of a spell being marked by moving in with a partner or by the children ageing past dependent age (or leaving the household for other reasons). We found that half of the lone mothers left lone motherhood within three years if they had never been married, around five years if divorced and closer to eight years if separated or widowed. These findings are similar, if slightly longer, than figures based on 1980 data (Ermisch, 1991a and 1991b). The long-term growth of lone motherhood is therefore due more to an increase in entries into lone motherhood than an increase in the duration of lone motherhood, although this data set cannot analyse any changes taking place in the 1990s. Overall, duration of lone motherhood seems to have declined slightly over time but this is because there are now more single lone mothers, who remain lone mothers for shorter periods than other types of lone mother. For any particular type of lone mother, duration appears to have increased slightly.

Using survival modelling techniques, housing tenure was shown to have an effect on the duration of lone motherhood: those in owner-occupied accommodation had much shorter spells than those in social-rented accommodation. The rate of local unemployment was also a significant factor – although its relationship to duration was rather complex.

The qualitative research included 28 women who were still lone mothers. A few of these were adamant that they did not want to find a partner. A few were very keen to find someone. The majority were more open-minded – a happy relationship was their ideal but they preferred lone motherhood to an unhappy one. Women generally felt they did not need a man, but would like one if 'Mr Right' or 'Mr Almost Right' came along. The ideal man for a happy relationship was considered to be someone with the following characteristics: kind; caring; non-violent; trustworthy; a good father; a breadwinner; willing to share the housework; and happy to allow them a degree of independence.

Six of the 44 lone mothers had had more children while still on their own but only one had deliberately planned to do so (she had thought that her boyfriend would live with her if she had a baby – but she was wrong). Two women became pregnant after having affairs with men who were married or cohabiting with other women. Sixteen women were no longer lone mothers at the time of the interview. Some of these had been very keen to find a partner. Others had been reluctant to leave lone motherhood but had, by chance, met a man with whom they felt very compatible. Some women moved in and out of lone motherhood on different occasions.

For those women who had been married or cohabited prior to lone motherhood, their post-lone mother relationships were very different from their earlier experiences. The main difference was that their current relationships were more egalitarian and provided more independence than they had previously had. These relationships were sometimes complicated however, when the new partner was also an absent parent.

Is life as a lone mother perceived as a problem?

The qualitative analysis showed that there were disadvantages to lone motherhood. Some women felt lonely and missed adult male company. Others found it a burden to have sole responsibility for decisions about finances, housing and children. The most serious problem for lone mothers, however, was lack of money. Those on benefit found it very difficult to manage. They also felt that there was a tension between wanting to go out and earn and support themselves through paid work and wanting to give their children as much of their time and personal attention as they could.

Policy researchers often focus on the negative side of lone parenthood, such as the poverty experienced by these families, but our analysis, in common with John McKendrick's research reported in Chapter 5 here, showed that life as a lone mother had certain advantages, in particular general autonomy over their lives and control of their finances. This echoes findings from the 1989 lone-parent cross section (Bradshaw and Millar, 1991: Table 2.16). Women who had previously been in couples said they no longer had to seek their partner's permission to do something. Nor did they have to cook, iron and so on for another adult. Gone, for some women, were the arguments and, in some cases, the violence. Direct access to money was also seen as an advantage of lone parenthood.

Reducing duration or alleviating the problems of lone mothers

So, lone mothers see some advantages to their way of life. In particular, those with boyfriends often felt they had the 'best of both worlds', for they were in control of their lives at home but also had access to an adult male. But there were also problems – mainly relating to their low level of income. The incomes of lone mothers could be raised through the benefit system although no political parties look likely to advocate this and there are some concerns (from those who see lone parenthood as morally or culturally problematic) that such increases in benefits would provide an incentive for other women to become lone mothers. But, as argued above, research does not back this point. Raising benefit levels for lone mothers is, however, merely attacking the symptom rather than the cause. It may be important to do this, but consideration should also be given to the employment opportunities of women and men (particularly young ones) and to the range of choices open to them.

A NOTE ON FATHERS

An important omission in this research, and from much other work, concerns the roles, attitudes and behaviour of fathers. Our research concentrated solely on the accounts of women since these play the main role in forming lone-parent families, but the actions and decisions of men will also be of importance in the process.

Relatively little research has been conducted into the situation of the fathers associated with single lone mothers, and in decisions about divorce, and so on. However, an area sometimes raised in discussion of family formation is the declining attractiveness of younger men as potential husbands, against a background of rising wage inequality for young workers, sizeable proportions unemployed or on training schemes, and an apparently rapid rise in young male suicides in the 1980s. Such a situation brings to mind a quote from the shepherd in Shakespeare's *Winter's Tale:*

> *I would that there were no age between sixteen and three-and-twenty, or that youth would sleep out the rest; for there is nothing in the between but getting wenches with child, wronging the ancientry, stealing, fighting ...*

Where research has been conducted on fathers, the results are often at odds with findings based on mothers (Bradshaw et al, 1997). However, it does seem that 'absent fathers' are a relatively disadvantaged group. Almost one-third of the mothers in the 1989 Lone Parent Survey (Bradshaw and Millar, 1991) said the absent parent was either financially 'hard-pressed' or 'not very well-off'. Of the lone mothers in the 1989 survey, 18 per cent described their partner's financial situation as inferior to their own, and 24 per cent described their partner's situation as being similar to their own.[5] The recent survey of non-resident fathers suggests as many as one-third of these men may be economically inactive (Bradshaw et al, 1997: Table 3). Moreover the changing economic fortunes of men do seem to be an important cause of changes in family status (Lampard, 1993). Future research could usefully explore the role of men in the creation and dissolution of lone parent families.

CONCLUSION

This chapter has sought to explore the reasons why some people become lone mothers, and why some leave this family type. Both quantitative and qualitative methods have contributed to this analysis. This research has been used to consider the likely effectiveness of measures designed to reduce the growth of lone motherhood. The analysis has suggested that lone motherhood is viewed as problematic by women but some women see it as less problematic than any available alternative. The main way of both reducing lone motherhood but also alleviating their problems is to improve

---

5. Don't know responses have been excluded in these analyses.

the employment opportunities of women in particular, and perhaps also of younger men. This is clearly a policy with wider implications – affecting all women and perhaps mothers in particular, rather than being based on specific policies for lone mothers as a group. This chapter has necessarily focused on the views of women and whether they see lone motherhood as a problem. Lone motherhood is seen as an example of the feminisation of poverty, but it is also important to consider how far one of the reasons for the growth of lone motherhood is the poor economic prospects of young men.

Chapter 4

Lone Mothers on Income Support in Northern Ireland: Some Preliminary Findings

Eileen Evason, Gillian Robinson and Kate Thompson

In this chapter, we briefly summarise early findings from a large-scale survey of lone mothers in Northern Ireland. The fieldwork was completed in December 1996. The survey was the main stage in an extensive programme of work commissioned by the social security statistics branch of the DHSS (NI). The survey was preceded by a literature review (Evason and Robinson, 1995a) and a focus group exercise (Evason and Robinson, 1995b). Also, on completion of the fieldwork, a short module on lone parenthood was included in Northern Ireland's general Omnibus Survey. The research may be considered timely inasmuch as the last major survey of lone parents in Northern Ireland was conducted in 1978 (Evason, 1980). Northern Ireland was included in Bradshaw and Millar's research (1991), but the number of lone parents interviewed (64) was too small for separate analysis and much of the work that followed was confined to Britain (Marsh and McKay, 1993b; McKay and Marsh, 1994; Ford et al, 1995). The motivation for the research did not, however, revolve purely and simply around the substantial gaps in our knowledge of the needs and circumstances of lone parents that had accrued by the mid-1990s. A major concern was the possibility that trends with regard to receipt of income support among lone mothers in Northern Ireland were diverging, to a greater extent than previously, from those in Britain.

TRENDS IN LONE PARENTHOOD IN NORTHERN IRELAND

As elsewhere, the proportion of families in Northern Ireland headed by lone parents rose significantly during the 1980s. Table 4.1 indicates that, as in Britain, lone parent families in Northern Ireland accounted for nearly one-fifth of all families by the early 1990s. The percentage rose to one quarter in 1995 – slightly above John Haskey's estimate of 24 per cent in Britain for the same year (see Chapter 2). This overall pattern conceals, however, a number of differences between the characteristics of lone parent families in Northern Ireland and Britain, some of which may help to account for the greater dependence on supplementary benefit/income support among lone parents in Northern Ireland noted in the past by, for example, Brown (1989).

Table 4.1: *Lone-parent families in Northern Ireland, 1991/2 and 1994/5, as percentage of all families*

	1991/2 NI	GB*	1994/5 NI**
All lone mothers	17	(18)	23
Single lone mother	6	(6)	7
Divorced lone mother	3	(6)	4
Separated lone mother	6	(4)	10
Widowed lone mother	2	(1)	2
Lone father	1	(1)	2
All lone parents	18	(19)	25
Base = 100%	1291		1266

Notes: *PPRU MONITOR No 1, 1992; **Continuous Household Survey, unpublished data.

A first obvious difference is that lone mothers are more likely to be separated rather than divorced in Northern Ireland. Divorce rates are lower here and thus the option of remarriage – a major route out of lone parenthood and poverty (Ermisch, 1986, 1991a; Millar, 1989; Bradshaw and Millar, 1991) – is of more limited significance. It should be noted that Northern Ireland's divorce legislation was, to a large extent, brought into line with the rest of the United Kingdom in 1978. More broadly, therefore, the profile is of interest as it underlines the point made elsewhere in this volume (Chapters 1 and 3) that seeking to reduce divorce rates is a doubtful strategy for curbing the growth of lone parenthood unless couples can be prevented from separating in the first place. In Northern Ireland the divorce rate is held down by cultural and religious perspectives, but this has not produced a lower volume of lone parenthood.

Further differences relate to family size and the ages of children in lone-parent families in Northern Ireland. Responsibility for the care of a child of preschool age has been repeatedly shown to be the most important single factor inhibiting employment among lone parents (see, for example, Duncan, 1991; Ermisch, 1991a; Marsh and McKay, 1993b). In 1993, 34 per cent of children in families in Northern Ireland in receipt of one-parent benefit (accepting the limitations of this as a measure) were aged four or under (DHSS (NI), 1995). The comparable figure for Britain was 27 per cent (DSS, 1994). With regard to family size, lone parents with three or more dependent children are less likely to be in full-time employment than those with one or two dependent children (Bradshaw and Millar, 1991). In 1993, 16 per cent of lone parents in receipt of one-parent benefit in Northern Ireland had three or more children with the corresponding figure for Britain being 11 per cent (DHSS (NI), 1995; DSS, 1994).

Finally, to all of these elements must be added the implications for Northern Ireland's lone parents of living in the region that has long had the highest unemployment and poorest day-care provision in the UK. Northern Ireland's state day nurseries were closed down at the end of the Second World War and no similar service has been developed since (Cohen, 1988). With regard to employment opportunities, it should be noted that to the region's long-standing problem of worklessness has been added the possibility that mechanisms such as competitive tendering have had a particularly sharp effect on women's employment opportunities in this part of the UK. Clearly, lone mothers cannot be insulated from these trends (Evason and Robinson, forthcoming).

THE STUDY

The differences and trends outlined above formed the background to the project. However, the trigger for a new study was provided by data suggesting a sharp increase in receipt of income support by lone parents in Northern Ireland. Between 1988 and 1993, the number of lone parents on income support increased by 70 per cent – a figure much above the rate of increase in the number of lone parents generally in Northern Ireland and the comparable figure for Britain of 44 per cent (DHSS (NI), 1995; DSS, 1994). In addition, though the samples are small, unpublished data from the Continuous Household Survey (CHS) for Northern Ireland suggested that by 1992 the proportion of lone parents dependent on income support had risen to 73 per cent and that between 1989 and 1992 the proportion of lone parents in full-time employment had declined from 18 per cent to 11 per cent – a much sharper drop than occurred in Britain (see John Haskey, Chapter 2 here and Jonathan Bradshaw, Chapter 9).

There are considerable problems with the data available for Northern Ireland in tracking through exactly what has been happening to lone parents over the past decade and, in fact, unpublished CHS data for 1994/5 present a less dramatic picture with regard to receipt of income support than those noted above. Not surprisingly, however, the core concerns of DHSS (NI) in 1994 related to the causes of rising dependence, barriers to employment among lone mothers, the effectiveness of the various incentives to seek employment within the benefits system and movement onto and off income support and family credit. These dictated the complex research design employed[1] and the restriction of the research to lone mothers who were single, separated or divorced. In the following paragraphs, some of the background information generated by the project is outlined and this is followed by an overview of the data obtained on needs and financial difficulties of lone mothers on income support.

Flows between benefits and out of lone parenthood

Table 4.2 details the original sample status by benefit status at the time of the interview for all the women interviewed, including those who had ceased to be lone mothers. The top half of the table shows that little movement occurred, particularly among income support claimants, between the time when the samples were drawn and the time of the interviews. Thus, 78 per cent of those selected as being on family credit were still on this benefit when interviewed. A rather higher proportion (88 per cent) of income support claimants reported no change in status by the time of the interview. The lower half of the table contains a number of points of interest. First, there is the pronounced movement of ex-family credit claimants towards income support and the significant number of ex-

---

1. Put briefly, the first stage in the project was a focus group exercise conducted in 1995. Some 39 lone mothers (20 income support and 19 family credit claimants) participated and the discussions ranged from knowledge of in-work incentives to experience of the Child Support Agency. The questionnaire developed subsequently was similarly broad, with an attempt being made to replicate as much of the preceding work in Britain as possible. The nature of the questionnaire; the fact that it was being developed in Blaise to enable computer assisted personal interviewing; and the sampling strategy employed (see below) meant that the time taken to develop the instrument was quite long. An extensive pilot in Spring 1996 led to considerable revisions and checking, particularly with respect to the routing. The main survey took place at the end of 1996. Given the objectives of the study and the interests of the sponsoring body, it was decided to draw four separate samples: lone mothers on income support (IS); lone mothers on family credit (FC); lone mothers who had left the income support register; and lone mothers who had left the family credit register. Further details on sampling design will be available shortly (Evason, Robinson and Thompson, forthcoming). Response rates varied across the four samples, but taking the four samples together the effective response rate was 70.5 per cent and a total of 1659 valid interviews were completed (response rates: IS 70.5%; FC 73.4%; ex-IS 66.9%; ex-FC 70.5%). These samples would not, of course, produce a representative sample of all lone mothers in Northern Ireland. We do, however, have a substantial volume of data from the first two samples, which relate to the majority of lone mothers in Northern Ireland at a particular point in time plus the data from the two other samples to enhance understanding of flows between benefits and routes out of lone parenthood.

income support claimants who had returned to this benefit. For the majority (60 per cent) of those leaving these benefit registers, the pattern is one of a revolving door rather than an escalator that moves women away from reliance on either benefit. Second, the table does show a significant proportion of women (22 per cent) as being on neither benefit but closer analysis indicates that this is primarily a consequence of moving out of lone parenthood itself. Some 300 women (18 per cent) were no longer lone parents at the time of the interviews with the main routes out of lone parenthood being reconciliation (32 per cent) and acquiring new partners (33 per cent).

Table 4.2: *Sample status by current benefit status, total sample (%)*

| Sample status | Current Benefit Status – total sample (row percentages) | | | |
	FC	IS	Neither	Total
FC	77.8	12.5	9.7	28.0
IS	5.6	88.1	6.3	26.0
Ex FC	15.1	48.0	36.9	25.1
Ex IS	35.5	23.0	41.5	19.9
All	34.2	43.9	21.9	100.0
Base	(567)	(728)	(364)	(1659)

Table 4.3: *Sample status by current benefit status, lone mothers only (%)*

| Sample status | Current Benefit Status – total sample (row percentages) | | | |
	FC	IS	Neither	Total
FC	82.6	13.4	4.0	31.2
IS	5.3	94.0	0.7	30.6
Ex FC	20.2	65.9	13.9	22.1
Ex IS	52.8	34.4	12.8	16.0
All	40.3	53.1	6.6	100.0
Base	(550)	(724)	(90)	(1364)

Table 4.3 shows that, once attention is confined to those who were still lone mothers at the time of the interview, the revolving door effect is much more pronounced. Only 7 per cent of the total sample were on neither benefit and, in all, 87 per cent of those selected because they had left income support or family credit were back on one or other of these benefits. It can be noted that 66 per cent of the ex-family credit claimants were on income support as, indeed, were one-third of those selected because they had left the income support register. The latter is a rather

higher proportion than that (14 per cent) reported by Bradshaw and Millar (1991: 15).

The result of these flows – and the stability of the income support sample itself – was that lone mothers on income support were the majority group (n = 724) in the total sample of lone mothers at the time of the interviews. Data on this subset of women are presented below with a distinction being made between those selected as being on income support and others on income support at the time of the interviews.

Characteristics of lone mothers on income support

Table 4.4 details the characteristics and other aspects of the circumstances of lone mothers interviewed. A number of observations can be made. First, the overall breakdown by marital status is broadly consistent with that for lone mothers generally in Northern Ireland – see Table 4.1 – but there is some variation between the two groups with those selected as being on income support being less likely to be single mothers. Second, the table indicates that the majority (85 per cent) of these lone mothers had had one spell of lone parenthood only and, interestingly, this is consistent with the data for Bradshaw and Millar's broader sample (1991: 7). The data on the duration of lone parenthood are, however, consistent with the discussion above on the more restricted routes out of lone parenthood in Northern Ireland. Three-fifths of these women had spent five years or more as lone parents, with the median duration being 60–72 months. This may be compared with 46 months in Bradshaw and Millar's (1991) stock sample, although more recent work (Marsh et al, 1997) suggests the duration of lone parenthood may be lengthening in Britain.

Third, the data on dependent children indicate that lone mothers selected as being on income support had larger families than other mothers on income support. Most significantly, nearly half of all of these women had at least one child of preschool age. In addition, the data on whether or not these lone mothers had planned their first pregnancies – see Figure 4.1 – demonstrate, yet again, the inadequacy of the crude stereotypes of single mothers that have featured in recent debates on lone parenthood. Single mothers are those least likely to plan their first pregnancy.

Receipt of income support and employment intentions

Table 4.5 indicates that, despite the heavier dependence on income support in Northern Ireland generally (Evason and Woods, 1995b), for these lone mothers receipt of income support is still, to a large extent, associated with becoming a lone parent. Only a minority (27 per cent) were already on income support when they became lone parents and the main reasons for the claim were loss of partner's income and pregnancy. It is noticeable that those selected as being on income support, generally older women with larger families had, in the majority of cases, claimed

Table 4.4: *Characteristics of lone mothers on income support (column %)*

	Selected as IS	Others on IS	Total
Marital status:	%	%	%
Separated	41.7	40.2	41.0
Divorced	19.3	16.3	18.0
Single	38.4	43.5	40.7
Causes first became lone parent:	%	%	%
Marriage breakdown	54.2	45.6	50.3
Relationship breakdown	10.7	10.6	10.6
Pregnancy/birth of child	33.6	42.0	37.4
Other	1.5	1.8	1.7
Age when first became lone parent:	%	%	%
19 or under	26.2	31.4	28.6
20–25	31.8	36.0	33.7
26–35	31.6	26.9	29.4
36 or older	10.4	5.7	8.3
Number of times a lone parent:	%	%	%
Once only	87.3	82.5	85.1
Twice	10.4	14.8	12.4
Three or more times	2.3	2.7	2.4
Total years as a lone parent:	%	%	%
Less than 2 years	11.0	6.9	9.1
Over 2 but less than 5 years	29.5	32.7	30.9
Over 5 but less than 10 years	34.1	41.8	37.6
More than 10 years	25.4	18.7	22.4
Number of dependent children:	%	%	%
One child only	31.8	38.7	34.9
Two children	37.7	35.0	36.5
Three and over	30.0	24.8	27.6
N/A	0.5	1.5	1.0
Youngest/only child under 5:	*47.8*	*46.8*	*47.4*
Base	(393)	(331)	(724)

throughout the the current spell of lone parenthood and this was typically their only spell of lone parenthood. Nearly half of these women had been on income support for more than six years. The duration of these claims does not, however, denote a preference, as such, for remaining outside the labour force. As Table 4.6 indicates, among those selected as being on

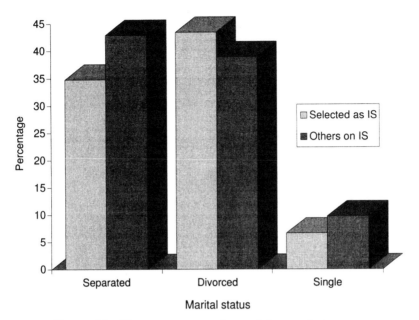

Figure 4.1: *First pregnancy planned, by marital status*

income support only a minority found being at home very satisfying. The majority were caught in a complex web of constraints: feelings of boredom and worries about money on the one hand and satisfaction that they were meeting the needs of their children and ought to care for them on the other. It is also noticeable that the preference for employment was much stronger among the other lone mothers on income support and this is a matter for further analysis. This variation is carried through in Table 4.7 but, even so, the majority of all of these women intended to seek paid, full-time (16 hours plus) employment at some point.

Finally, in this section, Table 4.8 details the main reasons for lone mothers not seeking employment at the time of the interviews. The emphasis on the need to care for children is predictable and the signifi-cance of ill health and disability is in line with other data (McKay and Marsh, 1994). The percentage of lone mothers who considered they would be no better off deserves further comment. As other work (Evason and Woods, 1995a) has shown, the gains from employment with in-work benefits may be narrower in Northern Ireland and a core theme in the focus groups exercise conducted as part of this research (Evason and Robinson, 1995b) was the frustration of women on family credit that they were little or no better off.

Table 4.5: *Receipt of income support (%)*

	Selected as IS	Others on IS	Total
Benefit status when last became a lone parent:	%	%	%
Already on IS	27.2	26.3	26.8
Claimed IS within three months	55.7	48.9	52.6
Claimed IS after three months	17.1	24.8	20.6
Base	(386)	(319)	(705)
Main reason first claimed IS as a lone parent:	%	%	%
Separation/divorce – loss of partner's income	55.2	37.9	47.3
Stopped work/moved from full- to part-time employment	6.6	21.2	13.3
Became pregnant	35.9	36.7	36.2
Other	2.3	4.2	3.2
Base	(393)	(330)	(723)
Has claimed IS throughout current spell of lone parenthood:	87.5	18.4	55.9
Base	(393)	(331)	(724)
On IS once only as lone parent	80.8	23.8	54.8
Base	(391)	(328)	(719)
Total time on IS as lone parent:	%	%	%
less than 2 years	9.7	26.3	17.3
2 years but less than 4 years	24.4	27.2	25.7
4 years but less than 6 years	16.5	17.5	17.0
more than 6 years	49.4	29.0	40.1
Base	(393)	(331)	(724)

Table 4.6: *Attitudes to work and the home*

	Selected as IS	Others on IS	Total
% strongly agree/agree			
I wish I were earning some/more money	89.1	94.3	91.5
I get bored being at home	71.2	81.8	76.0
I am happy to be at home as I think this is in the best interests of my children	51.5	26.4	40.1
I am happy to be at home and want to care full-time for my children while they are young	59.5	31.1	46.7
I often get depressed about not having a full-time job	46.5	60.4	52.8
As I am a lone parent I feel the children need me at home more	67.8	46.2	58.1
I feel out of things, not having a full-time job	52.7	64.8	58.2
Not having a full-time job is making me lose my confidence about ever getting back to work full-time	41.5	43.7	42.6
I really look forward to starting full-time work	59.2	72.9	65.4
I find being at home all of the time very satisfying	22.3	15.7	19.3

Table 4.7: *Employment intentions (column %)*

	Selected as IS	Others on IS	Total
	%	%	%
Currently looking for work (16 hours+)	5.7	16.4	10.5
Would like work within next year	20.3	23.9	21.9
Would like work eventually but not for over one year	48.1	38.4	43.7
Cannot/do not want to work now or in the future	20.3	14.8	17.8
Other/don't know	5.7	6.6	6.2
Base	(385)	(318)	(703)

Table 4.8: *Main reason for not currently seeking/wanting work (16 hours+) (column %)*

	Selected as IS	Others on IS	Total
	%	%	%
Would not be any better off	21.6	26.3	23.6
Need to look after children	51.5	39.3	46.4
Need to look after other relative or friend	3.3	3.1	3.2
Suffer from ill health/disability	13.9	15.3	14.4
Would not be able to find work	5.8	7.6	6.6
Other	3.9	8.4	5.8
Base	(361)	(262)	(623)

Aspects of living standards

The density of poverty and material hardship among lone parents in the UK is noted elsewhere in this volume (Chapters 1 and 9) and has been a constant theme in research in Britain (Bradshaw and Millar, 1991; Ford et al, 1995) and Northern Ireland (Evason and Woods, 1995b). In this project, living standards and degree of financial stress and difficulty were assessed with a variety of indicators. The questionnaire covered anxiety about bills, recent and current debts, reliance on assistance from informal and charitable sources and an amended version of the Mack and Lansley index together with a more open set of questions on perceived needs. In addition, the project sought to advance the debate through the inclusion of the general health questionnaire so that the link between financial hardship and psychological distress could be explored.

Table 4.9: *Lone parents who frequently worry about bills (column %)*

	Selected as IS	Others on IS	Total
Worries about bills	%	%	%
Never	7.5	7.0	7.2
Occasionally	26.2	21.6	24.1
Often/All the time	66.3	71.4	68.7
Base	(387)	(328)	(715)

In the data that follow it can be noted that there is some variation between the two groups of lone parents, with those selected as being on income support reporting less difficulty than other lone mothers on income support. Part of the explanation for this relates to problems that may occur when claimants move between benefits and fail to appreciate the impact receipt of family credit will have on their housing benefit entitlement. Of these other mothers, 53 reported that they had got into rent arrears when they had previously moved from income support to family credit.

Table 4.10: *Frequency of worries about bills: selected as income support only*

| | Number of dependent children | | | |
	1 child	2 children	3 or more	Total
Worries about bills	%	%	%	%
Never	8.3	9.5	4.9	7.5
Occasionally	40.7	18.2	22.9	26.2
Often/All the time	50.9	72.3	72.3	66.3
Base	(108)	(137)	(144)	(389)

| | Length of time on income support | | | |
	Under 2 years	2–5 years	5 yrs or more	Total
Worries about bills	%	%	%	%
Never	13.5	7.3	6.6	7.5
Occasionally	24.3	28.2	25.6	26.3
Often/All the time	62.1	64.5	67.8	66.2
Base	(37)	(124)	(227)	(388)

Table 4.9 indicates that, in line with British data (Ford et al, 1995), the majority of these lone mothers reported that they worried about bills often or all of the time. The level of anxiety increased sharply where there was more than one dependent child and there was some association between the level of anxiety and duration of income support receipt (Table 4.10). In common with other data for Northern Ireland (Evason and Woods, 1995b) in listing the bills – see Figure 4.2 – that caused most worry, the majority of these lone mothers referred to electricity or other fuel bills first. It can be noted that the cost of fuel in this part of the United Kingdom has featured heavily in numerous studies of low income households in Northern Ireland. In essence, the problem has been lack of access to one of the cheaper fuels – North Sea gas – and electricity prices which are substantially above the regions with the highest charges in Britain.

Table 4.11 indicates that the majority (57 per cent) of these lone mothers reported one or more debts over the preceding 12 months. Again, there

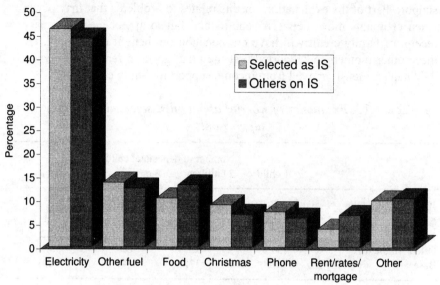

Figure 4.2: *Item cited first as causing worry*

Table 4.11: *Arrears: debts over preceding 12 months (column %)*

	Selected as IS	Others on IS	Total
	%	%	%
No debt	49.1	36.9	43.5
One debt	22.4	22.4	22.4
Two debts	14.2	15.4	14.8
Three or more debts	14.3	25.3	19.3
Base	(393)	(331)	(724)

Table 4.12: *Number of debts preceding 12 months by number of dependent children – selected as income support only (column %)*

	1 child	2 children	3 or more	Total
	%	%	%	%
No debts	57.8	46.0	45.5	49.1
One debt	26.6	17.3	24.1	22.4
Two debts	9.2	17.3	15.2	14.2
Three or more debts	6.4	19.4	15.2	14.2
Base	(109)	(139)	(145)	(393)

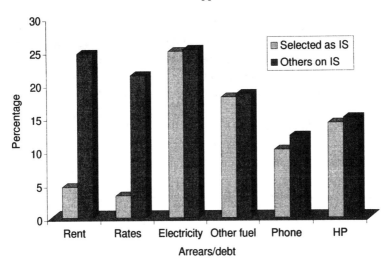

Figure 4.3: *Percentage of lone parents with arrears/debt over preceding 12 months (where total % exceeds 10% only)*

Table 4.13: *Lone parents currently owing money (column %)*

	Selected as IS	Others on IS	Total
	%	%	%
Currently in arrears	32.5	47.1	39.2
No arrears	67.5	52.9	60.8
Base	(388)	(329)	(717)
Amounts currently owed	%	%	%
£100 and under	34.7	21.5	27.3
£101 – £200	21.2	19.5	20.2
£200 – £500	16.9	29.5	24.0
£500 – £1000	13.6	20.1	17.2
Over £1000	13.5	9.4	10.9
Base	(118)	(149)	(267)
% with Social Fund repayment	59.5	58.1	58.8
Base	(390)	(329)	(719)
Level of Social Fund repayment	%	%	%
Weekly payment under £10	49.8	53.0	51.2
Weekly payment £10 – £19	42.4	43.2	42.7
Weekly payment over £20	7.8	3.8	6.0
Base	(229)	(183)	(412)

was some association between the level of difficulty reported and the presence of more than one dependent child (see Table 4.12). As expected, the most commonly cited difficulties related to fuel bills (see Figure 4.3) but, in support of the observations above, rent and rates figured more prominently in the responses of lone mothers in the 'others' category.

Table 4.14: *Runs out of money before next benefit payment is due (column %)*

	Selected as IS	Others on IS	Total
Runs out of money	%	%	%
Never	6.9	6.1	6.5
Occasionally	31.0	23.4	27.5
Often	24.1	25.8	24.9
Always	37.9	44.7	41.0
Base	(390)	(329)	(719)
*Strategies adopted when money runs out**	%	%	%
Borrows from family	72.5	74.1	73.2
Goes without	26.4	27.2	26.8
Borrows from friends	10.7	11.3	11.0
Other	9.1	5.5	7.4
Base	(363)	(309)	(672)

Note: *More than one could be selected.

Table 4.15: *Scores on Mack and Lansley index (column %)*

	Selected as IS	Others on IS	Total
	%	%	%
0	5.9	6.0	5.9
1 – 2	31.0	27.2	29.3
3 – 4	28.2	28.7	28.5
5 or more	34.9	38.1	36.3
Base	(393)	(331)	(724)

Table 4.13 indicates that two-fifths of these lone mothers owed amounts that 'should have been paid' at the time of the interview and, in the majority of such cases, the amounts owed exceeded £100. In addition, the majority (59 per cent) of these lone mothers were repaying loans from the Social Fund with the deductions at source accounting for a significant pro-

portion of total benefit in many cases. The introduction of the Social Fund posed particular problems for claimants in Northern Ireland generally (Evason et al, 1989) and the very heavy reliance on assistance from this source among these lone parents is in keeping with other data (Evason and Woods, 1995b).

Table 4.16: *Amended version of Mack and Lansley index (%)*

	Selected as IS	Others on IS	Total
Section 1			
Has meat/fish/vegetarian equivalent every other day	83.8	84.5	84.1
Has two meals per day	84.1	83.0	83.6
Parent skips meals never/occasionally	84.4	86.0	85.2
Has three meals a day for children	96.2	97.3	96.7
Has fresh fruit/vegetables every other day	84.1	84.5	84.3
Section 2			
Has sufficient beds for everyone in household	95.1	93.0	94.2
Has fridge	98.5	97.9	98.2
Has washing machine	96.4	93.3	95.0
Has carpet in living room	89.2	86.9	88.2
Has sufficient heat in living room	93.1	90.6	91.9
Has house well decorated	84.6	79.0	82.1
Section 3			
Cannot afford waterproof coats for everyone	43.8	40.4	42.2
Cannot afford two pairs all-weather shoes for children	46.7	46.8	46.7
Cannot normally afford new, rather than second-hand clothes	41.8	39.8	40.9
Cannot afford insurance for household contents	73.1	72.0	72.6
Cannot save at least £10 a month	80.5	84.5	82.3

Our data are consistent with this earlier research in indicating that along-side these formal debts the majority of these lone mothers also relied on informal help from friends and relatives. As Table 4.14 indicates, the majority of these lone mothers reported that they often/always ran out of money before their next benefit payment was due and the majority of those who did so borrowed from other family members and/or friends. In essence, many of these women were caught in the familiar cycle of starting the fortnight with less than their full benefit – in consequence of deductions at source from benefits and amounts that had to be repaid to relatives and friends – and borrowing again when they ran out of money before the fortnight ended. In addition, a minority (13 per cent) reported receipt of assistance from a charity over the preceding 12 months.

Table 4.15 details the scores of these lone mothers on the deprivation index used. Following Mack and Lansley's (1992) convention whereby the absence of three or more necessities is an indication of hardship, it can be noted that the majority of these families fall into this category. Indeed, over one-third scored five or more and may be considered to be in severe difficulty. There is also the possibility that this index understates the degree of hardship.

Table 4.16 indicates that only minorities of interviewees reported difficulties with the first two sets of items. It may be, however, that as a result of differences in culture, Northern Ireland interviewees are more likely to under-report shortages of food. Leaving this issue aside, it can be seen that the difficulties that were most commonly reported were in the third set of items and revolved around shoes, clothing and financial security.

Table 4.17: *Felt needs and family holidays (column %)*

	Selected as IS	Others on IS	Total
% reporting lack of items deemed essential for house	43.1	50.8	46.6
% reporting lack of items deemed essential for children	55.1	55.6	55.4
% reporting lack of items deemed essential for self	52.8	51.7	52.3
% never had a family holiday while a lone parent	55.9	51.7	54.0
Base	(390)	(329)	(719)

A focus on basic items was again evident – see Table 4.17 – where interviewees were asked whether they lacked items for the house, their children or themselves that *they* deemed essential. The reported deficiencies with regard to the house picked up the minorities lacking items in the second part of the index and, to a larger extent, items outside the index such as carpets for parts of the house other than the living room. Other difficulties related to clothing and footwear. Not surprisingly, over half of these lone mothers had not had a family holiday. The survey also considered briefly the circumstances of those who had ceased to be lone parents by the time of the interview. The majority (54 per cent) of these women reported that they were much or a bit better off than they had been when lone parents. The earnings of partners was the most commonly cited (55 per cent of cases) reason for feeling better off, suggesting that even in Northern Ireland, with lower wages and higher male unemployment, a major route out of poverty for lone parents is exiting from lone parenthood itself.

Psychological Problems

In many ways, the patterns of need and difficulty noted above are not new. In the past, we have lacked any indication of some of the broader implications of these patterns for those who are caring for a significant percentage of children in Northern Ireland. Table 4.18 details the results of administering the 12-item general health questionnaire (GHQ) (Goldberg, 1972) to these lone mothers. It can be seen that significant minorities of these women reported feelings of depression, strain and sleeping problems. Moreover, 57 per cent of those selected as being on income support and 56 per cent of the other lone mothers were above the cut-off point of 1–2 which may be used to identify 'cases' of mild psychiatric disorder.

Table 4.18: *Individual GHQ items*

Recently:	Selected as IS	Others on IS	Total
Less/much less able to concentrate	32.2	34.0	33.0
Lost more/much more sleep over worry	38.2	45.7	41.7
Felt playing less/much less useful part in things	21.2	24.2	22.5
Felt less/much less able to make decisions	14.4	15.7	15.0
Felt more/much more under strain	45.7	50.9	48.0
Felt more/much more couldn't overcome difficulties	29.8	34.3	31.8
Felt less/much less able to enjoy normal activities	28.0	34.2	30.9
Felt less/much less able to face up to problems	20.8	23.4	22.0
Felt more/much more depressed and unhappy	41.1	42.1	41.5
Felt more/much more loss of self confidence	31.6	37.0	34.0
Felt more/much more a worthless person	20.8	21.2	20.9
Felt less/much less happy all things considered	24.4	26.4	25.3

Table 4.19: *Mean score on GHQ by deprivation index score (column %)*

Deprivation Index Score	Mean GHQ Score Selected as IS	Others on IS	Total
	%	%	%
0	10.6	10.8	10.7
1–2	12.3	13.1	12.6
3–4	14.1	14.8	14.4
5 or more	17.9	18.2	18.0
All	14.6	15.4	15.0
Base	(388)	(326)	(714)

The overall mean GHQ score for these lone mothers was 15.0, a figure that is much greater than that reported in other studies undertaken in Northern Ireland (Cairns, 1988; Cairns and Wilson, 1985). This would indicate the very high level of psychological distress experienced by these lone mothers. Most importantly, Table 4.19 indicates the significant association between psychological distress and deprivation – with increasing psychological distress as material hardship increases.

CONCLUSION

Lone parent families now account for one-quarter of all families in Northern Ireland and these families are overwhelmingly headed by women. In 1995, three-quarters of all female lone parents were on income support or family credit. Our samples of lone mothers who were selected because they were on income support or family credit therefore provide us with information on the circumstances, needs and views of the majority of all lone parents in Northern Ireland. The data for those selected because they had left the income support and family credit registers are a rich source of information on flows between benefits and out of lone parenthood itself.

A number of issues have emerged from this preliminary analysis. The first and most obvious point is that the primary route out of receipt of either income support or family credit is moving out of lone parenthood itself rather than securing reasonably paid employment or increased maintenance or a combination of both. Those who remain lone parents move, to a large extent, between benefits – between low paid employment and no employment. Second, the data highlight the stability of the circumstances of the income support claimants. The majority had claimed income support throughout their current spells of lone parenthood and nearly half had been on income support for more than six years. These data indicate that a significant proportion of Northern Ireland's children live at or near the poverty line for very long periods. Third, the data suggested that the majority of these lone mothers wished to seek paid employment outside home at some point but were prevented from doing so at the time of the interviews by the now familiar constraints: the need to care for their children, ill health and disability and concern that they would be no better off.

The data on living standards indicate high levels of anxiety about bills and a substantial level of indebtedness, which has been exacerbated by the substitution of loans from the Social Fund for single payments. On the deprivation index used, the majority may be considered to be experiencing severe material hardship. Material hardship was, moreover, closely associated with psychological distress. The data suggest there is substantial volume of such distress among lone parents on income support in Northern Ireland and, most importantly, that the level of distress rises as material hardship increases.

Chapter 5

The 'Big' Picture:
Quality in the Lives of Lone Parents[1]
John McKendrick

POVERTY IN LONE PARENTHOOD

The association between poverty and lone parenthood, particularly lone motherhood, is long-standing. Millar and Bradshaw (1987: 234) find reference to it in the classical studies of poverty at the turn of the century (for example Rowntree, 1902) and note its prominence in the 'rediscovery of poverty' in the 1960s (for example Abel-Smith and Townsend, 1965). More recently, research has used absolute measures (based on a fixed poverty line) and relative measures (based on a flexible poverty line defined in relation to the average standard of living) to focus specifically on lone-parent poverty (for example Bradshaw and Millar, 1991; McKendrick, 1994a; Millar, 1987, 1989, 1992; Millar and Bradshaw 1987; Wright, 1992). Both approaches draw attention to the prevalence of poverty in lone parenthood in that they are over-represented among the ranks of the poor (incidence of poverty) and that their level of poverty is higher than that experienced by most other groups (average deprivation). With such conclusive evidence, it is hardly surprising that the reality of lone-parent poverty is accepted across the spectrum of political opinion.

There is, however, discord among commentators in their interpretation of the trajectory of lone-parent poverty. Wright (1992), in a cross-sectional comparative analysis of absolute lone-parent poverty between 1968 and 1986, demonstrated that while lone-parent poverty became more widespread and more intense, the gap between lone parent households and

1. Grateful thanks are extended to Nick Scarle for assistance rendered in the preparation of the illustrations and to Allan Findlay who offered much constructive advice at the stage of data collection. The manuscript is much improved due to the insightful comments of Jamie Peck and Fran Bennett and owes its existence to the persistence and patience of Reuben Ford and Jane Millar. The research was funded by the Economic and Social Research Council.

widespread and more intense, the gap between lone parent households and all other households closed considerably; absolute poverty fell by 73.5 per cent for lone parents, compared with 55.6 per cent for all households and 61.6 per cent for two-parent families (when the poverty line is drawn at 50 per cent below mean income). Wright also suggested that the growth in lone parenthood is responsible for increasing lone parents' share of poverty, but that growth in numbers *per se* had virtually no effect on the level of poverty (average deprivation) experienced by lone parents. Thus, Wright (1992: 22) concluded that 'significant progress has been made in the alleviation of (lone parent) poverty'. Contrary to this, Millar and Bradshaw (1987), in a longitudinal analysis of poverty in low income families between 1978 and 1980, reach the opposite conclusion; the financial position of lone parents deteriorated relative to two-parent households and relative to lone parents who repartnered. They suggest that the lack of adequate childcare provision, coupled with the low earning potential of lone parents (nine-tenths of whom are women), placed them in a supplementary benefit trap, which in turn accounted for their over-representation among the poor.

The debate on trends in lone-parent poverty is interesting, but can perhaps be resolved according to whether an absolute (Wright) or relative (Millar and Bradshaw) approach to poverty measurement is favoured (see Atkinson, 1987; Sen, 1983; and Townsend, 1985 for standpoint positions in this debate, and Doyal and Gough, 1991 for an attempt to move the debate beyond the binary divide). However, even if we accept that significant progress in alleviating lone-parent poverty has already been made, little comfort can be taken from, and no disputes contest, the large number of lone parents currently experiencing poverty in UK society and lone parents' markedly poorer existence *vis-à-vis* other family households in the UK (McKendrick, 1995, and see other chapters here). While the poverty facts are not disputed, significant differences of opinion are held with respect to the implications of poverty and the association between poverty and other problems of lone parenthood.

POVERTY AND THE PROBLEM OF LONE PARENTHOOD

There is no consensus over what constitutes the 'problem of lone parenthood', though all commentators consider that there is a problem of sorts. This point is not lost on Ford and Millar (Chapter 1 here) who recognise that conception of the problem varies between social groups, and over time and space. Similarly, McKay and Rowlingson (Chapter 3 here), explore the 'problems' of single lone parents apart from those of separated lone parents. Furthermore, while Ford and Millar present an expansive list of problems, which includes poverty, long-term changes to population structure, gender inequality, moral issues, 'cultural' issues, demands on fiscal resources and effects on children, Land and Lewis (Chapter 8) consider that the wider society perceives the latter three as the primary problem of lone parenthood in the 1990s. Yet, additional 'problems' should also perhaps be added to this list. McKendrick (1994a), for example, suggests that others' attitudes towards lone parents *per se* is a problem (in addition to poverty and the perceived problem of the number of lone parents). Reconciling the various interpretations of the 'lone-parent problem' would be a worthwhile exercise; however, it is more important to reflect on the interrelatedness of these problems and the consequent contradictions inherent in any attempt to use policy to address any particular problem. In the context of this chapter, it is therefore useful to reflect on the wider significance of the problem of lone-parent poverty.

In practice, policy objectives often seek to address several problems and, even if not, the strategies used to achieve a particular policy goal can have implications beyond its immediate objective. Take, for example, Ermisch's policy prescription outlined in his concluding chapter 'Prospects and Policies' in *Lone Parenthood: An Economic Analysis* (Ermisch, 1991a: 165): 'The issue of poverty and its primary source, the lack of a father's income, and the possible intergenerational effects of spending part of childhood in a one-parent family both point to the need for policies that reduce the number of one-parent families.'

Clearly, Ermisch positions himself against the lone-parent family, that is he perceives a need to reduce the number of lone-parent families, but also recognises that the poverty of lone parents is a problem. Although Ermisch does not decouple these problems in his policy prescription, there are still contradictions inherent in his prescribed solution. The threefold strategy he proposes contains elements that would appeal to commentators with markedly different outlooks on lone parenthood, specifically tightening divorce laws to reduce the number of lone parents (conceiving of lone parents *per se* as the problem); targeting benefits to those most in need (poverty as the problem); and, while the provision of child care facilities is raised as a means to increase labour market participation and hence reduce poverty levels, this is high on the list of priorities of those who argue that lone parents should be better accommodated in society (society *per se* as the problem). In tackling poverty, Ermisch is proposing measures that would inadvertently improve lone parents' standing in society. Clearly, lone-parent policy programmes can produce contradictory outcomes in terms of the policy-maker's outlook on lone parenthood.

Contradiction is also characteristic of debates around lone-parent poverty. The 'popular' belief that if welfare payments/benefits were made less attractive, more lone parents would enter the paid labour market and leave behind a life of poverty, would indeed be substantiated by some lone parents. However, for others (who gain low paid insecure employment) reducing welfare may only change the paymaster without increasing financial well-being, and for others still (who cannot find work) it would actually serve to intensify poverty (see Bryson in Chapter 10 here). Differential impact among the lone-parent population is not the only outcome that would arise from such a policy; a back-to-work solution to lone-parent poverty could exacerbate other problems of lone parenthood. It may only displace fiscal expenditure, rather than save money on welfare payments (particularly if workfare is part of the solution; Rose, 1995); if the lone-parent unit becomes financially stable then the (perceived) moral, cultural and population change problems associated with lone parenthood would become more difficult to address as the lone-parent family unit is strengthened in terms of economic well-being; the effects on some children could worsen, if preliminary research is correct to suggest that, in some localities, children's educational performance is adversely affected as a result of their parents working (O'Brien, 1997); gender inequality may not be breached if, as many expect (Marsh and McKay, 1993b), back-to-work solutions lead to marginal employment outcomes with poor long-term prospects, and would exacerbate the cultural problem of men's disenfranchisement as female lone parents compete for work with men (see also McKay and Rowlingson in Chapter 3 here). Poverty is a far more complex problem to address than the simple statistics of poverty lines and proportions in receipt of welfare benefits tend to suggest.

PROBLEMS OF RESEARCHING POVERTY (IN LONE PARENTHOOD)

Researching lone-parent poverty presents its own problems. Tedious, non-substantive problems that must be overcome at the present time include the prevailing unfashionability of referring to poverty in political and academic debate; the lack of interest in work that seeks to specify ever more precisely the incidence and intensity of poverty; and the methodological challenges that confront poverty research. None of these problems is insurmountable, although the methodological ones are particularly challenging, even to the point where they hamper the study of key issues, such as how to measure poverty in concealed lone-parent families – where lone-parent families live in households with other individuals/family groups (Millar and Bradshaw, 1987, at least refer to multi-unit households as a category in analysis, but ignore the different configurations of poverty within). Interesting contributions to the 'within-household allocation of resources' debate are awaited (Jenkins, 1991).

However, there are more fundamental problems with the study of (lone-parent) poverty. Applied poverty research tends to adopt a narrow focus for a complex phenomenon, using income-based measures and indices of material well-being to proxy for lone-parent poverty. This is useful in that it highlights the plight of lone parents in poverty; but it is also inadequate in that it fails to address the multi-dimensional nature of lone-parent poverty and tends to focus attention on narrow policy objectives (raising income levels) to the detriment of other solutions to lone-parent poverty. The root cause of poverty is not solely derived from income; town planning (Robertson, 1984), housing market dynamics (Bradshaw and Millar, 1991) and the geographies of local service provision (Donnison, 1982) all contribute to the impoverished existence of lone parents. More disposable income may be a solution to the problem, but the lack of money is not the only cause. Similarly, poverty has wide ranging impacts that affect many more aspects of lives than material well-being (McCormick and Philo, 1995; Evason et al in Chapter 4 here). In terms of policy objectives – and to return to Ford and Millar's introductory chapter here – policies such as the 'New Deal for Lone Parents', which aim to increase lone parents' participation in the paid labour force (to tackle lone-parent poverty), will fail unless attempts to challenge prevailing negative social attitudes toward lone parents (cultural and moral) are incorporated into a policy programme. For such policies to succeed, it is necessary to challenge the perception that lone parents are unreliable and feckless and to challenge the sentiment that lone parents should not be supported (even to enable them to support themselves) in any way whatsoever. A more holistic approach to the study of the conditions of lone parenthood is required.

Social inclusion/exclusion frameworks for research – now seen as the more acceptable face of poverty research – overcome these shortcomings by addressing a broader range of life experiences. However, this is still problematic in that it remains focused on overcoming problems faced by excluded groups. On one hand, this merely exacerbates the stigmatisation faced by 'excluded' groups (lone parents dependent on welfare), while on the other, it ignores positive aspects in the lives of those experiencing financial hardship. Thus, it ignores the independence, freedom, control over decision-making with regard to children, and peace of mind which lone parents value (McKay and Rowlingson in Chapter 3 here; Bradshaw and Millar, 1991, and Table 5.1). Indeed, by not recognising the positive aspects of life there is a danger that these may be compromised by anti-poverty strategies, for example, less control over their own lives may follow from a back-to-work solution which implies more reliance on others with respect to childcare and, of course, from the Child Support Agency's (CSA's) attempt to increase the role of absent fathers in supporting financially the lone-parent family unit (Clarke et al, in Chapter

14 here). These examples are illustrative of the need to take a wide ranging review of changes to the conditions of lone parenthood.

Table 5.1: *Best and worst things about being a lone parent (% of each group of lone parents)*

	Previous marital status			All lone parents
	Divorced	Separated	Single	
*Very best thing about being a lone parent**				
Independence	66	58	56	60
Freedom	35	30	26	31
Ability to make decisions for children	18	18	27	21
Peace of mind	20	18	10	15
Atmosphere in house	13	18	10	13
Money (coping/regular/having own)	14	13	10	12
More time for self/children	9	9	13	10
Generally like it	9	7	9	9
More self confidence	10	7	6	8
Nothing/don't know	13	15	14	13
Other	8	7	8	8
Base	(623)	(283)	(522)	(1428)
Very worst thing about being a lone parent				
Loneliness	57	50	43	48
Financial difficulties	46	41	46	45
No one to discuss problems with	31	37	26	30
Lack of adult conversation	14	13	8	12
Miss being part of a couple	12	17	9	12
Socially hard	12	15	1	12
Worrying as child grows up	9	13	9	10
Child needs other parent figure	6	14	7	8
Security (at night)	5	9	6	6
Nothing/don't know	4	5	8	6
Other	12	10	13	12
Base	(605)	(278)	(504)	(1387)

Note: *Respondents were permitted to record more than one answer.

Source: Bradshaw and Millar (1991).

QUALITY OF LIFE, A SOLUTION AND A PROJECT

A solution

While quality of life research is not without its problems (McKendrick, 1994a; Rogerson, 1989), or its critics (Bell, 1984), it nevertheless offers a solution to the limitations of poverty research outlined above. It is essentially an holistic approach in which the interconnectedness of life experiences are explored. This provides insight into the relative significance of life concerns to lone parents, for example the significance of poverty (financial situation) relative to health. It also presents an opportunity to consider both positive and negative aspects of life; the focus of study need not dwell on the latter, and prior assumptions may be challenged as the links between (assumed) pros and cons of life are explored. Furthermore, quality of life research offers the opportunity to examine the wider significance of a particular policy proposal on the lives of lone parents, for example, does access to childcare have benefits to lone parents over and above those pertaining to entry to the paid labour/reskilling market?

A project

The results presented in this chapter are drawn from a survey of 275 lone parents from central/southwest Scotland (the area previously known as Strathclyde Region). A questionnaire survey was devised following inter-views with individual lone parents and support groups; open-ended and broadly focused questions were used to prise out the general issues (domains) that concerned lone parents and specific points within each that were of particular note (subdomains). This is not insignificant since it means that the issues addressed in the survey were those that lone parents had identified as being significant to their lives. The survey itself was distributed to members of lone-parent support groups and was made available for self-collection and completion at libraries, doctors' surgeries and community centres throughout the study area. The main survey was preceded by a pilot, and was followed by a control sample survey in which an orthodox sampling frame was used to select a 'representative' sample of 35 lone parents from the study area (a survey of partnered parents was also undertaken at this point), a comparison of control and main survey samples instilled confidence in the main survey results. The survey addressed many aspects of lone parents' lives including, for example, migration over the life course of lone parenthood (McKendrick, 1983), a longitudinal review of quality of life over the life course of lone parenthood (McKendrick, 1994a) and migration and quality of life (McKendrick, 1994b). The broader project of which it was part also compared levels of poverty in lone-parent family households with that in two-parent family households in Strathclyde Region (McKendrick, 1995). The theoretical and method-ological underpinnings of this project are discussed in detail elsewhere (McKendrick, 1994a). The survey was carefully worded to emphasise that it was the responding lone parent's own opinions and experiences that were the subject of analysis. For the most part, the personal direction of the question toward the lone parent reinforced this point, for example, canvassing respondents on their relationship with their children: however, some questions will have been answered on behalf of the lone-parent family unit, for example, canvassing respondents on the healthiness of the local environment would entail an evaluation on how this environmental context affects the lone parent *and* her/his children. This does not produce a chaotic conception of a lone-parent quality of life: on the contrary, the schedule accounts for the full range of factors – personal and familial – that impinge on the quality of lone-parent life. Children's experiences of living in a lone-parent family are beyond the remit of this chapter (though see Clarke et al in Chapter 14 here for relevant commentary). For the purposes of this chapter, attention is turned to those aspects of the survey that sought to establish the importance of different life concerns to lone parents, the extent to which lone parents are satisfied with their experiences in each of these domains, and the net effect of these in a multiple-additive model of quality of life. The extent to which lone parents share a common experience of life, and the extent to which their experiences differ from partnered parents are also considered.

MAPPING THE QUALITY OF LIFE OF LONE PARENTS

Life concerns

Lone parents were asked to rate the importance of 14 domains on a five-point scale ranging from not at all important (one) to extremely important (five). Table 5.2 ranks these domains in order of importance, and provides information on the mean, modal response and the proportional distribution of opinion. Family life was considered by lone parents to be the most important aspect of their lives with 82 per cent rating it extremely important and a further 13 per cent rating it very important. Similar senti-ments were expressed for crime and control over their life, and to a lesser extent for health and housing. At the other end of the spectrum, there was less concern for leisure and others' attitudes toward them, particularly the latter where the most common opinion was that others' attitudes were 'not at all important' to them.

It is significant to note that for economic domains (work, financial situation and having opportunities to better themselves), less concern was expressed relative to the more personal domains (family life and control over life) and only comparable concern was expressed relative to domains pertaining to material conditions of life (housing, service provision); the thrust of much lone-parent policy is based on the need to improve their material well-being and to increase their labour market participation, yet other less tangible issues are deemed of more pressing significance by lone parents. The quality of life interpretation is not to suggest that these key policy goals should be reappraised; the relative insignificance of the economic domains does not imply that such factors are insignificant in the quality of life experienced by lone parents. Rather, it is a reminder that in developing policy, sight must not be lost of issues that matter most to lone parents.

Table 5.2: *The extent to which life concerns matter to lone parents: an overview (% of lone parents)*

Rank (Mean)	Domain	Mean	Mode	Very important	Extremely important
1	Family life	4.769	5	95	82
2	Crime	4.69	5	98	76
3	Control over life	4.673	5	95	75
4	Health	4.555	5	90	67
5	Housing	4.487	5	89	61
6	Financial situation	4.339	5	84	54
7	Having opportunities	4.077	5	74	45
8	Service provision	3.983	5	67	38
9	Neighbourhood	3.827	4	63	31
10	Advice and support	3.77	5	63	33
11	Work	3.607	4	56	26
12	Transportation	3.587	4	55	25
13	Leisure	3.283	3	41	21
14	Other people's attitude	2.726	1	31	15

Notes: Lone parents were asked to rate each domain using a five point scale, ranging from 1 (not at all important) to 5 (extremely important). In the table, 'very important', refers to the proportion of lone parents rating a domain either 4 (very) or 5 (extremely) on the five point scale. Base = 275 lone parents.

Source: LPQoL Questionnaires (pilot and main versions).

Life experiences

Having established the relative importance of domains, the next step is to consider lone parents' experiences of each domain (irrespective of how important these are deemed to be). As Table 5.3 illustrates, two indicators were used to 'measure' life experiences for each domain. One environmental and one personal/social one were considered for each domain, though different indicators were used for 'work' according to whether lone parents were in the paid labour market. As for domain importance, the indicators are ranked (in order of satisfaction), and information is provided of the mean and proportional distribution of opinion.

The first point to note is the satisfaction expressed by lone parents with their family life; when coupled with the knowledge that this domain is the one that is of most concern to lone parents, it implies a largely positive contribution by family life to the overall quality of life of lone parents. Equally notable, but for very different reasons, is the dissatisfaction expressed with their economic circumstances; of the seven issues with which lone parents were least satisfied, six of these relate to economic issues (two each for having opportunities, their financial situation and work for those who were not currently in employment). Lone parents' dissatisfaction with local employment opportunities, local employment training and the lack of local childcare provision emphasise emphatically the shortcomings of what is currently available to lone parents (which supports Ford's argument in Chapter 12 here). However, those lone parents in paid employment expressed a high level of satisfaction with their experience of work; perhaps challenging those commentators who are concerned for the quality of lone parents' employment experience.

A wealth of interesting insights can be gleaned from these results in addition to the key issues of economy and family. For example, relations with neighbours tend to be overlooked in debates over quality of life, or only referred to in exceptional cases where particular problems arise. For a population group so often on the receiving end of public criticism, it is interesting to note that lone parents expressed a high level of satisfaction in their relations with neighbours; it would appear that local/private relations run contrary to general/public ones. Donnison's (1982) concern that poor services are delivered to poor people does not resonate with lone parents' experience of their local health service, and the much verified point from national crime surveys that female lone parents are more fearful of crime than women in general, contrasts the level of satisfaction expressed by lone parents over safety inside their own home. It is not suggested here that the survey results are more valid than established findings, but they do challenge us to think these issues through once more with lone-parent lenses. Thus, women lone parents may indeed feel more vulnerable to crime in general, but given their life history they may feel less vulnerable in their own homes as a lone parent (here I am thinking of the adjustments of many lone parents to life after domestic violence –

Table 5.3: *Lone parents' satisfaction with specific aspects of their life:*
an overview (percentage of lone parents)

Rank (Mean)	Subdomain	Mean	Satisfied (%)	Dissatisfied (%)	Domain
1	Relationship with children	2.395	92	2	family
2	Family support in area	1.515	73	17	family
3	Doctor's service	1.406	74	14	health
4	Relations with neighbours	1.177	70	17	street
5	Travel to work time	1.153	66	21	work-in
6	Safety inside home	1.042	67	21	crime
7	Employment conditions	0.83	63	25	work-in
8	Housing appearance	0.676	63	27	housing
9	Public transport service	0.558	60	29	transport
10	Shops in local area	0.519	60	30	services
11	Healthy local environment	0.493	55	28	health
12	Physical condition of house	0.487	55	27	housing
13	Control over decisions	0.435	50	26	control
14	Advice and support of others	0.39	54	29	advice/support
15	Community spirit	0.134	45	31	street
16	Provision of leisure facilities	0.06	47	37	leisure
17	Vandalism in area	−0.124	41	42	crime
18	Reputation of area	−0.18	40	42	others' attitudes
19	Amount of spare time	−0.235	37	42	leisure
20	Pedestrian safety in area	−0.247	42	45	transport
21	Community groups in area	−0.433	28	46	advice/support
22	Local authority services	−0.495	33	49	services
23	Influence in local area	−0.837	20	51	control
24	Running costs of home	−0.925	26	59	financial
25	Local employment training	−0.971	21	59	work-out
26	Treatment of single parents	−1.078	19	59	others' attitude
27	Local childcare provision	−1.223	24	66	opportunities
28	Employment prospects	−1.239	18	65	work-out
29	Level of DSS support	−1.617	12	72	financial
30	What government is doing for you	−2.004	8	81	opportunities

Notes: Base = 275 lone parents. Lone parents were asked to express their satisfaction with each subdomain using a seven-point scale, ranging from −3 (very dissatisfied) to +3 (very satisfied). In the table, 'satisfied' refers to lone parents who responded positively (+1, +2, +3), while 'dissatisfied' refers to those who responded negatively (−1, −2, −3). Details of neutral experiences (0, neither positive nor negative) can be inferred from the results provided. Working and non-working lone parents were asked different questions about their experience of work (5, 7, 25, 28).

Source: LPQoL Questionnaires (pilot and main versions).

Bradshaw and Millar, 1991). These issues are explored in greater depth elsewhere (McKendrick, 1994a).

Key dimensions

In a multiple-additive model of quality of life, satisfaction with a life experience is weighted according to the importance given to that life experience; particular attention should be given to those domains that matter most to lone parents, that may make a particularly positive contribution to lone parents' quality of life (very important and a source of satisfaction), or a particularly negative contribution to lone parents' quality of life (very important, but a source of dissatisfaction). Table 5.4 is the product of two stages of survey data manipulation; the aggregation of (subdomain) indicators of satisfaction into a single satisfaction index, and the weighting of this index, by the importance accorded to that domain. Domains are ranked according to the proportion of the lone-parent population who experience a positive outcome.

Table 5.4: *Life concerns and life experiences: a synthesis of lone parent opinion (% of lone parent survey population)*

Domain Importance Satisfaction	QoL opinion profile				Base
	High Low	Low Low	Low High	High High	
Family life	8	2	3	87	244
Health	20	4	6	71	235
Crime	34	1	2	63	232
Housing	28	3	8	60	243
Control over life	49	2	3	47	171
Neighbourhood	20	8	30	42	222
Advice and support	29	14	22	36	167
Transport	23	20	23	34	227
Services	33	12	23	32	228
Work	26	30	18	27	183
Leisure	20	34	26	21	229
Financial situation	67	10	5	17	244
Others' attitude	24	46	22	9	217
Opportunities	67	21	5	8	241

Notes: Base = 275 lone parents. Lone parents are considered to perceive a domain to be of 'low importance' if they rated it to be at most quite important – 1–3 on the 5-point rating scale (high importance if 4 or 5 on the rating scale). Similarly, lone parents are considered to express 'low satisfaction' if the mean satisfaction is lower than zero (high satisfaction if greater than or equal to zero).

Source: LPQoL Questionnaires (pilot and main).

It follows from the earlier discussion that family life makes the most positive contribution to lone parents' quality of life, and having opportunities (closely followed by financial situation) makes the least positive contribution. Both are clearly issues that are worthy of further exploration. However, before so doing, it is useful to note that these are but three of six domains for which a clear lone-parent experience can be discerned; shared experiences are also evident for health, crime and housing (which are important and a source of satisfaction for lone parents). For the majority of the other domains, a wide spectrum of experience is reported by lone parents – no clear lone-parent experience emerges. Control over life is the exception that does not fit into either category; while always concerned with this issue, lone parents' experiences are split evenly between those who are satisfied and those who are dissatisfied. These discontinuities in life experience among lone parents raise the question of whether it is even valid to conceive of a lone-parent quality of life.

COMPARATIVE PERSPECTIVES ON QUALITY OF LIFE

A lone-parent quality of life?

The basic mappings of the quality of lone parent life, while allowing for some variation among lone parents, tend to focus on aggregate results. This is built on the assumption that lone parent is a meaningful social grouping – an assumption that (in Chapter 1) Ford and Millar challenge lone parent commentators to reconsider. The extent to which it is valid to conceive of a lone-parent quality of life can be evaluated empirically by considering whether there are consistent and substantial divisions in quality of life experiences between particular groups of lone parents.

It transpires that the economic status of lone parents is the major cleavage in terms of the quality of life. For almost every domain considered, working lone parents expressed more satisfaction than non-working lone parents (McKendrick, 1994a). Is this merely a key division among lone parents, or does it suggest that the quality of life of working and non-working lone parents are so far apart that it would be prudent to conceive of a quality of life for each group in turn? To justify the latter, not only must workers differ from non-workers; there must also be a basis of agreement among each group. The majority of working lone parents share similar experiences of overall quality of life (71 per cent of workers experienced a quality of life above the lone-parent average), as do non workers (64 per cent of whom experienced a quality of life below the lone-parent average). However, despite these cross-group differences there is no intra-group consensus, for example, almost two out of every five non-working lone parents experienced a quality of life above the lone-parent average. The 'minority' experiences are too large to be dismissed as anomalies. The inconsistencies undermine the case for subgroups.

However, the possibility that the economic status of lone parents is but one component of multivariate subgroupings (for example, dividing lone parents into groups based on economic status *and* age) within the generic lone-parent population must also be considered before reaching a decision on whether lone-parent quality of life is a valid concept with which to work. Once again, however, even though there is increased consistency of quality of life opinion within subgroups, there is still substantial divergence among the subgroup from the modal opinion. The most consistent opinion for non-earners under 30 years of age (lower than average quality of life), still omits one-third who considered that they had an above average quality of life. Thus, while the consistency of quality of life opinion is improved, it is still not sufficient to validate subgroups. There is more to be gained by researching lone-parent quality of life and exploring the differences of opinion among lone parents.

A parental quality of life?

Having established that it is better to pursue the quality of life of lone parents by generic rather than subgroup analysis does not confirm the utility of the lone-parent category; experiences among lone parents may exhibit more similarity than difference, but these experiences may be more accurately attributed to some wider grouping of which lone parents are a constituent part. The possibility that lone-parent quality of life is none other than parental quality of life is worthy of consideration. To this end, the life concerns and life experiences of partnered parents are compared with those of lone parents (Table 5.5a and 5.5b). Table 5.5a, in which life concerns are considered, provides information on the rank order of domains and on what proportion of each group considers each domain to be very important. Table 5.5b compares partnered parents and lone parents in terms of their life experiences, paying attention to what proportion of each group are satisfied with their experience of each issue.

Table 5.5 clearly demonstrates that lone parents and partnered parents share a similar outlook on life, but differ significantly in their actual experience of life; similarities are evident in terms of the relative importance (rank order of domains according to importance) and the absolute importance of domains (proportion of the population who consider that a domain is 'very important') although lone parents were less satisfied than partnered parents for each aspect of life that was surveyed.

Table 5.5a: *Life concerns and life experiences: lone and partnered parents compared (extent to which life concerns matter to parents and % who consider that domain very important)*

Rank (lone)	Lone parent	Domain	Partnered parent	Rank (partnered)
1	95	Family life	99	1
2	98	Crime	97	2
3	95	Control over life	91	5
4	90	Health	93	3
5	89	Housing	92	4
6	84	Financial situation	77	6
7	74	Having opportunities	55	8
8	67	Service provision	70	7
9	63	Neighbourhood	66	9
10	63	Advice and support	50	12
11	56	Work	61	10
12	55	Transportation	61	11
13	41	Leisure	36	13
14	31	Other peoples' attitude	21	14

Notes: Base = 275 lone parents and 160 partnered parents. Parents were asked to rate each domain using a five-point scale, ranging from 1 (not at all important) to 5 (extremely important). In the table, very important refers to the proportion rating a domain either 4 (very) or 5 (extremely) on the five point scale.

Source: LPQoL Questionnaires (pilot and main versions), 2PQoL Questionnaire.

Table 5.5b: *Life concerns and life experiences: lone and partnered parents compared (% satisfied with specific aspects of life)*

Rank (lone)	Subdomain	Lone parent	Partnered parent	Domain
1	Relationship with children	92	98	family
2	Family support in area	73	90	family
4	Relations with neighbours	70	77	street
7	Employment conditions	63	78	work-in
12	Physical condition of house	55	68	housing
13	Control over decisions	50	26	control
19	Amount of spare-time	37	72	leisure
21	Community groups in area	28	43	advice and support
27	Local childcare provision	24	39	opportunities
28	Employment prospects	18	29	work-out

Notes: Base = 275 lone parents and 160 partnered parents. Parents were asked to express their satisfaction with each subdomain using a seven-point scale, ranging from –3 (very dissatisfied) to +3 (very satisfied). In the table, 'satisfied' refers to parents who responded positively (+1, +2, +3). Working and non-working parents were asked different questions regarding their experience of work.

Source: LPQoL Questionnaires (pilot and main versions), 2PQoL Questionnaire.

Lone and partnered parents largely agree on the relative importance of domains. For ten of the fourteen domains, the rank order of importance for partnered parents never varies by more than two places from the rank order of lone parents. In absolute terms, the proportion of the populations who rate a domain very important typically differs by less than 10 per cent. The exceptions are advice and support (13 per cent more lone parents rate this very important) and having opportunities (19 per cent more lone parents rate this very important). This counters the earlier results (Table 5.2), which suggested that lone parents were relatively less concerned with having opportunities. That is, far from being satisfied with their lot, lone parents were more concerned (more than partnered parents) about having opportunities to better themselves. Thus, opportunities and advice and support are particularly significant issues for lone parents.

However, the most significant findings to arise from this analysis were those relating to family life. Despite the very high levels of satisfaction expressed by lone parents, significantly more partnered parents were satis-fied with family life. This is particularly notable in terms of parents' interactions with family who live locally; almost 20 per cent more part-nered parents were satisfied with the support provided by family who live locally. Thus, the high level of satisfaction experienced by lone parents was not unique. Indeed, if anything, lone parents' satisfaction with family life is misleading when set in a broader comparative context. Finally, there is one difference that is significant by virtue of its size alone: satisfaction with the amount of spare time available to the parent. Twice as many partnered parents were satisfied with this aspect of their lives (72 per cent compared with only 37 per cent of lone parents). Clearly, the time pressure faced by lone parents, reflecting their sole responsibility for family matters, is an area worthy of further investigation. More generally, the results point to substantial differences between lone parents and partnered parents; a lone-parent quality of life exists with regard to life experiences.

KEY CONCERNS

Overall quality of life

A summary index of life quality was estimated by taking one step further the 'key dimensions' synthesis referred to previously (Table 5.4). The 14 domain indices were aggregated into one summary index maintaining the principle that those domains that matter most to lone parents are accorded greater weight. Brief mention is made below of the summary statistic of life quality. However, more attention is paid to the divisions among the lone-parent population. If our concern is to improve lone parents' lives, then it is appropriate to consider which groups of lone parents are experiencing a higher quality of life (and thereafter to reflect on the significance of this and the implications that follow from it). Figure 5.1 presents a mapping of the factors associated with a higher quality of life for lone parents. As explained in the notes, the illustration disentangles those factors that may be of causal significance from those that are not, and draws attention to the relative importance of these factors.

The aggregate result is that lone parents' total life experience is neither markedly positive nor negative; the mean quality of life for the whole lone-parent population is +0.486 with 53 per cent experiencing a quality of life that errs toward satisfaction. Although there is evidence of significant variations in life experiences among lone parents (individual lone parents' mean quality of life ranged from −12.292 to +12.385, a range of 24.676 on the 71-point scale), the majority of lone parents experience a similar quality of life; the standard deviation from the mean is only 3.941 and the quartile distributions from the median of +0.227 are −2.143 (lower) and +3.091 (upper). Further support for the notion of a lone-parent quality of life is therefore provided. This strengthens the argument that it is valid for policy-makers, lone parent activists, academics and other social commentators to simplify the life experiences of lone parents by referring to a lone-parent quality of life. However, the most interesting finding pertains to the nature of lone-parent quality of life. Thus, despite being a deprived group lone parents do not, on the whole, report a negative experience of life. Of course, this does not imply that lone parents' lot cannot (or should not) be improved; every effort can (and should) be made to turn a neutral life experience into a positive life experience.

Why then do lone parents experience the quality of life they do? It has already been shown how being employed exerted a strong positive impact on the quality of life experienced by lone parents. The multivariate mapping in Figure 5.1 supplements our understanding of this issue. It is readily apparent that work status was the characteristic most closely associated with lone-parent quality of life (incidentally the premise of Bryson's analysis in Chapter 10 here), although it is suggested that lone parents' work status was, in turn, influenced by education level (educated parents being more likely to work) and demographic character (older lone parents being more likely to work). Together, this composite of work status, education status and age forms the key pathway through which quality of life differences emerge. It should also be noted how it leads to a whole series of divisions among lone parents in terms of quality of life, for example, because work status influences whether lone parents live in areas with deprivation (working lone parents being less likely to do so), deprivation area status was also associated with lone-parent quality of life (those residing outside deprivation areas were more likely to experience a higher quality of life). Similarly, the other area effect – residing in an area with fewer lone parents leads to a higher quality of life – owes more to the general environment in which lone parents live, rather than the presence of other lone parents. However, access to childcare is independently associated with a higher quality of life, which also adds further weight to the arguments of Ford (Chapter 12 here) and Bradshaw (Chapter 9 here) that childcare provision should be improved for lone parents.

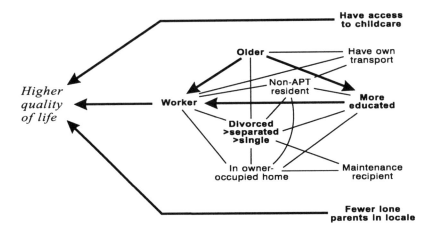

Notes: Base = 275 lone parents. The closer the variable is to the quality of life outcome, the greater the difference between variates of that variable. Variables, and relationships between variables, that help explain the quality of life outcome are represented in bold type. Variables that are associated with the quality of life outcome, but that do not help explain that outcome, are represented in normal type. Relationships between variables that do not help explain the quality of life outcome are represented in normal type. Inverse relationships between two variables that do not help explain the quality of life outcome are represented by broken lines. See text for further explanation.

Source: LPQoL Questionnaires (pilot and main).

Figure 5.1: *Explanations for the differences in quality of life experienced by lone parents*

Opportunities to 'better themselves'

This life concern was found to make a particularly negative contribution to the quality of lone-parent life; 67 per cent of lone parents were concerned with the issue, but were dissatisfied with the opportunities available to them (Table 5.4). It is thus worthwhile to reflect on the mapping of lone parents' satisfaction with these opportunities, which is presented in Figure 5.2.

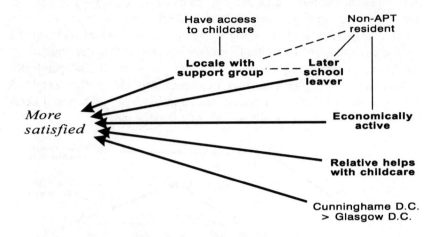

Note: See Figure 5.1 for source, cases and explanatory notes.

Figure 5.2: *Explanations for the differences in expressed satisfaction with the opportunities available to lone parents*

As for overall quality of life, a socio-economic composite (consisting of education status, economic status and area deprivation status) helps explain the level of satisfaction with opportunities. However, these are not the only significant explanatory components; two independent channels of influence, arising from childcare, are as significant: the presence of a relative as a childcarer, and the number of childcare opportunities in the local area. The role of childcare in enhancing opportunities is easier to comprehend than its broader role of enhancing life quality, which was referred to above. While living in an area with a lone-parent support group may directly increase opportunities by presenting a network of known childcarers, the results also suggest that the presence of the group *per se* is associated with better opportunities for lone parents; this is suggestive of the importance of lone-parent support groups in locales. Geographical significance seems also to extend to the macro-geographical scale; in contrast to previous research, which extols the virtues of (inner) city living for lone parents in that it affords better access to opportunities (Rose and Le Bourdais, 1988), there seems to be a higher level of satisfaction expressed by lone parents living outside the city. This is food for thought for geographers.

Family life

This life concern was found to make a particularly positive contribution to the quality of lone-parent life; 87 per cent of lone parents were concerned with the issue and satisfied with their experience of it (Table 5.4). As for opportunities, it is thus worthwhile to reflect on this issue at greater length. Once again, a mapping of family life is presented and discussed (Figure 5.3). However, the key issues worth exploring for family life are less to do with the divisions among lone parents as a more homogenous experience was reported; there is (relatively) less scope to improve the overall quality of life of lone parents via this domain. Attention is therefore paid to the changing nature of family life after the transition to lone parenthood (Figure 5.4) and the links between family and economy (Table 5.6).

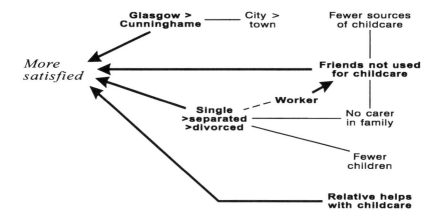

Note: See Figure 5.1 for source, cases and explanatory notes.

Figure 5.3: *Explanations for the differences in expressed satisfaction among lone parents*

Although it is the shared positive experience that is the key finding to emerge from lone parents' evaluation of their family life, it should be noted that there are still significant differences among lone parents in terms of their expressed satisfaction. Lone parents from the city (*vis-à-vis* smaller towns), those whose family plays a more central role in childcare, and lone parents who were never partnered, all express more satisfaction with family life. Once again, the results throw open the possibility that there is a geography of family relations worthy of closer exploration. They also draw attention to the significance of childcare in the wider family life of lone parents. Table 5.6 picks up on this latter point by presenting results that demonstrate that higher levels of satisfaction with local family support

98   *John McKendrick*

Relations with wider family

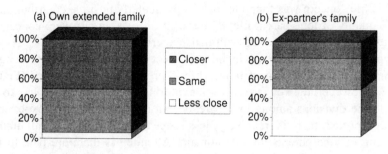

Happiness in the lone parent family

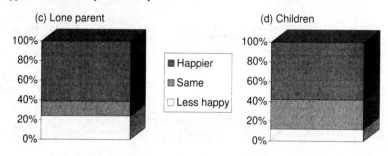

Parenting

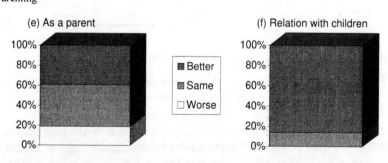

Notes: Base = 35 lone parents. Lone parents were asked to compare contemporary (as a lone parent) and life experiences to those before they became a lone parent. Parts d–f exclude those who became a lone parent on the birth of their first child.

Source: LPQoL Questionnaires (control).

Figure 5.4: *Changing experiences of family life on entry to lone parenthood*

were expressed when the lone parent's mother performed an active child-care role. Also presented are results that link economy and the family, drawing attention to the higher level of satisfaction expressed by working lone parents. These, of course, may be interrelated in that working lone parents may have more occasion to draw upon the services of relatives for childcare support.

Table 5.6: *The quality of local family support available to lone parents: variations by economic status and childcare arrangements, row % (lone parents)*

| | | Level of satisfaction with local family support | | |
		Dissatisfied	Neutral	Satisfied
Economic status:	Working	7	8	85
	Not working	28	15	57
Childcare resources:	Mother helps out	10	5	85
	No support from mother	22	17	61

Notes: Parents were asked to express their satisfaction using a seven-point scale, ranging from –3 (very dissatisfied) to +3 (very satisfied). In the table, 'satisfied' refers to parents who responded positively (+1, +2, +3).
1) $c2 = 16.30554$: $df = 4$: Sign. = 0.0003 : Base 239
2) $c2 = 13.98889$: $df = 4$: Sign. = 0.0009 : Base 200

Source: LPQoL Questionnaires (pilot and main versions).

These insights are significant, though they tend to detract from the key finding that lone parents were largely satisfied with their experience of family life. Figure 5.4 develops this theme a little further to present a more detailed look at lone parents' family life. The dynamics of family life relative to the life course transition to lone parenthood are the subject of concern; while transitions to lone parenthood may be linked to downward mobility in the housing market (Bradshaw and Millar, 1991) and may introduce problems regarding lifelong earning potential (Evandrou and Falkingham, 1995), it seems that it also leads to closer relations between the lone parent and the wider family, increased levels of happiness in the lone-parent family unit and better relations between the lone parent and her/his children (see Clarke et al in Chapter 14 here). A lone parent's lot, it would appear, is not all bad news in the eyes of lone parents themselves.

PLANES OF DIVISION

Attention is now turned from exploring the range of factors pertinent to understanding a particular issue (for example, work status and childcare status, family life), toward the wider impact of particular factors across a broad range of issues (for example, work status or family life and health). Following Ford and Millar's introduction in Chapter 1, it is particularly useful to consider the significance of work status and childcare status given the centrality of these issues to lone-parent policy debates. In addition, some thought is also given to the significance of the residential environment of lone parents. For each 'plane of division', comment is made when there is significant difference in experiences between groups of lone parents (for example, between those in paid employment and those who are not).

Work status

As has been referred to above, substantial differences in life experiences can be discerned between lone parents in paid employment and those who are not. As expected, these are evident for economic domains (financial situation, work and having opportunities) and 'material' domains (housing, health and services). However, the positive influence of work extends far beyond this, for working lone parents are more satisfied than non-working lone parents with family life (as previously discussed), advice and support available to them, and others' attitude towards them. According to the experiences of lone parents, it is an issue of far-ranging significance, which should add weight to the arguments of those concerned to encourage higher rates of paid labour market participation among lone parents.

Childcare status

Whether or not lone parents have access to childcare has a strong bearing on the level of satisfaction expressed for advice and support, control over life and having opportunities (and family life which was discussed previously). It was the factor that was most strongly associated with satisfaction for advice and support. Together, the results are suggestive of an important role for childcare in lone parents' lives – a supporting role that enables lone parents to capitalise on opportunities and thereby instilling a sense of control over their lives. It is an interesting but not altogether illogical paradox that by relying on others (for childcare support), a heightened sense of control emerges; without such support, lone parents are at risk from social exclusion in the broadest possible sense of engagement with wider society. Bearing in mind that these three issues are concerns that matter much to lone parents (Table 5.2) should add further weight to the need to consider childcare provision as a means to enhance the quality of life of lone parents.

Place of residence

Robertson (1984) is one of the few commentators to examine explicitly the significance of residential environment upon lone parents' lives (though see McKendrick, 1994a for a more detailed review, and 1995 for a discussion at the subregional scale of analysis). Once the interaction between personal and environmental variables is controlled (disentangling the effect of living in an impoverished neighbourhood from the effect of being a poor lone parent, for example), the residential environment is still found to have a bearing on lone parents' life experiences. Not unexpectedly, greater dissatisfaction is expressed with housing and services by lone parents living in deprived areas. Also, not unexpectedly, but nevertheless worthy of comment, is that these same lone parents also express greater dissatisfaction with health (links between poor environments and poor health resonate immediately). In each case (housing, services and health), residing in an area of deprivation is more closely associated with expressed dissatisfaction than any other factor. However, the significance of residential environment extends beyond these domains. Lone parents who live in deprived areas are also more dissatisfied with others' attitude toward them; this may be indicative of people's attitudes toward all residents of such deprived areas; however, it may also be attributed to the lack of understanding shown specifically toward lone parents in areas where they are prevalent (although contrast this with the findings of neighbourly relations from Table 5.3). A geography of social attitudes towards lone parents is raised as a possibility. Finally, where lone parents live in areas served by a local lone-parent support group, more lone parents express satisfaction with advice and support, and having opportunities to better themselves. The role played by such organisations is as yet too marginal in debates on how to improve a lone parent's lot.

POLICY POSTSCRIPTS

The contribution of this study of lone parents' quality of life to lone-parent policy debate (as with all quality of life work) is twofold. First, it aims to provide a context for policy debate. By necessity, policy debate is focused. However, it is important to grasp the wider significance of the particular policy proposal, both in terms of its relative significance to lone parents' lives and in terms of the wider (perhaps unintentional) effect that such a proposal may have. Second, and following on from this, quality of life research provides supporting evidence for policy proposals based on the broader impact that such measures are likely to have on lone parents' lives.

The paper established that it is valid to conceive of a lone-parent quality of life and that therefore it is valid to conceive of 'lone parent' as a unit of analysis. While differences were evident among lone parents, there was considerable shared experience of life – particularly for some domains – and consistent differences *vis-à-vis* partnered parents. It is significant that this more expansive review of matters that concern lone parents reaches such a conclusion, whereas more tightly focused policy studies (for example, McKay and Rowlingson in Chapter 3) tend to argue that lone parents' problems are shared with other groups in the population, albeit experienced by lone parents with greater intensity. This is not a 'circle that must be squared'; rather, it suggests that while much policy could be generic, there remain 'lone parent' issues, currently beyond the reach of social policy, which impinge upon their quality of life.

However, this is not to suggest that current policy priorities are mis-guided. Without question, the key division among lone parents is their economic status. Working lone parents reported more satisfaction across a wide range of life concerns; they report a higher overall quality of life. This chapter reinforces the importance accorded to this issue in contem-porary social policy (the 'New Deal for Lone Parents') and policy debate. The policy debate may be moving in the right direction, but as many have testified to date, there are considerable difficulties and contradictions to be faced and overcome in the process. A more expansive evaluation of policy initiatives is also required, as illustrated by the findings for childcare. Childcare was found to contribute in various ways to lone parents' lives, suggesting that the question of childcare is of much more relevance than (merely) as a means to increase lone parents' labour market participation.

In conclusion, it is important to return to the guiding premise of the chapter: the positive aspects of lone parents' lives must not be overlooked in attempting to improve their lot. Although lone parents fared less well compared with partnered parents, and although they are clearly a deprived group in terms of poverty experiences, it was nevertheless established that lone parents were not dissatisfied with their lives; indeed, if anything, lone parents' experiences tend to err toward satisfaction. Of particular note was the finding that lone parents were able to express considerable satisfaction with their experiences of family life. Further exploration of this issue draws attention to the uncharted territory of the geography of family life. The residential environments within which lone parents live their lives are not passive contexts; rather, the nature of the local environment contributes in various important ways to the lone parents' quality of life. Lone-parent policy must accommodate all such concerns: seeking to maintain the 'quality' that is already evident in lone parents' lives, broadening its focus to incorporate hitherto neglected but important issues (such as the local context of life), while engaging with mainstream social objectives. It is a tall order, but a new deal (of which the 'New Deal for Lone Parents' is but part) is well overdue.

Chapter 6

Marital Dissolution and Income Change: Evidence for Britain

Sarah Jarvis and Stephen P Jenkins[1]

The relationship between marital dissolution and the economic well-being of parents and their children is one of the central issues of British social policy. Being a lone parent is associated with a high risk of having a low income, not working and receiving social assistance benefits, as other chapters here reiterate. Policy responses have included the establishment of the Child Support Agency (CSA), changes to divorce law, and introduction of targeted job search programmes for lone parents. Unfortunately, empirical evidence for Britain about what happens to people's incomes when their partnerships dissolve is rare, and has largely been based on cross sectional data comparing married people and separated people at the same point in time.[2] This chapter provides new evidence about the income changes accompanying marital dissolution using a dataset that follows the same people over time, the British Household Panel Survey (BHPS).

Earlier studies of this kind for the United States, Germany and Canada typically use samples of all marital splits, that is samples including childless couples as well as couples with dependent children (see *inter alia* Burkhauser et al, 1990, 1991; and Finnie, 1993). In our own work with the BHPS using the same type of sample, we find, as these studies do, that separation is associated with substantial declines in income on average for separating women and children and that the incomes of separating men change much less (Jarvis and Jenkins, 1997). In this chapter, our analysis focuses instead on the subsample of couples who have dependent children

1. Research financed by the Joseph Rowntree Foundation. Financial and other research support were also provided by the Economic and Social Research Council, the University of Essex, and the British Academy. For comments and helpful discussions, we are grateful to conference and seminar audiences, our JRF project advisory group, and the editors.
2. An important exception is the longitudinal study based on divorce court records by Gregory and Foster (1990). For a critique of its methodology, see Jarvis and Jenkins (1997).

before they split, and we find that the differential income changes between fathers on the one hand, and mothers and children on the other, are even more marked. We also show that, although the tax-benefit system mitigates these differentials in outcomes, significant differentials remain. We document the changes in benefit receipt, labour market participation and maintenance transfers that occurred in parallel with the marital split.

DATA, DEFINITIONS AND METHODS

Our research is based on data from the first four waves (1991–4) of the British Household Panel Survey (BHPS). The first wave of the BHPS was designed as a nationally representative sample of the population of Great Britain living in private households in 1991, and had an achieved sample size of some 5500 households covering some 10,000 persons.[3] Original sample members in the BHPS (OSMs) are the adult respondents in the wave 1 sample and their children. All OSMs are 'followed' at the second and subsequent waves, and annual interviews are conducted with all adult members of households containing either an OSM or the child of an OSM. This 'following rule' is typical of household panel surveys and is designed to maintain representativeness of the population. Any person who joined the panel after wave 1 but subsequently stopped living with an OSM is not followed and interviewed again.

We define a marital split as a transition from a legal marriage or cohabiting union observed at the wave t interview to living apart from the wave t spouse at the wave $t+1$ interview, where t runs from 1 to 3. Our analysis is confined to couples who have dependent children, and whose children live with both parents (one of whom may be a step-parent) at wave t, and with one of their parents at wave $t+1$.[4] We document in detail what happened between waves t and $t+1$ to the incomes of (i) mothers (ii) fathers and (iii) their dependent children. The BHPS is, as yet, too 'new' to look at how incomes changed over a longer period, but since even brief poverty spells may have long-term effects, the short-term picture we provide is valuable.

We use three measures of economic status. The first is household *net income*, which is the sum across household members of income from employment and self-employment, investments and savings, private and

---

3. For a detailed discussion of BHPS methodology, representativeness, and the weighting and imputation procedures provided to account for differential unit non-response, attrition, and item non-response, see Taylor (1994) and Taylor (1996).

4. A dependent child is aged less than 16 years, or more than 16 years but under 19 years and unmarried, in full-time non-advanced education and living with their parents. We exclude from the analysis a small number of dependent children at t who are co-resident with a parent at $t+1$ but are non-dependent at $t+1$.

occupational pensions, other market income and private transfers (including maintenance income),[5] plus cash social security and social assistance receipts from the state, less income tax payments, employee national insurance contributions, and local taxes. This is the income measure used in official income distribution statistics in the UK (for example DSS, 1995b). The second income measure is *original income*, which is net income before taxes have been deducted and cash benefits added, that is income from the market. The third measure is *gross income*, which is original income plus benefit income from the state. All three income measures are measured prior to the deduction of housing costs.[6] By comparing the income changes using these different income measures we can look at the impact of the welfare state on post-separation income for fathers, mothers and children.

The time period over which income is measured is the month before the interview or the most recent relevant period (except for employment earnings that are 'usual earnings'), and we have converted all figures to a weekly equivalent basis, indexed to January 1995 price levels. We use an equivalence scale to adjust income for differences in the size and composition of households. The scale principally used is Britain's semi-official one, the so-called 'McClements (before housing costs)' equivalence scale, normalised so that the scale rate equals one for single adult households. Observe that changes in household composition occurring in parallel with a marital split can affect equivalent income via both changes in money income *per se* (changing the contributors to the household income pool) and changes in the equivalence scale rate. Since there is no unique 'correct' equivalence scale (Coulter et al, 1992a) it is important to investigate the robustness of results to the choice of equivalence scale. We do this by repeating our calculations for each of five members of the Buhmann et al (1988) family of equivalence scales (see below for further details).

Finally, and following standard practice, each person is attributed the income of the household to which he or she belongs. The implicit assumption is that incomes within households are pooled and equally shared, and

---

5. Maintenance payments have not been deducted from the measures of income for data consistency reasons (the requisite information is not available for wave 1). We are confident that this does not lead to bias because the amounts of maintenance paid are typically not large and relatively few liable non-custodial parents pay maintenance. Conclusions are unaltered if calculations are repeated for wave 2–4 data using income measures from which maintenance payments have been deducted. See Jarvis and Jenkins (1997) for full details.

6. In Jarvis and Jenkins (1997) we also report income change calculations based on an 'after housing costs' income measure. Husbands do not do as well as estimated using a 'before housing costs' income measure, but the differences are relatively small and the substantial differential between the experience of men and women remains.

this may of course not reflect actual practice. For example, a woman who had a less than equal share of household income when she was married might in fact increase her own income when her partnership dissolves (even if total household income were to fall). We do not address this issue here: see Jarvis and Jenkins (1997) for further discussion.

Sample numbers and characteristics

The numbers of separating fathers, mothers and children who experienced a marital split in waves 1 to 4 of the BHPS are given in Table 6.1. The first row shows the number of separating fathers, mothers, and children

Table 6.1: *Numbers of parents experiencing a marital split*
(BHPS, waves 1–4)

Parents experiencing a marital split between waves t and $t+1$	Husbands	Wives	Children
1. Original sample members at wave t eligible to be interviewed at wave $t+1$	116	117	232
2. As (1) and with an interview at wave $t+1$ of any kind (full, proxy or telephone interview)	69	107	197
3. As (2) and has valid original and gross income data at waves t and $t+1$	66	104	189
4. As (2) and has valid net income data at waves t and $t+1$	51	85	151

Note: For the definitions of an original sample member, a marital split, and original, gross and net income, see text. The children column refers to the children of couples experiencing a marital split (see text). Row 1 excludes cases where neither partner of the splitting partnership provided an interview at $t+1$.

where at least one partner was traced at the wave after the split. If both spouses in a partnership leave the panel (namely attrit), we cannot tell if they also split up. Separating fathers were considerably more likely to attrit than mothers: interviews were conducted with approximately 60 per cent of fathers, but 90 per cent of mothers. The sample is reduced further by incomplete response during interviews (see the third and fourth rows), but this occurred at similar rates for men and women. The relatively high attrition rate for separating men is common to other panel studies of this kind (see for example Burkhauser et al, 1990). Comparisons with our earlier work (Jarvis and Jenkins, 1997), which used a sample of all separating men, reveal that men with children were more likely to attrit than men without children. This may be partly attributable to the establishment of the CSA in the early 1990s.

Attrition will bias the results of our analysis if there is a correlation between characteristics associated with attrition and income change. However, our earlier work using a sample of all marital splits suggests that attrition is not a serious problem (Jarvis and Jenkins, 1997). Although there were some small demographic differences between the sample of all persons who experienced a marital split and all persons who provided interview data, the distributions of income were remarkably similar for the two groups. In our analysis we account for non-random attrition by using the BHPS longitudinal enumerated individual weights for wave t+1 in our calculations.

A further issue raised by Table 6.1 concerns the small sample numbers, particularly for men. Small samples are typical for panel data analyses such as ours, and numbers are further reduced by the focus on marital splits involving dependent children. We attempt to minimise sampling errors by limiting the number of subgroup breakdowns, and in order to minimise the influence of outlier values, we present information about medians rather than means.

INCOME CHANGES ACCOMPANYING A MARITAL SPLIT

Income changes are summarised in several ways in Table 6.2, for each of the original, gross, and net income measures. In discussing the results in more detail we focus on net income, for this is the measure of economic status most commonly used in Britain, but it is clear that the same story could be told using the gross and original income estimates.

The first two rows of the table show the average (median) incomes before and after the marital split for separating mothers, fathers and children. We see that while the pre-split incomes of fathers and mothers are broadly similar, mothers and children suffer substantial declines in real net income after the split (about £20 per week on average), whereas the real income for fathers increases (by about £10 per week).[7]

Approximately two-fifths of men in our sample experienced a decrease in net income following a marital split, compared with two-thirds of women and children (Table 6.1, third row).[8] If we examine the distri-

---

7. Average pre-split incomes for husbands and wives are only broadly equal rather than exactly equal because of sampling error and differential attrition.

8. Our estimates are based on a sample that includes a small number of people who are living with a new partner at wave *t*+1, and it would be interesting to explore whether post-split incomes are higher for this group: some North American studies have shown that repartnering is associated with higher income, especially over the longer term (see for example Duncan and Hoffman, 1985; and Finnie, 1993). When we exclude the persons who repartner from our calculations, we find that the estimates change very little, but in the expected direction.

bution of income changes (fourth row), we find that the median change in net income for fathers is a 14 per cent increase, but for mothers it is a 17 per cent decrease. Since most children live with their mothers rather than their fathers after their parents' partnership dissolves, children experience falls in net income of a similar magnitude to mothers. To put these figures into perspective, note that the median net income change between wave 1 and wave 2 for all couples with children was an increase of 3 per cent.

Table 6.2: *Comparison of pre- and post-marital split incomes for separating husbands, wives and children (BHPS, waves 1–4)*

	Husbands	Wives	Children
Original Income			
Pre-split median income (£ per week)	136	149	102
Post-split median income (£ per week)	164	35	17
Percentage with income decrease	40	80	78
Median percentage change	25	−74	−77
Gross Income			
Pre-split median income (£ per week)	149	161	126
Post-split median income (£ per week)	181	107	95
Percentage with income decrease	38	69	63
Median percentage change	13	−25	−21
Net Income			
Pre-split median income (£ per week)	116	120	110
Post-split median income (£ per week)	128	99	92
Percentage with income decrease	41	66	67
Median percentage change	14	−17	−14

Note: Original, gross and net income defined in text. Incomes equivalised using the McClements scale, and indexed to January 1995 price levels. Data weighted using BHPS longitudinal enumerated individual weights for wave *t*+1.

There is considerable heterogeneity in income changes about these averages for all three subgroups. Calculations supplementing those presented in Table 6.2 show that one-quarter of mothers experienced an increase in their net income of at least 19 per cent and another quarter experienced net income falls of at least 38 per cent. Although the median net income change for separating fathers was positive, about 40 per cent of this group experienced an income fall, and one-quarter experienced income falls of at least 29 per cent. However, one-quarter experienced income increases of at least 47 per cent. Thus, while there is much heterogeneity in income change accompanying a marital split, the distributions of changes for mothers and children are clearly displaced leftwards in the direction of relative disadvantage compared with the fathers' distribution.

CHANGING INCOMES OR CHANGING NEEDS?

When couples with children split up they typically form two households of different sizes (particularly in the short term), with the larger household usually headed by the mother, who takes primary responsibility for the care of the children. (Approximately 95 per cent of children in our sample live with their mother post separation.) Separating married men with children are the subgroup likely to experience the largest decrease in household size between wave *t* and *t*+1, and are the group with the largest income gains on average (Jarvis and Jenkins, 1997). This raises the issue of whether our income change estimates, and the differentials between the sexes, are the result of pure income changes or of household composition-related changes. We therefore investigate now whether our picture of differential income changes is simply the result of making the particular assumptions about economies of scale which are incorporated in the McClements equivalence scale. To do this, we have recalculated the income change statistics using a range of equivalence scales from the Buhmann et al (1988) class, characterised by the formula:

household equivalence scale rate = (number of household members)$^\theta$, $0 \le \theta \le 1$.

The smaller the value of θ, the greater the extent to which 'two can live as cheaply as one', ie the greater the economies of scale in the equivalence scale. This parametric scale provides a good approximation to most equivalence scales in use, including the McClements scale for which the corresponding θ value is between 0.6 and 0.7 (Coulter et al, 1992b; Jenkins and Cowell, 1994).

Figure 6.1 shows how the estimate of the median change in net income accompanying a marital split varies with the choice of equivalence scale, plotted using five values of θ ranging from zero (corresponding to no adjustment to money incomes, ie infinite economies of scale) to one (the per capita scale rate case). Tthough the choice of scale makes a large difference to the size of the differential between fathers on the one hand and mothers and children on the other, the differential itself clearly remains. As expected, the choice of scale has a greater impact on income change estimates for fathers, for whom the median net income change ranges from a one-third decrease (if $\theta = 0$) to a one-fourth increase (if $\theta = 1$). For mothers and children, the median change is always negative and, even in the per capita case, the average decrease is one-fourth for mothers and one-fifth for children. Figure 6.1 shows that the estimate of fathers' median income change is negative only when θ is less than 0.5 (i e less than the θ value corresponding to the McClements scale). In sum, though our estimates are sensitive in absolute terms to changes in the equivalence scale, the differential between fathers and mothers and children is not. And the differential is substantial for the mostly commonly used equivalence scales (corresponding to θ values between 0.25 and 0.75).

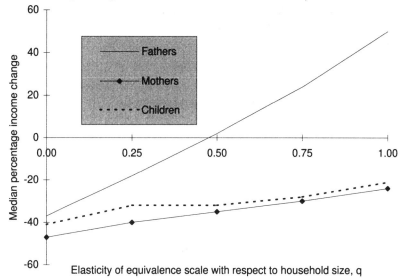

Figure 6.1: *Median percentage income change estimates: sensitivity to changes in economies of size parameter*

The calculations also tell us that were we to look simply at money income changes – the case where incomes are not adjusted for differences in needs (θ = 0) – virtually all separating parents would experience a decrease in money income. But as the weight given to the needs of additional household members is increased, for fathers the impact of 'needs'-related changes (typically a decline in the number of dependents) tends to offset the money income changes, whereas this is not the case for mothers or children.

THE ROLE OF THE WELFARE STATE

In this section, we consider how the relationship between marital splits and income changes is affected by tax and benefit policies. We follow Burkhauser et al (1990, 1991) in using comparisons between our three different income measures (net, original and gross) to assess the influence of taxes and benefits on the income differentials identified above. Clearly, this provides only 'first approximations of the net influence of govern-

Sarah Jarvis and Stephen P Jenkins

ment. This must be the case since it is implicitly assumed that no behavioral changes would take place in the absence of government intervention' (Burkhauser et al, 1990: 322n).

Table 6.3: *The impact of government cash benefits and direct taxes on the incomes of separated mothers and of children, relative to separated fathers (BHPS, waves 1–4)*

	Gap between median income changes			% of gap closed by policy		
	(1)	(2)	(3)	(4)	(5)	(6)
Equivalence scale	Original income	Gross income	Net income	Cash transfers	Cash transfers, direct taxes	Direct taxes
				$100*[1-\frac{(2)}{(1)}]$	$100*[1-\frac{(3)}{(1)}]$	$100*[1-\frac{(2)}{(2)}]$
			Mothers relative to fathers			
McClements	99	38	31	62	69	18
Buhmann et al						
$\theta = 0$	57	25	10	56	83	60
0.25	77	36	22	53	71	36
0.5	69	51	37	26	56	28
0.75	121	73	54	40	55	26
1	152	96	74	37	51	23
			Children relative to fathers			
McClements	102	34	28	67	73	18
Buhmann et al						
$\theta = 0$	60	17	4	72	93	76
0.25	86	23	14	66	77	31
0.5	75	42	34	54	63	19
0.75	128	63	52	46	59	24
1	154	93	71	40	54	24

Notes: The first three columns are derived from Table 6.2 and additional calculations for alternative equivalence scales and show the arithmetic difference between the median percentage income change for men and the median percentage income change for women (top panel) and children (bottom panel).

In Table 6.3 we summarise the differential income changes of separating mothers relative to fathers (first panel) and children relative to fathers (second panel). First we calculate the simple arithmetic difference between the median percentage income change for fathers and mothers, and fathers and children (columns 1–3). To assess the impact of the welfare state we then compute the proportion of the gap that is closed by (i) cash transfers (the difference between original and gross income), (ii) cash transfers and direct taxes (the difference between original and net income) and (iii) direct taxes (the difference between gross and net income).

Column 4 suggests that the size of the income change gap for mothers relative to fathers that is reduced by cash transfers is larger the greater the economies of scale, ranging from around one-third (37 per cent if θ = 1) to one-half (56 per cent if θ = 0), and a bit larger for the McClements scale (62 per cent). The same pattern emerges when we look at the reduction in the gap for children relative to fathers, but here the percentage reductions are slightly larger.

We can also examine the combined impact of direct taxes and transfers (Table 6.3, fifth column) and of direct taxes alone. It is clear that if one takes a broader definition of the welfare state, including taxation as well as transfers, then policy is more successful in reducing the gap between the sexes: figures in the fifth column are always larger than their counterparts in the fourth column. It is also clear that for mothers and children, cash transfers play a greater gap-reducing role than direct taxes (compare fourth and sixth columns) for all equivalence scales besides the no-adjustment case (θ = 0).[9] In the next section we look at the role played by cash transfers more directly, documenting changes in the receipt of welfare benefits accompanying a marital split.

CHANGING INCOME SOURCES: THE GOVERNMENT, THE LABOUR MARKET AND FORMER PARTNERS

One of the key factors underlying the differential income changes experienced by men and women when they separate is the change in the pattern of receipt of income from different sources. Of particular policy interest is the extent to which becoming a lone parent reduces labour market participation and increases dependence on social assistance benefits. Here we concentrate on three of the major sources of people's incomes: the labour market, the government and transfers from other members of their family. We first document in turn the changes in the incidence of social assistance benefit receipt, participation in paid work, and the receipt and payments of maintenance income.

The first two panels of Table 6.4 document how reliance on social assistance benefits changes with a marital split. The first section refers to income support or receipt of both unemployment benefit and income support. (Since the family is the unit of assessment, receipt refers to receipt by either spouse.) We find that before the split a slightly higher

---

9. Table 6.3-type calculations are reported by Burkhauser et al (1990) using panel data for Germany (1983–6) and for the USA (1981–5), but comparisons between our results and theirs are compromised by the fact that their samples refer to all marital splits, rather than only dissolutions involving dependent children, as here. (There are also some other differences in definitions used and differences in time period covered.) For a comparison of results using a sample of all marital splits, see Jarvis and Jenkins (1997).

Table 6.4. *Welfare benefit receipt, participation in paid work, and maintenance before and after a marital split (BHPS, waves 1–4)*

Column percentages	Husbands	Wives
*Income support or unemployment benefit with income support**		
not receiving at *t*, not receiving at *t*+1	68	41
not receiving at *t*, receiving at *t*+1	7	30
receiving at *t*, not receiving at *t*+1	5	5
receiving at *t*, receiving at *t*+1	19	25
*Housing benefit, income support or unemployment benefit with income support**		
not receiving at *t*, not receiving at *t*+1	62	38
not receiving at *t*, receiving at *t*+1	9	30
receiving at *t*, not receiving at *t*+1	5	4
receiving at *t*, receiving at *t*+1	24	28
Paid work		
not working at *t*, not working at *t*+1	21	45
not working at *t*, working at *t*+1	4	5
working at *t*, not working at *t*+1	14	19
working at *t*, working at *t*+1	61	30
Receives maintenance at t+1		
yes	1	14
no	99	86
Receives maintenance at t+1 (husbands and wives with dependent children at t+1)		
yes	5	24
no	95	76
Payment of maintenance (husbands and wives with dependent children at t)		
not paying maintenance at *t* or *t*+1	73	95
not paying maintenance at *t*, paying at *t*+1	24	3
paying maintenance at *t*, not paying at *t*+1	3	2
paying maintenance at *t*, and *t*+1	1	0

Notes: *Benefit receipt refers to receipt by the respondent or respondent's spouse. Data weighted using BHPS longitudinal enumerated individual weights for wave *t*+1.

proportion of mothers were in receipt of benefit compared with fathers (30 and 24 per cent respectively), but this differential widened considerably after the split, when 55 per cent of mothers but only 26 per cent of fathers reported receipt of these benefits. Almost one-third of separating mothers move on to benefit, compared with just 7 per cent of fathers. A similar picture emerges when the definition of benefit receipt is widened to include housing benefit. In this case, almost 60 per cent of women are in receipt after the split but only 30 per cent of men.

Before the marital split, 75 per cent of fathers were working compared with 47 per cent of mothers (where 'working' is defined as employment or self employment, whether part or full time), reflecting the fact that mothers typically have primary responsibility for childcare. After the split, only around 65 per cent of fathers worked and 35 per cent of mothers, so that separation appears to disrupt mothers' careers more than fathers' careers.[10]

Receipt of maintenance from a former partner is potentially an important source of income for lone mothers. As in other UK studies, we find that the incidence of maintenance receipt is low. Only about one-quarter of mothers receive some maintenance after the split (compare Bradshaw and Millar, 1991, with McKay and Marsh, 1994, who report figures of between one-quarter and one-third).

The incidence of maintenance payment is summarised in the bottom panel of Table 6.4. Given the relatively low labour market participation rate of mothers post-separation, receipt of support from their former partner may be crucial in preventing a large decline in income. We find that only about one-quarter of fathers were paying maintenance after the current marital split (a few were paying maintenance to other former partners before the split). This proportion matches the percentage of mothers receiving maintenance cited above.

Our results show that marital separation is accompanied by substantial changes in incomes for mothers, reflected in a relatively high incidence of social assistance receipt, low labour participation rates and a low likelihood of receiving maintenance. Fathers are at lower risk of an income decrease and are more likely to have paid work after their partnership breaks down. Concern about the adverse effect of separation on mothers and children has prompted the government to increase in-work benefits for families with children (such as family credit), to establish the CSA

---

10. Some readers may find the proportion of fathers not working prior to the marital split, 25 per cent, to be very high. The figure reflects the relative youth of our sample who are at relatively high risk of unemployment (Jarvis and Jenkins, 1997). Also the period covered by our data covers the trough of the macro-economic cycle followed by slow recovery.

and, more recently, to offer additional job search resources to single parents. Arguably, these initiatives have not yet had significant success.

Perhaps the most pressing policy issue concerns lone mothers who receive social assistance benefits after they separate from their former partners. The CSA has concentrated its efforts on the former partners of these women, but under the current rules separated mothers receiving income support receive no net gain from higher maintenance as their benefit is reduced pound for pound. Gains for those receiving family credit are limited to the amount of the maintenance disregard. Hence, although the gap between the incomes of separated fathers and mothers is reduced where the CSA successfully mandates payment, this is achieved by making absent fathers poorer rather than by making lone mothers better off.

Given the manifest difficulties involved in enforcing maintenance payments, perhaps a more effective strategy would be to concentrate on policies aimed at raising lone mothers' labour market earnings. However, raising participation requires not only that that appropriate jobs are available, but also that women can afford to take them and also that they can pay for suitable childcare when they are working.

SUMMARY AND CONCLUDING COMMENTS

We have provided new evidence for Britain about the financial consequences of marital separation for parents and their children using a nationally representative longitudinal survey. Marital splits are associated with substantial declines in real income for mothers and children on average, whereas fathers' real income on average changes much less. A focus on average income changes disguises heterogeneity in outcomes – there are gainers as well as losers among fathers, mothers and children – but the income distributions for separated mothers and children are nonetheless distinctly displaced in the direction of disadvantage relative to the distribution for separated fathers.

These broad conclusions are robust to the choice of income definition and to the degree of economies of scale built into the household equivalence scale. And, although there is significant attrition from the BHPS, by separating fathers in particular, and although our sample numbers are relatively small, these factors are unlikely to change our conclusions about the differential income changes between separating fathers and mothers.

We have also documented the extent to which the British welfare state mitigates the differential impact of marital splits on mothers' and children's incomes relative to fathers'. Although the welfare state significantly reduces income differentials, substantial differentials remain, and comparisons with our earlier work based on the sample of all separating couples suggest that separating mothers experience greater income falls than childless separating women (Jarvis and Jenkins, 1997). Our analysis of the pattern of receipt of incomes from social assistance benefits, paid work and former partners are indicative of well-known inequalities between fathers and mothers in the labour market and in the home (Holden and Smock, 1991). These include the greater career labour market attachment of fathers compared with mothers, the greater earnings of working fathers than working mothers, mothers' greater responsibility for caring for children (especially after the marital split), and the failure of many separated fathers to pay sufficient maintenance to their former partner to support their children.

Chapter 7

Small Fortunes: Spending on Children in Lone-Parent Families

Sue Middleton and Karl Ashworth

Much available evidence about the living standards of children in lone-parent families, as in other types, has been extrapolated from studies of family income and consumption. It is assumed that an individual family member shares the same standard of living as the family as a whole and, therefore, children's living standards mirror those of their parents. If this assumption is correct, and given that lone-parent families on average have lower living standards than two-parent families, then children in lone-parent families must experience a lower standard of living than those in two-parent ones. Yet, small-scale studies suggest that equal sharing of living standards among family members is open to question; parents, particularly lone ones, are said to sacrifice their own consumption in order to protect and improve their children's living standards (Dobson et al, 1994; Dowler and Calvert, 1995; Kempson et al, 1994; Middleton et al, 1994). A lack of direct evidence about the resources that are allocated to children within families has made it impossible to test these findings by comparing the living standards of children in lone and two-parent families.

The findings of a survey funded by the Joseph Rowntree Foundation and undertaken by the authors in 1995 allow such comparisons to be made. This nationally-representative survey was the first in Britain to focus on the lifestyles and living standards of individual children, rather than of the whole family.[1] In this chapter, we describe some of the survey findings about the living standards of children in lone and two-parent families. The figures are based on survey data relating to 526 children living in lone-parent families and 713 children in two-parent families. These data have been weighted to be representative of all children in Britain and, with a few noted exceptions, the figures presented here are weighted.

---

1. Further details of the survey are available from the authors.

In the first section, we compare average spending on children from birth to 17 years for a range of regularly purchased goods, services and activities. We examine the financial contribution made by people other than parents to children's budgets, and show how average spending on children in lone and two-parent families varies by the number of children in the family; age; income support receipt; labour market activity; whether or not the mother smokes; and use of childcare. We conclude this section with descriptions of a model that takes into account the effect of all these characteristics on spending.

All our figures are weekly average amounts, following the conventions of household expenditure surveys, such as the Family Expenditure Survey (FES). It should be borne in mind that these average amounts conceal wide variations in spending which, again, will be the subject of later reports (Middleton and Ashworth, 1997).

In the second section of the chapter we outline some implications of the spending comparisons for social policies that provide support for families bringing up children, in particular for lone parents. Assumptions about the relative costs of children are made in all such social policies and our evidence enables us to test some of these assumptions by exploring how well they match the reality of average spending on children.

AVERAGE SPENDING ON CHILDREN

An average child receives 'regular' spending of £47.20 a week from parents between birth and her/his seventeenth birthday. Other people (absent parents, grandparents, other relatives, friends and the child her/himself) contribute a further £5.72 on average, or 10 per cent of total spending.

Our figures do not include everything that is spent on a child. We have chosen to concentrate on spending that might be expected to occur at least annually: food; clothing and shoes; nappies; school; activities; other regular spending on items such as toys, books, toiletries and video rental; Christmas; holidays; birthdays; telephone calls; baby sitting; and childcare. Spending on 'capital' items such as furniture, bedding and baby equipment is not included and will be the subject of later reports.

What is spent on an individual child in a family might be expected to vary by the total number of children in that family — the more children, the less we might expect to be spent on one individual child. Therefore, in much of what follows comparisons are made between children in one-child families (only children); two-child families; and families with three or more children.

Figure 7.1 shows that a child living in a lone-parent family can expect to receive lower average spending than a child living with two parents and the same number of siblings. However, the differences are quite small. Overall, lone-parent children receive about 10 per cent less than two-parent ones. The difference is smallest for children in two-child families (1 per cent) and largest for those in families with three or more children (17 per cent). Despite their lower incomes, lone parents seem to manage to spend similar average levels as two parents, but this becomes more difficult when there are three or more children in the family.

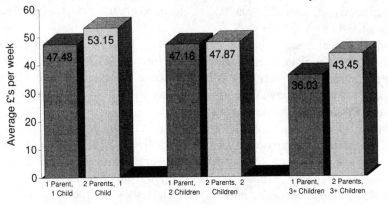

Figure 7.1: *Parents' weekly spending on children*

Table 7.1 shows how parents allocate spending to different areas of children's budgets. Children in lone-parent families receive lower spending on all items except telephone calls, other regular purchases, other money and baby sitting. However, the differences are small for most budget areas. Lone parents apparently succeed in maintaining spending on most budget areas by sacrificing holidays, on which lone-parent children receive 40 per cent less spending; and spending on the child's birthday, 21 per cent less. Children in lone-parent families also receive 19 per cent less spending for childcare. We return to the issue of childcare later in this section.

It seems that children in lone-parent families with three or more children fare particularly badly in comparison with their counterparts in two-parent families on most budget areas. Whereas only children in lone-parent families receive lower spending than those in two-parent families on seven of the 13 budget items, lone-parent children in three child families receive less on 11 of the budget areas. They receive slightly more spending only on telephone calls and school.

Average spending on school of £3 per week covers spending on items such as educational and leisure trips, sport, books and extra lessons. It does not include the cost of school uniform, transport or meals. Parents of secondary aged children spend almost £6 per week on school. In a recently published report, we have shown that children in lone-parent families receive almost as much spending as those in two-parent families, with parents concentrating on providing money for items that might be regarded as integral parts of the school curriculum, such as educational trips and extra lessons (Middleton and Ashworth, 1997).

Table 7.1. *Children's budgets*

	Child in:	
	Lone-Parent Family £'s per week	Two-Parent Family £'s per week
Food	17.06	18.62
Clothes and shoes	4.43	4.49
Nappies	0.90	1.05
School	3.09	3.53
Activities	4.47	4.59
Telephone	0.40	0.26
Other regular purchases	4.46	4.07
Other money	0.70	0.69
Holidays	3.17	5.27
Christmas	2.90	3.29
Birthdays	1.34	1.69
Baby sitting	0.60	0.55
Childcare	2.68	3.30
Total	46.20	51.40

Who contributes

The contributions that other people make to spending on children in lone and two-parent families changes the picture slightly (Figure 7.2). Children in lone-parent families receive almost 50 per cent more from others than those in two-parent families, with children in lone-parent families with three or more children receiving most. The financial contributions of grandparents, absent parents, other relatives, friends and the child's own spending reduces the difference in parents' average spending between children in lone and two-parent three-child families (17 per cent) to less than 3 per cent.

Grandparents make the largest contribution to spending on children in most family types, and spend more than absent parents on children in lone-parent families. On average, grandparents spend almost twice as much (£2.07 per week) on a lone-parent child as an absent parent (£1.14 per week). Spending by absent parents does not include maintenance or child support payments, which we have included as part of family income. Therefore, spending by absent parents reflects additional money spent on the child, perhaps on access visits.

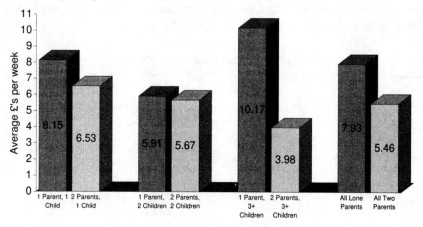

Figure 7.2: *What other people spend on children*

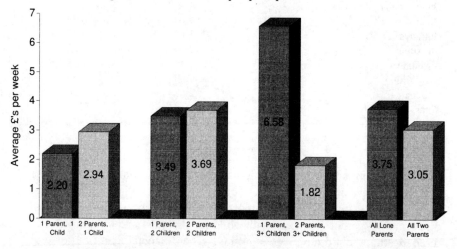

Figure 7.3: *What secondary aged children spend*

Grandparents spend much more on 'only' children, whether in a lone or two-parent family, than on a child with siblings. But, as Figure 7.2 shows, a child in a lone-parent, three-child family receives much more from other people in total than children in any other family type. This anomaly is accounted for by the much larger amounts secondary-aged children in these families are contributing to their own budgets (Figure 7.3).

Evidence from our earlier qualitative work suggested that older children from less affluent homes were less likely to be given control over their own budgets than those from richer homes, thereby restricting their opportunities to learn budgeting and financial management skills. At first sight, Figure 7.3 suggests that secondary-aged children in lone-parent families spend more on themselves than those in two-parent families. However, this is only the case for lone-parent children in three-child families who spend over three times as much as their counterparts in two-parent families. In other family types, children in two-parent families spend slightly more on themselves than those in lone-parent families. The explanation for this is unclear. It may be that older children in lone-parent three-child families are more likely to have part-time jobs, perhaps appreciating the need to contribute to the family budget more than children in other family types (this is explored further in Middleton and Croden, 1997).

Average spending and age

In general, spending increases with age, although not by as much as might have been anticipated (Figure 7.4). Ignoring spending on childcare for the time being, preschool children in both lone and two-parent families receive least, and secondary-aged children most. Lone parents spend 15 per cent more on babies than on preschool children, and 22 per cent more on primary than preschool children. In contrast, babies in two-parent families receive only 6 per cent more than preschool children, and primary children 11 per cent more than preschool children.

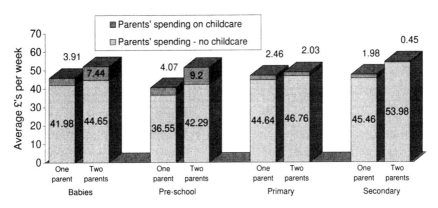

Figure 7.4: *Age and parents' spending on children*

However, the pattern of lone parents increasing spending on successive age groups by larger percentages than two parents is reversed at secondary school age. Lone parents spend only 2 per cent more on secondary-aged children than on primary children, whereas secondary-aged children in two-parent families receive 15 per cent more.

The largest difference between spending on children in lone and two-parent families occurs for secondary-aged children, with children in lone-parent families receiving 16 per cent less than those in two-parent families. The smallest difference is between spending on babies, who receive only 6 per cent less in lone parent than in two-parent families.

Taking account of spending on childcare changes the picture somewhat. Lone parents still spend least on preschool children and most on secondary-aged children, with the biggest increase in spending between the preschool and primary age groups. However, preschool children in two-parent families receive only 1 per cent less spending than babies. As Figure 7.4 shows, the reason for this is the higher levels of spending on childcare for babies and preschool children in two-parent families. Average amounts for childcare for primary children are similar for lone and two-parent families, but lone parents spend much more on care for secondary-aged children than two-parent families. Including spending on childcare, therefore, tends to increase the spending gap between babies and preschool children in lone and two-parent families; has little effect at the primary age; and decreases the gap for secondary-aged children.

However, very few parents pay for childcare so the average amounts spent by those who do pay are very much larger than the figures presented here. We return to a comparison of the use and cost of childcare later in this chapter.

Average spending and income support receipt

Some 65 per cent of lone-parent households in our weighted sample were on income support, representing 68 per cent of lone-parent children. Only 9 per cent of children in two-parent families were on income support. Figure 7.5 shows that differences in average spending between children in lone and two-parent families are reduced by taking into account whether the family is in receipt of income support. Children in lone-parent families on income support receive 6 per cent less spending than their counterparts in two-parent families; children in lone-parent non-income support families receive 6 per cent more spending than those in two-parent families not on income support.

It seems that living in a family that is on income support is more important than whether or not a child lives with one or two parents. Children in lone-parent families on income support receive 23 per cent less on average than those not on income support. Two-parent children on income support receive 13 per cent less than those not on income support. We also examined differences in average spending according to the number of

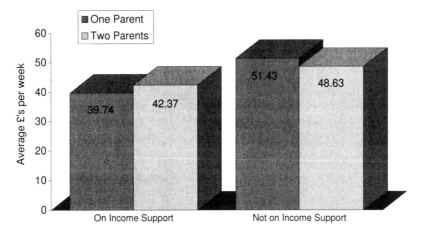

Figure 7.5: *Spending and income support*

children in the family. Although numbers in some cells are small, it seems that whether or not the family is on income support is more important than family size and number of parents, with the exception of lone-parent, three-child families. This is not to say that living in a lone-parent family has no effect on spending since, as we have seen, a far greater percentage of children in lone-parent families are on income support than in two-parent families. Therefore, a much larger proportion of children in lone-parent families will experience the lower average spending that seems to occur when a child lives in a family on income support.

Average spending and labour market activity

Figure 7.6 shows how spending on children varies according to the labour market activity of their parents. Before spending on childcare is taken into account, a child living with a lone parent who is in full-time work receives 5 per cent more spending than a child living with two parents who are both in full-time work; 18 per cent more than a child with two parents of whom one works full time and one not at all; and 36 per cent more than a lone-parent child whose parent does not work.

Children in two-parent families with no working adult receive 16 per cent less than those with two parents who are working full time. Children with one parent who is not working full time receive lower spending than children in two-parent families where both adults do not work full time, but the differences are generally small. Taking spending on childcare into account increases differences in spending between the children of full-time working parents and other children. Children with one parent working full time receive 67 per cent more average spending than children with one non-working parent and 45 per cent more than children with two parents, one working full time and one not working. Children with two parents working full time receive 55 per cent more than children with two non-working parents.

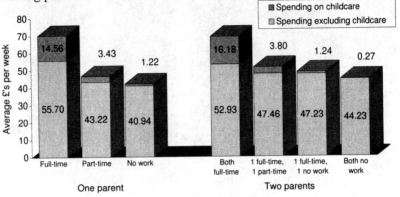

Figure 7.6: *Spending and labour market activity*

It seems that, as for income support receipt, living with adults who are in full-time work is more important for spending on children than whether the child is living with one or two parents. Again, this is not to say that children living in lone-parent families are as well off in spending terms as those in two-parent families. Far more two-parent families have at least one parent in work than do lone-parent families. A greater proportion of children in lone-parent families will receive the lower average spending that we have shown to be associated with being out of work, than will children in two-parent families.

Average spending and smoking

In their study of smoking among low income families, Marsh and McKay (1994: 79) found that: 'whereas many low income parents will say that they themselves go without in order to be able to buy cigarettes, they will suggest that they try to protect their expenditure on their children from the effects of their buying cigarettes. The evidence suggests that in many cases they do not succeed.' Their evidence was based on a definition of hardship as 'an enforced lack of socially perceived necessities' (Mack and Lansley, 1985, quoted in Marsh and McKay, 1994: 58). Marsh and McKay suggest that while smoking was not the sole cause of hardship among low income families, it did increase hardship equally among adults and children, independently of other factors that cause some families to be poorer than others. We collected information about the smoking behaviour of adults in the households in our survey. While the measurement of hardship among children is outside the scope of this paper, we decided to explore whether smoking has any effect on average spending on children in lone and two-parent families.[2]

Among our respondents, 57 per cent of lone parents smoked, as did 27 per cent of mothers in two-parent households, compared with 55 per cent and 38 per cent in Marsh and McKay's study. Lone-parent mothers were slightly less likely to smoke the more children they had, whereas mothers in two-parent families with three or more children were more likely to smoke than those with one or two children.

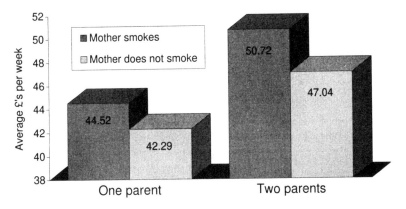

Figure 7.7: *Smoking and parents' spending on children*

Figure 7.7 suggests that whether or not the mother smokes makes very little difference to what is spent on a child. If anything, it would appear that children whose mothers smoke receive slightly more spending than children whose mothers do not smoke. Children in lone-parent families whose mothers smoke receive 5 per cent more than those whose mothers do not smoke. Mothers in two-parent families who smoke spend 8 per cent more on their children than those who do not smoke. Only lone mothers with one child, and two-parent mothers with two children, spend less on their children if they smoke than if they do not smoke and the differences are very small. (The effects of smoking on average spending are investigated further below.) This seems to suggest that mothers who smoke do not do so at the expense of their children. This supports the findings of qualitative studies, which have suggested that poor mothers who smoke go without food for themselves in order to do so (Dowler and Calvert, 1995). In fact, they may spend more on their children because they smoke,

2. We intend to revisit this issue in more detail in a later paper, which will incorporate a similar definition of hardship to that used by Marsh and McKay.

feeling that if they are 'treating' themselves they must also treat their children (Dobson et al, 1994).

Average spending on childcare

We have already seen the extent to which spending on childcare by working parents in both lone and two-parent families increases spending on children. Slightly more children in two-parent families (43 per cent) than in lone-parent families (35 per cent) regularly receive care from someone other than their mother. Reuben Ford's work on the use of childcare by lone parents (Ford, 1996) found that just over two-thirds of working lone parents use childcare and that around three in ten pay for childcare (42 per cent of those who use any childcare). The average amount paid for childcare in 1994 in his study was £33.20. He also suggests that out-of-work lone parents would be less likely than workers to intend to use their parents as carers for their children.

Our survey produced similar results. Of the 31 per cent of lone parents who work, whether full or part time, 59 per cent use childcare. Some 28 per cent of working lone parents pay for childcare, 47 per cent of those who use childcare at all. The average amount paid is slightly lower than in Ford's study, at £31.88 per week. Non-working lone parents in our study are only half as likely (17 per cent) as workers (34 per cent) to have their child cared for by a family member (this category includes other family members as well as grandparents).

Our study enables us to explore differences in the use and costs of childcare for children in lone and two-parent families. We decided to compare children in lone-parent families whose mother works full or part time with children in two-parent families where both parents work full time or one parent works full time and one part time. In other words, children in both family types will have parents who work for at least part of the time and might, therefore, be expected to need childcare. Of children living in two-parent families, 56 per cent have parents who both work full time or one full time one part time, compared with 31 per cent of children living in lone-parent families where the parent works full or part time. For simplicity in what follows, children in lone-parent families where the mother works full or part time are simply referred to as 'children in lone-parent working families'; children in two-parent families where either both work full time or one works full time and the other part time are 'children in two-parent working families'.

Some 32 per cent of children in two-parent working families receive childcare from someone other than their mother, compared with 59 per cent in lone-parent working families. Children in two-parent working families are slightly less likely to receive paid childcare; only 24 per cent

(43 per cent of two-parent children who receive any childcare) compared with 28 per cent in lone-parent working families (47 per cent of those who received childcare at all).

Children with two full-time working parents are slightly more likely to be cared for by other family members (65 per cent) than those in lone-parent families (58 per cent). Children in two-parent families are less likely to receive care from friends, or what we have chosen to call 'formal' care (childminders, nannies or nursery care). Not surprisingly, children in two-parent families are much more likely to receive care from their father than are children in lone-parent families.

When children do receive paid childcare, average costs are 12 per cent higher for those in lone-parent working families (£31.88 per week) than for children in two-parent working families (£28.35 per week). This is because children in lone-parent families are more likely to receive formal care, which, as Figure 7.8 shows, is more expensive than paid care provided by family or friends.

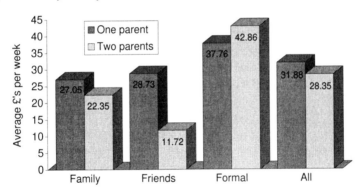

Figure 7.8: *Spending on childcare by working parents who pay*

The average costs of having a child cared for by family or friends are also lower for children in two-parent working families. Reasons for this await further investigation, but it may be that children in these families receive fewer hours of paid care than those in lone-parent working families.

Although differences in the use and costs of childcare between children in one and two-parent working families are small, the type of childcare that children receive varies much more. Children in lone-parent working families are more likely to receive formal care and less likely to be cared for by other members of their family. Children in one-parent working families are much more likely to be cared for by childminders than those in two-parent working families, who are almost twice as likely to receive nursery care (Figure 7.9). No children in one-parent working families receive before or after school care and only 6 per cent of children in two-parent working families receive such care.

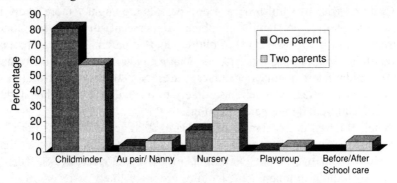

Figure 7.9: *Sources of formal childcare for working parents*

A multivariate analysis of average spending

So far in this section we have examined the extent to which spending on children in lone and two-parent families varies according to each of a range of social, economic and personal characteristics. We have shown that in general:

- children in lone-parent families receive only slightly less average spending than children in two-parent families;
- children with more siblings receive less than those with fewer or no siblings;
- older children receive more average spending than younger children;
- children in families on income support receive lower spending than those in families not on income support;
- children whose parent(s) are not working receive lower spending than those whose parents are working;
- whether mothers smoke or not makes very little difference to spending on children;
- there are only slight differences between spending on childcare for children in lone and two-parent working families.

We have not yet taken into account the interaction between each of these characteristics and average spending. In other words, what are the driving factors towards children receiving more or less spending and which characteristics are most likely to affect average spending on a child?

We have explored these interrelationships by means of a regression model. This describes how parents' spending on children is linked to each characteristic in the model, holding 'constant' other characteristics. By allowing each characteristic to vary in turn, we can build up a picture of which characteristics are most important in explaining variations in spending on children in lone and two-parent families.

Our model examined sequentially the relationship between spending and family type; whether or not someone in the household (not just the mother) smokes; the number of children in the family; whether or not the child's family is in receipt of income support; and age of the child (Table 7.2). Two sets of models were produced, including and excluding spending on childcare. These models were than extended to take into account parents' labour market activity, at which stage income support status was excluded from the models, and not working became the reference category (Tables 7.3 and 7.4). Income support status was excluded at this stage because the majority of families with no worker were also claiming income support.

Table 7.2 shows the percentage differences in spending on children, which are explained by each characteristic in the model.[3]

Table 7.2: *Spending on children (% differences explained by each characteristic)*

| | Including childcare % | | | | | Excluding childcare % |
	A	B	C	D	E	
Lone parent	90*	90*	90*	105	105	96
Smoker		93*	93	97	97	99
2 children			86*	87*	87*	89*
3+ children			70*	71*	71*	74*
On income support				73*	73*	88*
Age					100	101*
Constant	3.97	3.82	3.98	3.97	3.97	3.75
R^2	0.01	0.01	0.04	0.09	0.09	0.06

Note: *is significant (P <.05).

Models A to E in Table 7.2 show differences in spending including childcare. The first model (Model A) includes only family type and shows, as reported earlier, that a child in a lone-parent family receives lower spending than a child in a two-parent family. However, only 1 per cent of

---

3. We have chosen to present the tables in this way, rather than include coefficients and standard errors, for ease of interpretation. These can be obtained from the authors.

variation in spending (R^2 = .01) is explained by family type, which means that differences in spending must be mainly related to characteristics other than whether the child lives with one or two parents.

Model B then takes into account whether someone in the family smokes. While smoking does lead to lower average spending on children, it is not as important in explaining differences in spending as whether the child lives in a lone or two-parent family. In other words, differences in spending are more likely to be related to family type than to parents' smoking.

The next model (Model C) takes into account the number of children in the family. A child with one sibling will receive significantly lower spending than a child with no siblings (86 per cent). Having two or more siblings reduces spending to 70 per cent of what is spent on an only child. Adding number of children into the model increases the overall percentage difference explained to 4 per cent (R^2 = .04). Parental smoking no longer has a significant effect on spending.

Model D takes into account whether the child lives in a family that is on income support. Income support receipt is more important in explaining spending differences than family type, which is no longer statistically significant. In other words, low income better explains the relationship between spending on children than whether or not they live in lone or two-parent families. However, this model still only accounts for 9 per cent of differences in spending (R^2 = .09). Our final model (Model E) shows that age of the child is unimportant in explaining differences in spending, including childcare.

In summary, differences in spending, including childcare, appear to be driven by income constraints and resource demands, rather than living in a lone or two-parent family, or having a parent who smokes. In other words, it is the prevalence of income support receipt among lone-parent families that explains lower spending on children in these families, rather than being in a lone-parent family *per se.*

We then examined spending excluding childcare costs. The results are similar except for age of the child. When childcare spending is excluded, older children are seen to receive significantly more spending than younger children. This is because younger children inevitably receive more spending on childcare than older children, therefore including childcare in the model masks higher spending on older children.

The second set of models take into account the effect of parents' labour market activity for spending on children in lone and two-parent families in turn (Tables 7.3 and 7.4). For children in lone-parent families Model A, which includes childcare spending, explains 13 per cent of differences in average spending (R^2 = .13) (Table 7.3). A child in a lone-parent family receives much higher average spending when the parent works, either full or part time. Children living in a family with three or more children have lower average spending and, again, there are no effects for age or parents' smoking.

When childcare is excluded, only family size differentiates between spending. It appears that much of the extra spending on a child whose lone parent works is accounted for by childcare costs. In other words, children in one-parent working families do not necessarily receive higher spending on budget areas that directly benefit them, such as food, clothing or activities. Rather, most of the higher income that work brings is swallowed up by the costs of childcare, particularly for younger children.

Table 7.3: *Spending on children in lone-parent families and labour market activity*

	Including childcare (%)	Excluding childcare (%)
Smoker	96	99
2 children	89	91
3+ children	70*	70*
Full-time worker	162*	116
Part-time worker	125*	114
Age	100	101
Constant	3.75	3.63
R^2	.13	0.7

Note: *is significant (P <.05).

The model for children in two-parent families produces similar findings (Table 7.4). Children in families where both parents work full time, or one works full time and one part time, receive higher spending than children in families where either both parents are out of work or only one is working full time. Taking childcare spending into account again suggests that a substantial proportion of the extra spending that younger children in working families receive is accounted for by childcare costs.

In conclusion, it seems that differences in spending on children are explained only partially by the characteristics included in these models. We intend to expand our analysis to include other characteristics, such as differences in attitudes to parenting. However, it seems that living in a lone-parent family matters to a child in spending terms only in that this is related to a low family income. While children in a lone-parent family receive lower spending than children in two-parent families, this appears to be the result of the large proportion of lone parents who are on income support or not working. Spending on a child in a lone-parent family decreases significantly only when there are three or more children in the family and this is more important than whether or not the parent smokes. In fact, smoking does not affect what is spent on children in either family type to any significant extent. Finally, much of the extra spending on children in working families is accounted for by the costs of childcare, rather than on items of direct benefit to the child.

Table 7.4: *Spending on children in two-parent families, and labour market activity*

	Including childcare (%)	Excluding childcare (%)
One smoker	99	99
Both smoke	100	96
2 children	88*	88*
3+ children	76*	77*
Both in full-time work	154*	111
1 full time/1 part time	119*	107
1 full time/1 not working	107	105
1 or both/part time	106	100
Age	100	102*
Constant	3.77	3.65
R^2	.08	.05

Note: *is significant (P <.05).

THE POLICY IMPLICATIONS OF AVERAGE SPENDING

Evidence about what parents spend on children can be used to evaluate social policies designed to assist families bringing up children. Assumptions about the relative costs of children are made in a range of benefits and allowances for children living in lone and two-parent families. For example, the provision of an additional premium for lone parents on income support was predicated on the belief that lone parents experience proportionately greater financial demands than two-parent families; income support allowances for children assume that older children cost much more than younger children.

In this section, we explore what average spending patterns can tell us about the relative costs of children of differing ages in lone and two-parent families and how these compare with the assumptions in income support and family credit allowances. We also consider the relative costs of children in a much used measure of childhood poverty, the government's households below average income (HBAI) statistics. Finally, we consider the implications of spending on, and use of, childcare for policies designed to assist lone parents back into work, in particular the childcare disregard in family credit calculations.

Average spending and age relativities

Assumptions about the relative costs of children are usually expressed in 'equivalence scales'. The most common form of equivalence scale assigns a value of 100 per cent to a married couple and then calculates the proportion of income or expenditure needed by, for example, a single adult or a child of a particular age to reach a similar standard of living. (For a detailed discussion of the use of equivalence scales in estimating children's living standards, see Banks and Johnson, 1993.) We have calculated equivalence scales for children implied by average spending by assigning a value of 100 per cent to the oldest age group in our sample – 16 year-olds – and working out equivalences for younger children accordingly.

Income support allowances

The amounts allowed for children in income support calculations assume that age affects the cost of a child. For income support purposes, children are divided into those aged under 11 years old; 11 to 15 years; and 16 to 18 years old. Income support also makes additional sums available to families with children through a family premium and, where appropriate, a one-parent premium.

We have calculated a notional income support allowance for each child in the sample, taking into account both the basic child allowance and an amount for family and one-parent premia.[4] We then worked out the average income support allowance for children in each of the income support age bands. Figure 7.10 compares these notional income support allowances with parents' average spending on children in lone and two-parent families.[5]

Income support allowances meet between 48 per cent (under 11 year-old child in a two-parent family) and 75 per cent (16 year-old in a lone-parent family) of average spending by parents.

The allowances meet a larger percentage of spending on children in

---

4. Family and one-parent premia were introduced in recognition of the additional costs to an adult of running a family. It might be argued, therefore, that including a proportion of these sums as income notionally available to be spent on children artificially inflates the amounts allowed for children in benefits. However, to exclude premia completely would have led to criticisms that we were underestimating the amount of benefit income notionally available to children.
5. Spending figures exclude childcare.

lone-parent families than in two-parent families for each age group.
The reason for this is that, as we have shown, spending on children
varies only slightly between children in lone and two-parent families.
The extra premium for lone parents means that the notional allowances
for children in such families are higher and, therefore, meet a greater
proportion of spending than for children in two-parent families. However,
if the one-parent premium element of notional allowances is removed,
income support allowances would meet only 50 per cent of spending
on lone-parent children under 11 years and 58 per cent for children
aged 11 to 15 years. This would produce greater equity between children
in lone and two-parent families, although we might question whether
social policy should aim to achieve equality of deprivation. Parents have
to find the difference between what is allowed for their children in
income support allowances and what they actually spend. For those on
income support the difference has to come from the allowances
they receive for themselves. Removal of the one-parent premium might
lead to a situation in which lone parents are either forced to reduce
spending on their children or to make even greater sacrifices in their own
consumption.

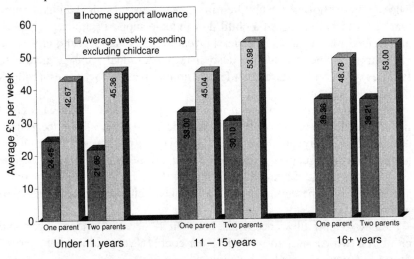

Figure 7.10: *Income support and parents' spending on children*

It can be argued, of course, that means-tested benefits are not intended to
provide average living standards but a minimum safety net. However,
Figure 7.10 also suggests that the amounts allowed for children of differing ages in income support calculations do not reflect differences in
spending. For children in both lone and two-parent families, income

support assumes that younger children cost much less than older children. For example, under 11 year-olds in a lone-parent family are assumed to cost only 67 per cent as much as a 16 year-old. The relative costs implied by spending suggest that younger children cost only slightly less than older children; under 11 year-olds in a lone-parent family receive 87 per cent of spending on a 16 year-old. This confirms the findings of other studies, which have also suggested that the costs of children do not vary by anywhere near as much as is suggested in income support allowances (see, for example, Berthoud and Ford, 1996).

We have repeated this exercise using income support allowances excluding family premia, and for children on income support. Whichever comparison is made, average spending figures suggest that younger children, particularly those in two-parent families, are disadvantaged in income support calculations when compared with older children. This will not only affect children on income support. Income support allowances are also used by the Child Support Agency (CSA) in calculating main-tenance levels for children, which must also disadvantage younger children.

Even if income support allowances for children cannot be raised overall, some reconsideration of the levels for children of differing ages would seem to be necessary. This would not, of course, assist the parents of older children on income support who would see their benefits decrease as the benefit levels allowed for younger children increased. However, redistri-bution would mean that income support allowances more accurately reflect what parents are actually spending on children in different age groups.

Income support levels are also often used as a proxy 'poverty line'. In other words, children living in families on income support are defined as 'poor'. Since income support allowances assume larger cost differentials between children of differing ages than those implied by average spending, using income support as a measure of childhood poverty might seriously underestimate the numbers of young children who are poor.

Family credit

Family credit is a benefit that tops up the wages of low-paid families who work for more than 16 hours a week. Since many lone parents wish to work less than full time and are often in low-paid employment, family credit was expected to be of particular value in assisting lone parents back into work.

Family credit allowances for children, like income support, make assumptions about the relative costs of children of differing ages. Again using 16 year-olds as the base age group, Figure 7.11 suggests that the equivalences used in family credit calculations relatively disadvantage younger children even more than those for income support. For example, family credit assumes that a child aged under 11 years costs only around half as much as a child aged 16 years, whereas spending on children aged under 11 years in a two-parent family is 85 per cent of what is spent on an equivalent 16 year-old and, for an under 11 year-old in a lone-parent family, 87 per cent.

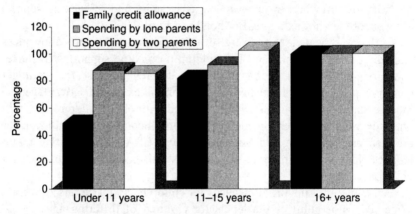

Figure 7.11: *Family credit and parents' spending equivalences*

As for income support, the distribution of family credit allowances between children of differing ages might usefully be reconsidered.

Households below average income

Equivalence scales are also employed in measuring the living standards of children by the government's HBAI statistics (DSS, 1996). Again taking 16 year-olds as the base age group, we have recalculated the HBAI equivalence scale for younger children in lone and two-parent families and compared these with the relativities implied by average spending (Figure 7.12). For each age group, and for children in both lone and two-parent families, the equivalent income produced by the HBAI scale is much lower than the average spending scale. This is so for all children in the younger age groups, in particular children aged under two years, and between five and seven years, in lone-parent families. Again, this implies that estimates of children's living standards using HBAI statistics might seriously underestimate the numbers of younger children who are poor.

Readjusting equivalence scales within an existing poverty measure would not, of course, decrease the total numbers of children who are poor. The numbers of older children measured as poor would simply decrease as the numbers of poor younger children increased. But readjusting equivalence scales would mean that poverty measures give a more accurate representation of poverty among British children.

Childcare

The issue of available and affordable childcare for working parents has been high on the policy agenda for some time. The argument has developed that work is the answer to the problems of parents on income support, particularly lone parents, but that many of the jobs available are likely to be low paid. If working while children are young is to be made financially worthwhile, then parents need assistance with childcare costs. (The issue of whether it is equitable, or in the interests of children, to expect lone parents to work, when mothers in two-parent families on income support are not expected to do so, is outside the scope of this chapter.) The childcare disregard in family credit calculations aims to provide such assistance for working families where the parent is low paid and working for more than 16 hours per week. In 1995, when our survey took place, family credit calculations could disregard up to £40 per week of earnings to meet the costs of childcare. This produced a net benefit of up to £28 per week. The disregard was subsequently increased in April 1996 to £60 per week, a net benefit of £4210. The government has announced a further increase in the disregard to £100 per week, a net benefit of £70, for families with two or more children.

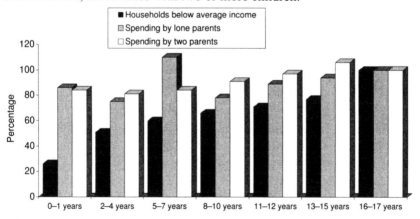

Figure 7.12: *Households below average income and parents' spending equivalences*

In the spending models described earlier, we have seen the extent to which additional spending received by the children of working parents is accounted for by the costs of childcare. Among working parents who pay for childcare these costs average £31.88 per week for a child in a lone-parent family and £28.35 per week in a two-parent family. The maximum net benefit of the childcare disregard would meet 88 per cent of the average childcare costs of one child in a lone-parent family and 99 per cent in a two-parent family. Therefore, while the childcare disregard would have come close to meeting the average childcare cost for one child in 1995, it would have been of no assistance in paying for the care of second or subsequent children.

Further, the disregard is only available to parents who use registered childcare. As we have seen, many working parents prefer to pay family or friends to look after their children and, hence, would not be eligible for the disregard.

The average cost of 'formal' or registered care is higher; £37.76 per week for a child in a lone-parent family and £42.86 per week in a two-parent family. The disregard would have met only 74 per cent or 65 per cent of these costs respectively. The numbers of lone mothers in our survey working full time (more than 30 hours per week) and using formal care are small. However, spending by such mothers averages £41.81 for an only child, and £28.99 for a child in two-child families. If it is assumed that childcare costs for two children are twice that for one child, or £57.98, the disregard would have met only 48 per cent of these costs, or 67 per cent of the cost for an only child.

It seems that the childcare disregard and, in particular, the recently announced increases for families with two or more children, could be an important source of help for working lone parents. However, research suggests that few parents are aware of its availability or of the net benefit it can provide (Ford, 1996). In addition, the disregard is not payable for the type of childcare most parents choose, that is, friends or family.

CONCLUSION

In Chapter 1, Reuben Ford and Jane Millar questioned whether defining families according to whether they have one or two parents is useful or helpful in social policy terms. The findings in this chapter suggest that, in terms of average spending on children, it is neither. Average spending varies most by whether the child is living on income support in a family where parents are not working, rather than whether they are living with one or two parents. In other words, lone parenthood may be useful only in so far as it is associated with low income, rather than as a concept in itself.

Chapter 8

The Problem of Lone Motherhood in the British Context

Hilary Land and Jane Lewis

Lone motherhood has been and remains an emotional subject, especially in the English-speaking countries. In other European countries the problems arising from the new pluralism in family forms have not created the same sort of moral panic. Rather, the main fault line is identified as that between the single-earner and dual-earner family. In France, where social security policy has historically sought to redistribute between families with and without children, rather than between the social classes, the focus is firmly on care and provision for children.

In Britain, lone mothers have been marked out for more attention, particularly in the past decade. Lone motherhood began to move up the policy agenda in the 1970s as the growth in their numbers, their increasing propensity to become dependent on means-tested benefits and the entry of unexpectedly large numbers of lone mothers into council housing at the end of the decade made them more visible to policy makers. But, in the late 1980s and 1990s, the problem of lone motherhood has again been redefined, such that concern about the poverty of lone mothers and their children has been substantially eclipsed by concern about:

- the level of public expenditure needed to support lone-mother families;
- the dangers posed by the antisocial behaviour of unattached young men; and
- the fate of children in lone-mother families in terms of educational achievement, criminality and propensity to divorce in their turn.

In the hope of informing the policy debate in this difficult area, the Joseph Rowntree Foundation agreed to fund a historical study of the problem of lone motherhood (Kiernan et al, forthcoming). Our objectives have been to examine the nature of the problem of lone motherhood in the context of the changing marriage system and to trace the treatment of lone mother families with regard to social security and housing policies. Our aims have been to expose the dimensions of the problem and to examine some popular ideas about how we got to where we are.

MOTHERS AND THE MARRIAGE SYSTEM IN THE TWENTIETH CENTURY: CHANGES IN BEHAVIOUR

The popular wisdom locates the beginnings of the late twentieth century growth in lone-mother families rather loosely in the 'permissive' years of the late 1960s, which implies that a more draconian approach to marriage and divorce law and to the treatment of lone mothers might be the answer, for example by making divorce more difficult (which the 1996 Family Law Act seems set to do), and by interpreting equity between one and two parent families to mean a levelling down of benefits for the former.

In fact, there have been two major changes in the marriage system in the postwar period. First, there was in the 1950s and 1960s a widespread separation of sex and marriage. The increase in sexual activity outside marriage resulted in a sharp rise in both the extramarital and marital birth rates during the 1960s. This contrasts with the war years, when the marital birth rate fell and the extramarital birth rate increased because so many marriages were thwarted by wartime disruption and to a lesser extent by death. The pattern for the 1960s also differed from that of the period since the mid-1980s, when the extramarital birth rate rose dramatically and the marital birth rate fell. In other words, the 1960s were different. Increased sexual activity resulted in an increased pregnancy rate, but there was still a tendency to marry. It is perhaps therefore not so surprising that there was seemingly little panic about what amounted to a significant increase in the separation of sex from marriage. The fact that a majority of premarital conceptions were legitimised and that divorce rates were low, resulted in a series of optimistic statements from investigators about family stability.

Second, since the beginning of the 1970s there have been marked changes in marriage patterns, with substantial declines in marriage rates, less marriage and older marriage, a dramatic rise in divorce rates that levelled off from the 1980s and the emergence of widespread cohabitation. Declining marriage and increased childbearing outside marriage have been inextricably linked to the growth of cohabitation, which was probably at its nadir during the 1950s and 1960s. Increases in divorce, cohabitation and childbearing outside marriage have thus all contributed to the separation of marriage from parenthood.

CHANGES IN ATTITUDES TOWARDS SEXUAL MORALITY

Behind these changes in behaviour lies an equally profound set of changes in attitudes towards sexual morality, which have resulted in the almost complete erosion in the stigma attaching to divorced and unmarried mothers. Unlike behaviour, this shift may be traced back to the 1960s.

At the beginning of the twentieth century most commentators saw marriage as a social discipline and a duty. Marriage was an institution regulated by a strict moral code. Beginning in the interwar years, there was a movement to attack the hypocrisy of an externally imposed moral code, which turned a blind eye to gross transgression as long as it did not become public, and which insisted on evidence of gross moral fault before it would permit divorce. Reformers began to argue in favour of a new, higher morality from within, to be based on love. After the war, anxiety about 'rebuilding the family' overcame calls for reform and the 1956 Royal Commission on Divorce (Cmd 9684) took a very conservative position, insisting on the importance of the public purposes of marriage. But in the 1960s doctors and churchmen began to stress that love was the only proper basis for personal relationships and to agree that the morality of sex had little to do with marriage; sex could be moral or immoral in or outside marriage. In the influential view of the Bishop of Woolwich's 1963 book, *Honest to God*, neither divorce nor premarital sex could be labelled as 'wrong' unless they were lacking love. The idea was not to give wholesale approval to premarital and extramarital sex, but the new attitudes could be used to justify more radical behaviour.

The Finer Report (DHSS, 1974) on one-parent families recognised that in a liberal democratic society, government could no longer seek directly to control marital and reproductive behaviour because it could not allow the rich to remarry and further reproduce while restricting the behaviour of the poor. Finer accepted the revolution in sexual morality and also accepted that it meant that part of the cost of the breakdown of marriage had to fall on public funds. In the 1990s there is little public appetite for a return to a traditional moral code under which hypocrisy was rife, the rich were treated differently from the poor and men were treated more favourably than women.

SOCIAL POLICIES AND LONE MOTHERS

Lone mothers are potentially the sole carers and sole supporters of their children. Historically, social provision has in many western countries been based on the assumption of a 'male breadwinner model' (Land, 1980; Lewis, 1992); within such a model women with children and without men become a social problem. The terminology used to describe lone mothers has often reflected this way of thinking. Thus, in the late 1960s the term 'fatherless families' was often used.

In the case of lone mothers, there are three main possible sources of income: the labour market, the absent father or their own families and the state. During the twentieth century, lone mothers in all western countries have been able to reduce their dependence on men and to increase the amount of income they obtain from the labour market and the state. All lone mothers 'package' income from different sources, but the way in which they do so has varied considerably over time and from one country to another. In the case of the relatively small number of lone fathers, governments have expected them to work and to maintain a housekeeper if necessary to care for the children. Between 1918 and 1988 the tax system recognised this in the form of tax relief. The expectation reflected both the idea that men should provide as breadwinners and the reality that they are paid more than women and are more strongly attached to the labour force.

Within the context of assumptions about male breadwinning, government has been faced with the decision of whether and how far to step in to replace the male earner, in other words, how far to treat lone mothers as mothers and how far to treat them as workers. Historically, countries in which the male breadwinner logic has been strong have tended to make a dichotomous choice in this respect. Thus, in Britain under the Poor Law (which was finally abolished in 1948), lone mothers tended to be treated as workers and were told to keep as many of their children as they could by wage earning. The rest would be cared for by the state. Widows were treated most leniently, with shortfalls in income often made up by 'outdoor relief' in the form of cash or kind. Unmarried mothers were treated the most harshly because of their moral taint and relief was usually only given to them inside the workhouse. Separated women (divorce was relatively rare until after the Second World War) would often be refused help for a period of time, to make sure that there was no collusion between husband and wife to defraud the authorities.

In Britain, women campaigned for 'mothers' pensions' or 'mothers' endowment', renamed children's endowment or allowances in Britain during the interwar years (Koven and Michel, 1995). In the USA, they were conspicuously successful and by 1920 some 40 states offered mothers' pensions. However, in Britain, governments fought shy of allowing claims on the basis of motherhood and in 1925 finally agreed to mothers' pensions only for widows, paying them on an insurance basis to the wives of men who had been insured. It was thus possible to fit widows into a social security system based on the male breadwinner model, but divorcees and unmarried mothers were more difficult to accommodate.

The claims of these women as mothers were recognised explicitly in Britain only after the Second World War, when under the National Assistance Act of 1948 they were not required to register for work if they had dependent children under 16. Thus, by mid-century, lone mothers were treated as mothers, though public opinion and policy makers reserved disapproval of mothers who had paid work while their children were very young. Sir William Beveridge's 1942 blueprint for postwar social reform insisted on the 'vital importance' of women's work in the home, and Beveridge struggled to find a way of insuring against divorce as a risk, but concluded that this was impossible when one party was inevitably going to be blamed (before 'no-fault' divorce) and when it might be possible for women to get maintenance under private law as well as drawing insurance benefits as of right. Ideas about the desirability of keeping mother and child together also acquired greater importance (although John Bowlby (1951), the leading proponent of the theory of maternal deprivation, favoured adoption for children born outside marriage).

In the late twentieth century, as lone mothers have become more visible as both their numbers and autonomy have increased, it is possible to see the pendulum swinging back again towards treating them as workers rather than as mothers. When lone mothers reached the top of the policy agenda at the end of the 1980s, the problem was defined largely, though not exclusively, in terms of public expenditure costs, and the first policy response was to seek more maintenance from fathers. With the failure of the child support legislation, attention has switched in the 1990s to the only remaining source of income for lone mothers: the labour market. However, we would question how successful the dichotomous treatment of lone mothers as either *mothers* or *workers* can ever be.

SOCIAL SECURITY AND EMPLOYMENT

An important part of the background against which social security, housing or employment policies developed in the postwar years is the growing interest policy makers showed in lone mothers. This was determined in part by their growing visibility, as well as their growing numbers. Lone mothers had literally been 'concealed' in their parents' households where, in addition to accommodation, grandmothers provided childcare for those able to find employment. Not until unmarried mothers began to leave the parental home and were joined in the 1960s by growing numbers of women leaving the marital home did policy makers begin to get a measure of them. At the same time, the social taboos, which were both a cause and a consequence of these changes and which sustained their invisibility and muted the voices of the women themselves, became weaker.

Hilary Land and Jane Lewis

The position of lone mothers in the social security system had improved greatly as a result of the postwar welfare reforms. Lone mothers with a school-age child were not required to register for work to claim state means-tested benefits. Eligibility rules and levels of benefits were determined by national scale rates and claimants were no longer required to return to their area or parish of origin to claim assistance. The obligation on adult children to maintain parents and vice versa and on grandparents to maintain grandchildren ended. This meant that the unmarried mother who returned to her parents' home was entitled to claim benefit for herself and her child(ren) as a non-householder, irrespective of the economic status of her parents. Conversely, *their* benefit status was unaffected.

Table 8.1: *Trends in the number of part-time and full-time employees in employment (Great Britain)*

Year	Full time (000s)	Part time* (000s) Total of which female		Ratio of full time to part time
1951	19 239	832	779	231:10
1961	19 794	1 999	1 851	99:10
1971	18 308	3 341	2 757	55:10
1981	16 407	4 442	3 789	37:10
1991	16 817	4 615	4 114	36:10
1996	16 308	5 181	4 393	31:10

Note: *Except for 1951, part-time work is defined as working less than 30 hours a week.

Source: Select Committee on the European Communities, 1982; Employment Committee, 1990; *Labour Market Trends*, March 1997, p 109.

British governments both before and after the Second World War were clear that married mothers of young children should be providing full-time care for them in their own homes. Certainly, it was not the responsibility of the state to enable them to combine full-time employment with motherhood. However, it was taken for granted that lone mothers, especially unmarried ones, would choose to take full-time employment, relying either on their own mothers or friends to provide childcare or on local authority daycare services, which, although reduced in size after the war, gave priority to the children of lone parents. Throughout the 1950s and 1960s, the government was committed to a policy of full employment. There was a shortage of labour, especially in the expanding health, welfare and education services. Women's labour and skills were regarded as an under-utilised but much needed resource. In addition to recruiting full-time workers, especially for the NHS from overseas, the government exhorted managers in both the public and private sectors to arrange hours of employment to suit women with family responsibilities.

At first, by encouraging part-time employment, policy makers were concerned with enabling married women to combine their 'domestic duties' with paid employment. By the end of the 1960s, the focus broadened to include mothers of young children, though the official view, reflecting public opinion, was that it was undesirable for married mothers with pre-school children to take full-time employment. The growing proportion of mothers taking up paid work relied extensively on informal sources of childcare – mainly their own mothers, their husbands or friends and neighbours. At this time, the majority of unmarried mothers were living with their parents and over half of all employed lone mothers relied on their own mothers for childcare both for preschool and school-age children. During the 1970s, both the labour movement and the re-emerging women's movement raised the question of the state's responsibility to provide childcare services and argued for extending collectively funded nursery provision. The official view, endorsed by the Finer Committee in its report in 1974, was that central and local government should support the development of childminding rather than day-nursery provision. Part-time employment had continued to grow and, though mothers joined the labour market in ever growing numbers throughout the 1970s, the proportion employed full-time fell rather than increased, as Table 8.2 shows.

Table 8.2: *Proportion of mothers in paid work by age of youngest child 1949–95*

Age of youngest child	Work status	Date (end December)					
		1949	1959	1969	1979	1990	1995
0–4	Full-time	9	8	8	7	13	17
	Part-time	5	7	14	19	28	31
	All	14	15	22	26	41	48
5–10	Full-time	–	20	23	18	19	22
	Part-time	–	24	33	45	47	43
	All	–	44	56	63	66	67
11–15	Full-time	–	36	31	31	32	34
	Part-time	–	30	29	47	46	41
	All	–	66	60	78	78	75

Source: Equal Opportunities Commission (EOC), 1986, p 87; Central Statistical Office, 1997.

Until the end of the 1960s only a minority of lone mothers depended on means-tested social security benefits (17 per cent in 1961). Living within the family, their need for childcare and accommodation was of no concern to the policy makers or politicians. In so far as they were a problem, lone mothers (especially unmarried ones) came to the attention of the welfare and children's departments at local government level. In the mid-1960s, poverty among families with children was 'rediscovered' and the question of how the state should adjust family income to family size was high on the policy agenda for the first time since the introduction of family allowances in 1946. Initially, the focus was on two-parent families with an employed father, but by the end of the 1960s the poverty of children of lone mothers was drawing increasing attention. Discriminating between children on the basis of the marital status of their parents no longer seemed appropriate. Illegitimacy became less stigmatised in private law and the Finer Committee was established to review policies towards lone parents, with a brief to consider how to achieve parity between children in one- and two-parent families.

Family allowances had been increased by the Labour government in response to concern about child poverty. The Conservative government elected in 1970, however, chose a more selective method of supporting the children of low wage earners and in 1971 introduced the means-tested family income support (now family credit). Lone parents were treated on a par with two-parent families. They also considered the introduction of a tax credit scheme that would have linked the tax and benefit system. The Finer Committee reported in 1974, by which time there was a Labour government. Barbara Castle, then Secretary of State for Social Services, was unable to accept the committee's proposal for a guaranteed maintenance allowance on the grounds of cost. However, she did introduce measures that helped lone parents in employment and encouraged those on benefit to supplement their income by earning. Child benefit replaced family allowances and tax allowance for all children in 1978, with lone parents receiving it for their first child a year earlier. The 1970s ended with the prospect that the number of lone parents dependent on benefit might fall, although it was emphasised that lone mothers should be able to choose whether or not to seek paid employment.

The cohabitation rule, which presumed that a woman cohabiting with a man was and should be supported by him, was challenged more frequently. Cohabitation was becoming more common and in any case the women's movement was challenging the assumption of dependency within marriage.

The economic social policy priorities of the 1980s were very different. A commitment to full employment had already been abandoned by the previous Labour government, but the Conservative government elected in 1979 had a very different attitude towards taxation and public expenditure. Social security in general was high on the Conservative government's agenda throughout the 1980s because of its concern to curb public expenditure. In the early 1980s, the government was preoccupied with young people, the unemployed and the escalating costs of residential care for old people. Its major review of social security conducted in 1985 contained little discussion about lone parents and predicted little change in the numbers dependent on benefit in the future (Land, 1986). However, as the economy went into recession at the end of the 1980s, the number of lone parents dependent on income support grew rapidly and the numbers in

Table 8.3: *Numbers of lone parents claiming means tested assistance 1951–93*

Year	Number (000s)	% of total claimants*
1951	41	4.1
1961	76	4.1
1971	213	7.3
1980	320	10.2
1986	578	11.7
1988	694	15.9
1990	774	18.5
1993	989	17.4

Note: *National assistance until 1966, supplementary benefits until 1986 and currently income support.

Source: Annual Report of SBC for 1980; Annual Reports of DHSS for 1986, 1988; and DSS for 1993.

full-time employment fell to 16 per cent in 1990, compared with 22 per cent in 1979 and 25 per cent in 1971. This was alarming for a government committed to cutting public expenditure. Even more alarming was the dramatic increase in the total numbers of lone parents, especially the never-married, combined with the declining proportion of benefits recovered from fathers. For the first time in debates about lone parents, fathers moved from the shadowy periphery to centre stage. Absent fathers attracted the adjectives 'feckless' and 'runaway'. With these images in mind, Parliament passed the Child Support Act in 1991. In contrast to earlier postwar debates, when the solution to the 'problem' of lone mothers was to encourage and facilitate their ability to support themselves and their children 'single-handed' by taking up paid employment (not noticing this depended heavily on the availability of 'free' family childcare), the solution was to seek resources from fathers, moreover biological fathers, irrespective of marital status.

The Child Support Act proved to be far more controversial than had been anticipated, as other chapters in this volume show and as the liable relative officers of the former National Assistance Board and Supplementary Benefit Commission could have predicted. Many fathers, especially those with second families, were neither able nor willing to provide substantial support for the children and mothers with whom they were no longer living. Those who had never lived with the mother of their child or children were even less willing to do so. The formula for calculating the amount of child support was opaque and the administrative procedures complex. It quickly became clear that fathers could not, after all, be relied on to reduce most lone mothers' dependence on income support. The government turned therefore to the only other source of income available for lone mothers, namely earnings. Lone mothers as well as two-parent families were encouraged to move from income support to family credit by the reduction in the number of hours of employment to qualify for family credit from 24 to 16 in 1992. Childcare disregards were introduced in 1994 in family credit, but only a minority were able to benefit from them. The Labour government elected in 1997 built on the more proactive responses being developed by the Conservative government in the form of providing lone mothers with advice and support in moving off income support. It recognised very quickly the need for an expansion of affordable childcare, especially for those with children of school age. Lone mothers will still have a 'choice' about whether or not to take up paid work, but the clear expectation is that once children are in school they will be expected at least to explore the possibilities of returning to paid employment.

HOUSING

Lone parents were of no particular concern to those responsible for housing policies in the early postwar years. Those who could find no room in the private sector or within the family home could easily be ignored by local authority housing departments. By the early 1960s, homelessness and the shortcomings of the private rented sector were becoming issues of public concern. The treatment of homeless families by local authority welfare departments attracted adverse media attention. Lone parents did not attract special attention, despite evidence that they were over-represented among homeless families. Homelessness in the 1960s was seen by many to *cause* family breakdown rather than the converse, because of the policy of welfare departments to split families in homeless family hostels (Greve,

1964). The debates about homelessness during the 1970s were very different from those of the 1960s, for they took place against the background of the rediscovery of domestic violence, described as 'domestic friction' in debates in the 1960s. Overall, lone parents' access to local authority accommodation did improve during the 1970s and in some ways this compensated for the contraction of the private sector. By the middle of the 1970s, lone parents were receiving more assistance with their housing costs through changes in the systems of rent and rate rebates, thus making rented accommodation more affordable. Family law changed, giving divorced or separated wives greater chances of continuing to occupy the matrimonial home and in some cases a share in the equity of the house once a marriage ended. As the number of divorces increased rapidly during the 1970s, this was an issue of growing significance. Important changes also occurred in private law, which strengthened lone parents' ability to keep a roof over their head.

In 1977, the Housing (Homeless Persons) Act was passed with all-party support. For the first time, local authority housing departments became responsible for housing the homeless and had a duty to provide accommodation to an applicant who was unintentionally homeless, in priority need and had a local connection. The subsequent Code of Guidance made it clear that women who left home because they had experienced, or were at risk of, violence fell within the definition of unintended homelessness. Cohabitees, carers of dependent children or adults who were not necessarily related by blood or marriage, were included. By the end of the 1980s, over 40 per cent of householders renting from local authorities were women compared with just over 30 per cent at the beginning of the decade. This is not surprising given that homelessness was becoming a more important route into public sector housing.

In contrast to the concern of the politicians and policy makers to put lone parents on a par with two-parent families in the public sector in the 1970s, the current concern is to reduce their access to such housing. It was alleged that lone parents had had priority over two-parent families in the allocation of public housing and that this must be reversed. Under the 1996 Housing Act, those who are accepted as genuinely homeless (defined more strictly) no longer have a right to permanent housing: the arrangement of a short-term tenancy is all that is required of a local housing authority.

The dislocation of lone mothers from both formal and informal sources of support, particularly care, as well as from employment opportunities, can only result in trapping lone parents and their children more firmly on income support. Housing, employment and childcare are inextricably linked, but policy makers in the 1990s have failed to see this because the focus of concern has become the demise of the 'traditional' two-parent family. In contrast with the debates of the 1960s, the recent focus has been on the behaviour of the parents, rather than the needs of the children.

CONCLUSION

The current debates about lone mothers and their claims on the benefit system need to be put in the context of changes in employment and family structures, which have occurred in the last ten years. In the second half of the 1980s, the UK had one of the fastest rates of growth in economic activity rates among women with children under ten years old in the EU. By 1991, over half were in paid employment but, as Table 8.2 shows, it was part-time employment that had continued to increase. Lone mothers have not shared in this increase in economic activity rates and, unlike the 1950s and 1960s, their employment rates are no longer higher than those of married mothers. Also, in contrast to the earlier decades, part-time jobs have been structured more with employers' than employees' needs in mind. There has been a shift in the occupational structure of the employed population towards highly paid non-manual occupations and away from low-paid manual occupations. Among employed women, by 1990 83 per cent were in the service sector and 13 per cent in the manufacturing sector. Inequalities between the highly paid and low paid grew (the ratio of the lowest decile to the highest decile of gross hourly earnings for women changed from 2.6 to 3.2 between 1983 and 1993). Mothers in professional or managerial occupations were more likely to be in paid employment than mothers in unskilled manual occupations and for the first time more likely to be employed full time when their children were under five years old. For example, in the period 1990 and 1992, nearly a third of mothers in professional or managerial occupations worked full time and over a quarter part time. The comparable proportions for mothers in unskilled manual occupations were 1 per cent and nearly half (Holtermann, 1995: 26). More children were growing up in a family where no one was in paid employment. Between 1979 and 1990/1, the proportion of children living in a family with no one in full-time employment had risen from 18 per cent to 26 per cent (DSS, 1995b). On the other hand, more children in two-parent families were growing up with *both* parents in paid employment (Holtermann, 1995: 37). The increase was particularly noticeable among couples with preschool children – from 29 per cent in 1980 to 44 per cent in 1991. Unlike lone mothers, these families could afford to pay for childcare, and daycare provision in the private sector grew dramatically. Day nursery provision in the private sector declined and lone mothers, increasingly dependent on the social housing sector for accommodation, had little choice over where they lived. Those who did not live near relatives or friends who could provide childcare 'free' or at a low cost, had little option but to stay on benefit. One study found that 27 per cent of lone parents and a third of couples were spending between a quarter and a half of the mother's take-home pay on childcare. Morever, the cash volume of paid-for childcare had increased over fourfold among mothers of preschool children between 1980 and 1990 (Marsh and McKay, 1993).

It is clear from comparative studies that lone mothers in the UK are less likely to be in paid employment and more likely to be poor than lone mothers in other EU countries. As Bradshaw et al (1996: 76) have argued, this is because there is 'an ineffective child maintenance regime, non-existent training and into-work advisory services, poor maternity and parental leave provision and a housing benefit system which results in sharp increases in housing costs upon leaving income support' (see also Chapter 9 here). They also point to the high level of childcare costs compared with most other countries where childcare costs are subsidised. The growing recognition by government of the importance of childcare provision in enabling lone mothers to become less dependent on benefit is to be welcomed. However, until the needs of children and their mothers are given higher priority not only within social security policies but also in housing, employment, wages and transport policies, and until the complexity of family life is recognised more fully, both within these individual policies and in the way they interact, lone mothers will continue to be seen as 'a problem'.

Chapter 9

International Comparisons of Support for Lone Parents

Jonathan Bradshaw

Comparative research in social policy is still in its infancy. While there is a body of comparative research relevant to social policy for lone parents (Roll, 1992; Mitchell and Bradshaw, 1993; Duskin, 1990; OECD, 1993; Whiteford and Bradshaw, 1994; Bradshaw et al, 1993; Eardley et al, 1996; Shaver and Bradshaw, 1995; Bradshaw et al, 1996a and 1996b; Ditch et al, 1995 and 1996, Duncan and Edwards, 1997) it is not easy to use it to learn simple lessons for how policy might develop in Britain. Nevertheless, I think there are three very clear conclusions to be drawn for Britain from recent comparative research on the topic:

- the risk of poverty among lone-mother families is exceptionally high in Britain;
- the labour supply of lone mothers is exceptionally low in Britain; and,
- despite some shifts in attitudes to lone mothers' employment in recent years, our policies are still a confused product of competing ideologies about the respective roles of women as mothers and workers.

This chapter presents evidence on these points from my own recent comparative research. However, first the next section compares the numbers and characteristics of lone parents cross-nationally.

LONE PARENTS: NUMBERS AND CHARACTERISTICS

The comparative analysis of social policies affecting lone-parent families is hampered today, as it was when Roll (1992) wrote her report for the European Union, by the absence of reliably comparable data on the prevalence and characteristics of lone-parent families in different countries. In our recently published study of lone-parents' labour supply in 20 countries (Bradshaw et al, 1996a and 1996b), we sought to collect comparable data from national informants on the prevalence of lone-parent families using the definition established by the Finer Committee (1974):

> *a mother or a father living without a spouse (and not cohabiting) with his or her never-married dependent child or children aged either under 16 or from 16 to (under) 19 and undertaking full-time education.*

The attempt was a failure. From their own published sources, the national informants were able to match this definition in only nine out of the 20 countries. Germany, France, Ireland, Austria, Portugal, Japan and New Zealand were not able to provide data that matched the age cut-off for children. Thus, for example, the children in Ireland and Austria were defined as under 15 years. Germany and Portugal counted lone parents with any never-married children regardless of age. France included all children under 25. The Netherlands and Norway count as lone parents cohabiting couples with children where the man is not the father of the children. Spain, Luxembourg, Portugal and Italy were not able to identify lone parents who are living with their families. No doubt, for some countries these problems arise because of variations in the definitions used in published data and it would be possible to produce more comparable data with direct access to the data sets. However, it is clear that, in some countries, the source of intercensal estimates of the prevalence of lone parents are just not adequate for the purpose. McCashin (1997), for example, has undertaken a careful analysis of the sources of data on the prevalence of lone parents in Ireland and concluded that the Irish Labour Force Survey, which is the main source of most estimates of prevalence, does not ask enough questions about relationships within a household to ensure that lone mothers living in their parents' household are counted.

Bearing in mind these reservations, the prevalence of lone-parent families using these most recent national sources of data is given in Table 9.1 and compared (for EU countries) with three estimates published by Eurostat and derived from the Community Census Programme.

- the first is for children of any age except for Luxembourg (under 25), Finland and Sweden (under 18);
- the second is for children under 15; and
- the third for children under six.

Then, these are compared with estimates derived from the European Employment Survey for children under 15.

Then data are presented from the first sweep of the European Household Panel Survey. This may become the best source of comparable data on

Table 9.1: *Estimates of the prevalence of lone parent families from various sources*

	Col 1	Col 2	Col 3	Col 4	Col 5	Col 6	Col 7
Belgium	11 (1992)	21	15	15	9	13	11
Denmark	19 (1994)	18	20	14	–	19	15
Germany	19 (1992)	19	15	14	10	12	10
Greece	11 (1991)	11	6	3	3	5	3
Spain	7 (1991)	13	–	–	2	4	3
France	12 (1990)	16	11	8	9	12	9
Ireland	11 (1993)	18	11	9	7	11	9
Italy	6 (1992)	16	–	–	4	6	4
Luxembourg	7 (1992)	19	12	11	6	6	4
Netherlands	16 (1992)	16	12	11	7	10	8
Austria	15 (1993)	19	–	13	9	–	–
Portugal	13 (1991)	13	9	6	4	6	5
Finland	16 (1993)	19	–	10	12	–	–
Sweden	18 (1990)	18	–	14	–	–	–
UK	21 (1992)	22	19	19	18	18	15
Australia	18 (1994)						
Japan	5 (1990)						
New Zealand	25 (1992)						
Norway	21 (1993)						
USA	29 (1991)						

Notes:

Col 1 = Lone-parent families as percentage of all families with children;

Col 2 = Lone-parent families as percentage of all families with children 1990/91;

Col 3 = Lone-parent families with children under 15 as a percentage of all families with children under 15, 1990/1;

Col 4 = Lone-parent families with a child under 6 as a percentage of all families with a child under 6, 1990/1;

Col 5 = Lone-parent family with a child under 15 as percentage of all families with children with a child under 15, 1995;

Col 6 = Lone parent with a child under 16 as a percentage of all families with a child under 16 1994; and

Col 7 = Percentage of children under 16 living in a lone parent household.

Sources:

Col 1 = National informants using national sources; Bradshaw et al 1996;

Col 2 = Eurostat: Demographic Statistics 1995 Table j–8;

Col 3 = EC: Demographic situation Eurostat (1994) Table 16;

Col 4 = EC: Demographic situation Eurostat (1994) Table 16;

Col 5 = Labour Force Survey 1995 Eurostat (1996) Table 114;

Col 6 = Computed from table 3d–1 supplied by Eurostat from the ECHP 1994; and

Col 7 = Computed from Table 6-1 supplied by Eurostat from the ECHP 1994.

lone parents (short of the next census), but children in this analysis were defined as under 16 only and it is not possible to identify lone parents living in multi-unit families using the 1994 data, though it may be possible for 1995.[1] Also, the Netherlands treats cohabiting parents with no child from their present partnership as a lone parent. Finally, the table presents data on the proportion of children under 16 living in lone-parent families.

The figures in the first column of Table 9.1 indicate that the proportion of lone-parent families varies from 29 per cent in the USA, 25 per cent in New Zealand and 21 per cent in Norway and the UK, to only 5 per cent in Japan, 6 per cent in Italy and 7 per cent in Luxembourg and Spain. In some cases, the estimates summarised in the other five columns broadly agree with the data provided by the national informants: this is true for the UK, Sweden and Denmark. But, in other cases there appear to be large differences in estimates, which require further investigation.

THE EMPLOYMENT OF LONE PARENTS

If it is hard to compare the prevalence of lone parent families between countries, it is well nigh impossible to compare their characteristics. Estimates of lone fathers as a proportion of lone parents are available. The UK has one of the lowest proportions at 9 per cent, Greece has 25 per cent and Germany 17 per cent (see Bradshaw et al, 1996, Table 2.1). However, comparable data on the marital status, age of mother, ages of children and number of children are more difficult to obtain. Table 9.2 below provides some data from the early and provisional analysis of the European Community Household Panel (ECHP) for 1994. It confirms the finding in Bradshaw et al (1996) that the UK has a comparatively large percentage of lone parents with young children (under three) and a comparatively low proportion of lone parents with only one child.

It is also difficult to make comparisons between the proportions of lone mothers in employment outside the home in different countries. Some estimates exclude the self-employed, definitions of full-time and part-time work differ and it is not always clear whether estimates include or exclude lone mothers on parental leave and or unemployed and receiving benefits. Some evidence from the ECHP is given in Table 9.2 above. The next three figures, derived from Bradshaw et al (1996) show that out of 20 countries:

---

1. One possible indication of lone-parent families 'hidden' in multi-unit households is the proportion of children living in atypical households and other households undefined in the ECHP 1994. It can be seen below that the variations are substantial. The percentage of children living in multi unit households in 1994 was Belgium (4%); Denmark (2%); Germany (4%); Greenland (17%); Spain (14%); France (4%); Ireland (10%); Italy (16%); Luxembourg (16%); Portugal (17%); Portugal (17%) and the UK (8%).

Table 9.2: *Some characteristics of lone-parent families: evidence from the ECHP, 1994*

	Col 1	Col 2	Col 3	Col 4	Col 5	Col 6
Belgium	4	58	55	62	3177	3815
Denmark	11	65	69	74	4311	4487
Germany	17	62	70	56	3467	3738
Greece	4	63	67	40	2582	2819
Spain	4	56	61	30	2498	3277
France	9	63	71	50	4300	4855
Ireland	17	41	23	28	1789	2447
Italy	7	66	61	42	2118	2804
Luxembourg	14	68	76	47	7466	8010
Netherlands	3	52	36	48	2416	3179
Portugal	7	53	69	63	1817	2100
UK	20	50	41	58	3559	4287

Notes:

Col 1 = Percentage of lone-parent families with a child younger than three;

Col 2 = Percentage of lone-parent families with only one child;

Col 3 = Percentage of lone-parent families with earnings;

Col 4 = Percentage of married/cohabiting mothers with earnings;

Col 5 = Equivalent household income of all lone-parent families in pound sterling purchasing power parity per month; and

Col 6 = Equivalent household income of employed lone-parent families in pound sterling purchasing power parity per month.

Source: Tabulations provided by Eurostat.

1. The UK has the second biggest difference (after New Zealand) in the proportion of lone mothers and married/cohabiting mothers in employment (Figure 9.1).
2. The UK has the fourth lowest proportion of lone mothers employed (after Ireland, New Zealand and the Netherlands) (Figure 9.1).
3. The UK has, with New Zealand, the second lowest proportion of lone mothers employed full time (Figure 9.2) and the second lowest proportion employed full time as a proportion of those employed (Figure 9.3).

Why is this?

There is no doubt that variations in the characteristics of lone-mother families explains some of the variation in employment levels, particularly for the UK. Thus, the UK has relatively high proportions of single lone mothers, young lone mothers, lone mothers with preschool children and a low proportion of lone mothers with only one child. However, although

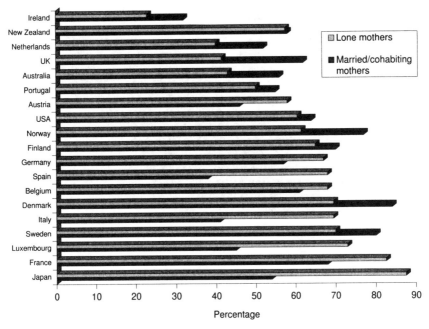

Figure 9.1: *Percentage of lone mothers and married/cohabiting mothers in employment*

there is considerable variation in the characteristics of lone-mother populations, we concluded in our study (Bradshaw et al, 1996) that these differences are not the sole or sufficient determinant of variation in lone mothers' employment patterns. For example, France, Sweden and Belgium have lone mother populations with characteristics similar to our own, yet they all have very high employment rates and even when you control for mothers' age, the number of children and the age of the youngest child, the UK still has lone mother participation rates that are lower than most other countries. So, other factors are also responsible for the employment position of lone mothers in the UK.

Why should we be concerned about the failure of lone mothers in the UK to obtain access to employment? The primary interest of the Conservative governments in the 1980s and early 1990s, and one that led them to abandon an often repeated stance of neutrality on the issue of employment, was a concern with the public expenditure costs of support-ing the seemingly ever-increasing population of lone mothers on income support, family credit and housing benefit. Indeed, that cost was one of the reasons why they were never able to reduce taxation (albeit minor com-pared with the costs of unemployment). Of course, their failure to achieve cuts in public expenditure and taxation can be claimed as a reason for them losing the election in 1997. So, politically, it is an important issue.

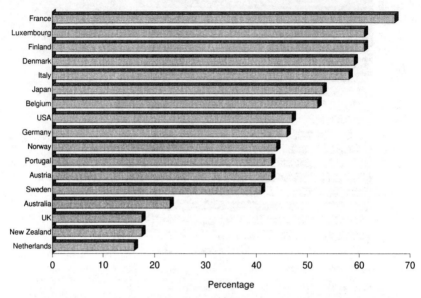

Figure 9.2: *Percentage of lone mothers in full-time employment*

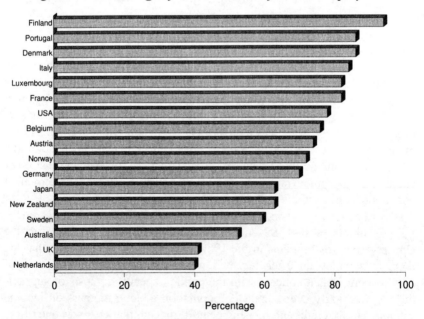

Figure 9.3: *Percentage lone mothers who are employed full time*

However, my reason for being concerned with lone mothers' labour supply has nothing to do with public expenditure. It is derived from comparative data on poverty, which is presented in the next section. However, before presenting it, it is important to emphasise that 'getting lone parents into work' should never become the only concern of policy in this field. The focus should surely be the interests of nearly three million children living in lone-parent households. There are very strong arguments that it is in the interest of those children, at least for a time after the breakdown of a marriage or cohabitation, that their mother is not hassled to take paid work and there may be other times when it might be in the interests of the lone mother, her children and the community that she is not required to combine paid work and caring responsibilities – particularly if that paid work does not actually result in any improvement in the children's living standards or quality of life. It would be a disaster if social policy in Britain were to follow the US welfare reforms where the imperative to get lone mothers off the rolls is likely to drive many already impoverished children further into hardship.

LONE PARENTHOOD AND POVERTY

This section of the chapter draws on the Luxembourg Income Survey to present evidence on the prevalence of poverty among lone parents in different countries and how that varies according to whether or not they are in employment.

Figure 9.4 shows that circa 1990 (in fact 1991 for the UK) the proportion of lone-parent families in the UK in pre-transfer poverty (that is with equivalent incomes below 50 per cent of the median before taking taxes and benefits into account), is higher at 69 per cent than in any other of the 19 countries for which data were available in the Luxembourg Income Survey. After the impact of taxes and benefits, 30 per cent[2] of lone parents in the UK are still living below this poverty threshold. This is a smaller proportion than in the USA, Australia, Canada and Germany (in the last of these, the proportion in poverty actually goes up as a result of the transfer system!).

---

2. This figure is different from and lower than the 56 per cent given in Table 1.1 of Bradshaw et al (1996). There are three reasons for this: the previous table was based on the 1990 Family Expenditure Survey and this one is based on the 1991 FES; the previous one used a threshold of 50 per cent of *mean* income and this uses 50 per cent of *median* income; and there is no doubt that estimates of poverty rates are particularly sensitive to the threshold used in the UK, not least because so many lone parents are dependent on income support. Thus, if we had used a threshold of 40 per cent of median income, the proportion of lone parents in post transfer poverty would have been 19 per cent and if we had used the 60 per cent threshold the proportion of lone parents in post transfer poverty would have been 51 per cent.

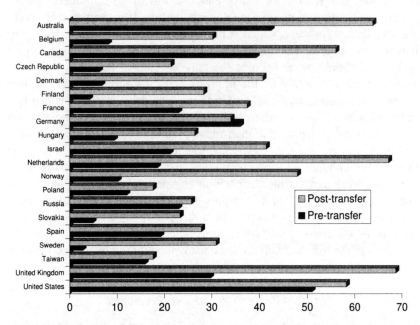

Figure 9.4: *Percentage of lone parents with incomes below 50 per cent of median. Circa 1990. Luxembourg Income Survey*

Figure 9.5 takes lone mothers only and compares the post-transfer poverty rates (equivalent incomes below 50 median income after taking taxes and benefits into account) according to whether or not the lone mother has any income from employment. In all countries, the proportion of lone mothers in poverty falls if they are in employment. In the UK, the poverty rate falls from 47 per cent if lone mothers are in employment to 9 per cent if they are not. This is not the biggest proportional fall as a result of employment – look at the fall in the Czech Republic and Sweden. However, employment is not a guarantee of avoiding poverty in any country and the poverty rates among employed lone mothers in the UK are still comparatively high. Nevertheless, employment is a substantial improvement over non-employment.

We have also undertaken a similar analysis with children as the unit of analysis. Figure 9.6 compares the proportion of children living in families with lone parents in poverty (with equivalent income below 50 per cent of *mean* income). Overall, 47 per cent of the children of lone parents in the UK are in poverty. If the lone parent has no earnings, that proportion is 64 per cent and if the lone mother is in employment the proportion is 28 per cent.

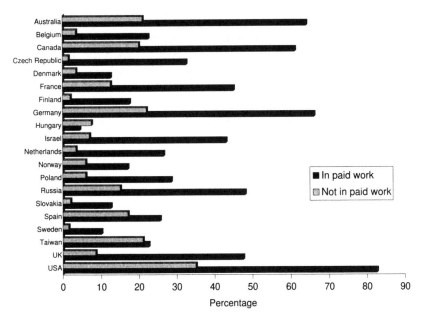

Figure 9.5: *Percentage of lone mothers with income below 50 per cent of the median. Circa 1990. Luxembourg Income Survey*

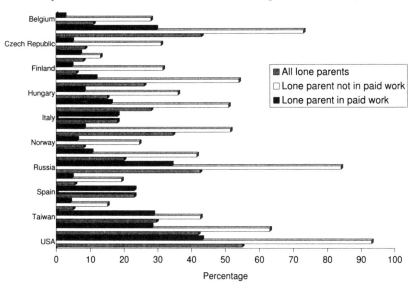

Figure 9.6: *Percentage of children living in lone-parent families with incomes below 50 per cent of average income. Circa 1990. Luxembourg Income Survey*

POLICY IMPLICATIONS AND OPTIONS

In the light of this, most of the rest of this chapter will be concerned with what lessons from abroad can be learned about how we might increase the labour participation rates of lone mothers in the UK. However, before concentrating on that, there are some points to be made about the relative living standards of lone parents dependent on income support. This is particularly important in the context of the action of the government to abolish the lone parent premium in income support and thus arguably to make the first ever deliberate real cut in the real level of the Beveridge safety net. There are three points to make.

First, we have observed in Figure 9.4 the high poverty rates among lone parents in the UK who do not have employment (and are therefore very likely to be dependent on income support). In Table 9.3 we compare the net disposable income of a lone-parent family with one child aged seven receiving social assistance. The relative generosity of countries varies to some extent according to whether the comparisons are made before or after housing costs. If they are made before housing costs, the southern European countries are discounted (because they do not have developed social assistance schemes) and the UK comes well down the league table just ahead of Ireland and France. If they are made after housing costs, the relative position of the UK improves, but income support is still £200 per month less than *Socialhilfe* in Germany for the same family and about £100 per month less than social assistance in Sweden, the Netherlands and Denmark.

As well as being concerned about the absolute level of income support, there may be concern about its relationship with net incomes in work – the replacement rate. These are also compared in Table 9.3. It can be seen that before housing costs the UK lone parent has one of the lowest replacement rates in the EU and after housing costs it is still comparatively low.

The decision to abandon the lone parent premium and abolish one-parent benefit was justified to 'enable the Secretary of State better to consider . . . the relative level of support provided to lone parents as against that for two-parent families with children' (note to the SSAC from the DSS on restricting benefits for lone parents, 1996). As far as social assistance is concerned, this balance is compared in the final column of the table, which shows the ratio of the net disposable income of a lone parent with one child to a couple with one child. The relativities vary a good deal – in Portugal, a lone mother receives 103 per cent of a couple (ie more). In Denmark, a lone parent receives only 63 per cent of a couple. At 79 per cent, the ratio in the UK is lower than in Belgium, Germany, France, Italy, the Netherlands and Portugal.

Table 9.3: *Comparisons of the level of net disposable income of lone parents not in employment and receiving social assistance*

	Col 1	Col 2	Col 3	Col 4	Col 5
Belgium	534	322	90	85	100
Denmark	585	477	91	92	63
Germany	543	543	77	104	88
Greece	55	−167	19	−	−
Spain	240	−35	53	−	−
France	316	211	56	55	92
Ireland	331	298	47	47	66
Italy	56	49	12	11	100
Luxembourg	649	403	81	85	70
Netherlands	542	445	84	87	92
Austria	398	221	74	78	77
Portugal	249	181	89	85	103
Finland	419	353	73	75	68
Sweden	463	463	95	136	77
UK	355	355	49	65	79

Notes:

Col 1 = Net disposable income of a lone parent with one child aged 7 receiving social assistance in pound sterling purchasing power parity per month 1995. Before housing costs;

Col 2 = Net disposable income of a lone parent with one child aged 7 receiving social assistance in pound sterling purchasing power parity per month 1995. After housing costs;

Col 3 = Replacement rates: net disposable income on social assistance as a percentage of net disposable income of the same lone parent employed for half national average male earnings. Before housing costs;

Col 4 = Replacement rates: net disposable income on social assistance as a percentage of net disposable income of the same lone parent employed for half national average male earnings. After housing costs; and

Col 5 = Net disposable income of a lone parent with one child as a proportion of the net disposable income of a couple with child both receiving social assistance.

Source: Ditch et al, 1995.

So, the cut in the level of income support is hardly justified by comparative research – indeed it is not justified by any research – in fact it is an(other) example of policy making inspired by Institute of Economic Affairs ideology rather than the research evidence. It is an assault on the living standards of the poorest children in Britain.

EMPLOYMENT

The comparative study of lone mothers' employment published in 1996 (Bradshaw et al, 1996a) sought to learn lessons from abroad for the UK. In that study, we attempted to cover the main factors that might explain variations in labour supply in different countries, including the characteristics of lone-mother families, labour demand and the state of the labour market, education and training services that might assist lone parents, socio-cultural factors such as attitudes to the respective roles of mothers as workers and carers, the availability and cost of childcare, maternity and parental leave provision, earnings, family benefits, child support regimes, income taxation, social assistance rules, housing benefit systems, health and education costs, replacement rates and marginal tax rates.

Here, it is not possible to rehearse all the evidence, but what can one say about the UK position? There is a coherent story to tell. As has been said, the characteristics of UK lone mothers are consistent with, but do not themselves fully explain, the low rates of employment. Compared with other countries, the demand for female labour is quite high; both female earnings and the rate of taxation are middling; in-work benefits are high, especially given that low earnings and socio-cultural influences tend to encourage mothers' employment, particularly when the child begins school. These factors might be expected to encourage lone mothers' employment, but they are offset by a relatively liberal work test in income support, an ineffective child maintenance regime, non-existent training and into-work advisory services, poor maternity and parental leave provision and a housing benefit system that results in sharp increases in housing costs associated with coming off income support – particularly for owner occupiers. A key factor affecting lone mothers' labour supply behaviour appears to be the very high level of childcare costs in the UK. These, unlike most other countries, are not subsidised (except since 1994 in the family credit disregard). The result of all this is that after housing costs, replacement rates are high and after childcare costs they are much higher than any other country.

It is possible to produce this kind of coherent explanation for each country in the study. However, it is much more difficult to extract a more general set of explanations of lone parent labour supply covering sets of countries. It might be expected that countries with high proportions of lone mothers in employment would have relatively high wages, high child benefits, a strong maintenance regime, strong availability for work tests, low income tax and low housing costs associated with moving off social assistance into work, good quality child care, low replacement rates and low marginal tax rates. There is no high participation country that meets all those criteria. Nor do any of the low employment countries meet all the opposite criteria.

Perhaps, the countries that are most similar to each other are the southern EU ones and Japan: they all have relatively low proportions of lone mothers; Spain, Italy, Portugal and Japan all have high proportions of lone mothers in employment and they tend to work full time. Also, in these countries the proportion of lone mothers employed is much higher than that of married mothers. All these countries have weak or non-existent social assistance regimes – effectively, there is no alternative to work or family support. With the exception of Italy, they all have high proportions of lone mothers living in multi-unit households, indeed living with their mothers who are not in employment. Thus, informal childcare is substituting for formal childcare – lone mothers are employed because their mothers are not.

This pattern is likely to change rapidly and it is not a model to which northern European countries return. Indeed, it is not possible to learn easy lessons from abroad about lone mothers' employment. It is unlikely that there are single or simple measures that can be employed by the UK, for example to increase the employment of their lone parents. The employment levels of lone mothers will be influenced by their characteristics, the state of the labour market, public attitudes to mothers' employment, maternity and parental leave, the level of in-work incomes and the benefits available out of work, the rules governing labour participation, the effectiveness of the maintenance regime, the treatment of housing costs and health and education costs. It does look as if the level of child benefits matters, but probably the most important factor of all is the availability of good quality, flexible and affordable childcare.

CONCLUSION

There is some evidence that proportions of lone parents claiming income support in the UK are falling. As Table 9.4 shows, the number of lone parents on income support in May each year as a proportion of John Haskey's latest annual 'best estimates' of all lone parents (see Chapter 2) indicate that the proportion of lone parents on income support has been declining since 1992.

However, it is unclear whether this is due to policy efforts, or to a general improvement in labour demand. The UK has become more intent on encouraging lone mothers into employment with new policy measures. These include the CSA and its in-work disregard, the reduction in hours for family credit, the childcare disregard in family credit, the back to work bonus, the child maintenance bonus, the limited nursery vouchers scheme, an expansion of holiday daycare, the 'new deal' for lone parents and the

168   *Jonathan Bradshaw*

mean-spirited decision to abolish the lone-parent premium in income support.

Table 9.4: *Proportion of lone parents on income support*

1990	1991	1992	1993	1994	1995	1996
64%	67%	69%	68%	66%	63%	(59%)*

Note: *1996 author's estimate based on extrapolating the rate of increase in the prevalence of lone parents.

Nevertheless, more radical measures are called for than the portfolio already on offer. These should include:

1. A *guaranteed* maintenance scheme for those in employment;
2. a less sharp taper in housing benefit and/or a return to bricks and mortar subsidies in social housing – and a mortgage benefit;
3. easier access to and better quality of training;
4. measures to increase labour demand;
5. a more thoroughgoing and better resourced advisory service;
6. a tougher work test for lone mothers on income support;
7. higher in-work benefits (including the retention of one parent benefit);
8. but, most important of all, there is a need to invest in good quality, flexible and affordable childcare, including holiday care and after school care. Childcare alone will not solve the problem but without it other measures will prove fruitless.

Chapter 10

Lone Mothers' Earnings[1]

Alex Bryson

Lone mothers' low and declining employment rates have attracted the attention of policy-makers and academics alike. This is understandable given the consequential rise in the proportion claiming welfare benefits, and the negative impact of joblessness on lone mothers' wellbeing (Bryson et al, 1997). However, similar attention has not, as yet, been paid to lone mothers' *earnings*. It is important to know what affects lone mothers' earnings because:

- their earning potential is a key determinant of their employment rates (Ermisch and Wright, 1991; Jenkins, 1992);
- the wellbeing of lone mothers and their families rises (falls) with earnings (Bryson et al, 1997); and
- higher earning capacity is the surest way to guarantee lone mothers' financial independence in the longer-term, permitting them to work without the assistance of wage subsidies.

This chapter analyses earnings of a nationally representative cross section of lone mothers in 1991. The data are longitudinal, allowing analyses of cross-sectional data and wage progression over a four-year period, during which time there were changes in personal and household circumstances (including (re)partnering) and in the benefit system.

The chapter focuses on three issues. First, it examines the impact of human capital (qualifications, training and work experience) on earnings. The questions here are whether lone mothers reap the full rewards of investing in their earning potential and, if not, how policy can help facilitate this process. Second, it focuses on the effect of family credit on

1. The author is grateful to the Joseph Rowntree Foundation for funding the study and to the Department of Social Security for permitting access to the data.

earnings and earning progression. The concern here is that family credit may trap lone mothers on low earnings. As Reuben Ford and Jane Millar note in Chapter 1 above, 'Trapping lone parents onto low wages and long-term dependency on family credit may seem little improvement over the current position of lone parents trapped on income support – with the added disadvantage that their time for parenting is reduced.' Finally, the effect of family responsibilities is briefly considered.

THE DATA AND HYPOTHESES

The data track a nationally representative cross section of lone mothers in 1991 over four years, with data collected through face-to-face interviews in 1991, 1993, 1994 and 1995.[2] Table 10.1 shows the characteristics of the sample.

Table 10.1: *Lone-parent characteristics as used in final earnings models*

	Persistent workers	All workers, 1991	Whole sample, 1991
Age in 1991:	%	%	%
Under 25 yrs	11	17	17
25–29 yrs	14	19	22
30–34 yrs	23	20	20
35–39 yrs	21	19	17
40+ yrs	32	24	23
Qualifications in 1991:			
No qualifications	24	31	43
Low school qualifications	26	31	29
Vocational qualifications	20	17	14
Advanced school qualifications	10	6	4
Post-school qualifications	11	8	5
University-level qualifications	8	7	5
Increased qualifications between 1991–5	26	19	17
Ever been on job-related training	63	44	37
Undertook job-related training, 1993–5	49	27	20
Type of employer in 1991:			
Public sector	32	28	17
Commercial	58	62	36
Other	5	6	4

---

2. They were collected under the DSS-funded Programme of Research into Low Income Families, based at the Policy Studies Institute. For a full description of the PRILIF data see Marsh et al, 1997.

(*Table 10.1 continued*)	Persistent workers	All workers, 1991	Whole sample, 1991
Missing data (%)	5.00	5.00	43.00
Employer employs 10+ people (%)	73.00	71.00	–
Missing data (%)	2.00	5.00	–
Trades union member in 1991 (%)	27.00	20.00	12.00
Months spent in 1995 job	54.81	–	–
Weekly net wage (£s):			
1991	110.08	100.22	–
1995	137.77	–	–
Hourly net wage (£s):			
1991	3.94	3.62	–
1995	5.17	–	–
Weekly hours:			
1991	28.30	28.06	–
1995	30.00	–	–
Under 30 hours per week in 1995 (%)	43.00	–	–
Received family credit in 1991 (%)	23.00	19.00	9.00
% time spent in full-time jobs, 1991–4	69.67	47.55	28.39
% time spent in part-time jobs, 1991–4	10.79	10.75	8.41
Housing tenure in 1991: (%)			
Owner	47.00	37.00	27.00
Social renter	38.00	44.00	55.00
Other tenure	15.00	20.00	17.00
Partnerships in survey period: (%)			
Partner with no job in 1991–2	5.00	6.00	6.00
Partner with no job in 1993–4	7.00	8.00	8.00
Partner in full-time job in 1991–2	10.00	8.00	6.00
Partner in full-time job in 1993–4	14.00	10.00	7.00
Months as a lone mother to 1991	62.80	55.04	58.05
Route into lone motherhood: (%)			
Single never-married mother	13.00	19.00	24.00
Separated from marriage	21.00	19.00	16.00
Divorced	44.00	38.00	34.00
Separated from cohabitation	18.00	20.00	21.00
Widowed	4.00	3.00	5.00
Maintenance payable in 1991: (%)			
Over £25 per week	16.00	14.00	10.00
Under £25 per week	22.00	21.00	17.00
None	62.00	65.00	72.00
Ever been on Income Support before 1991	58.00	67.00	78.00
Brought up with both parents (%)	80.00	67.00	65.00
Region, 1991: (%)			
Southeast	19.00	21.00	22.00

(*Table 10.1 continued*)	Persistent workers	All workers, 1991	Whole sample, 1991
West	8.00	6.00	5.00
Wales	4.00	3.00	5.00
Midlands	19.00	19.00	17.00
East Anglia	9.00	6.00	6.00
Northeast	15.00	16.00	16.00
Northwest	18.00	18.00	16.00
Scotland	9.00	11.00	14.00
Attitudes in 1991: (see text)			
Work commitment (1–6 scale)	3.94	3.89	3.71
Home orientation (1–5 scale)	2.30	2.44	2.66
Number of children in 1991: (%)			
One	58.00	60.00	49.00
Two	30.00	27.00	31.00
Three or more	12.00	14.00	19.00
Age of youngest child in 1991: (%)			
Under 5 years old	27.00	39.00	46.00
5–10 years old	39.00	35.00	31.00
11–15 years old	25.00	20.00	18.00
16–18 years old	9.00	5.00	4.00

In this chapter we use these data to explore three hypotheses:

Human capital

There is substantial evidence that wages are determined, in large part, by levels of qualifications, training and work experience (Polachek, 1995). But, is this the case for lone mothers? Or, does their experience of lone motherhood (with its exposure to hardship and competing family responsibilities) mean women who are, or have recently been, lone mothers do not benefit from the educational and job investments they make, or are unable to invest sufficiently to make much difference to their earning capacity?[3]

The data include information on actual full-time and part-time work

3. Other research shows lone mothers have low levels of human capital relative to other workers and potential workers. Although low human capital may result from lone motherhood if it reduces the investments (financial and otherwise) mothers make in their earning potential, it is also possible that a low earning potential may result in selection into lone motherhood in the first place. Jenkins, Ermisch and Wright (1990) find some limited evidence to support the 'selection' hypothesis among ever-married lone mothers.

experience over the survey period collected retrospectively at each interview; job-specific human capital, namely experience of job-related training and job tenure; and qualification levels. In addition, age is used as a proxy for longer-term experience.

Family credit

By definition, a working lone mother is *the* family breadwinner and will need a 'family wage'. In practice, half of those working 16 hours or more rely on family credit to supplement their wages (Marsh et al, 1997). The reliance on family credit arises because most lone mothers can only command fairly low hourly earnings, while responsibilities for young children limit the hours they can work. Recent research shows family credit substantially improves lone mothers' chances of entering employment (Bryson et al, 1997). But is there a price attached?

There will be a price attached if recipients accept wages lower than they could reasonably be expected to command given their other characteristics and attributes. Family credit provides the opportunity to accept low-waged work, or to work relatively short hours, because wages are topped-up according to an assessed needs level. Family credit may offer the opportunity for a lone mother to (re-)enter the labour market by undercutting competing labour, and on terms that may allow her to match work with family commitments. It might not be surprising, then, if lone mothers on family credit receive lower wages than might otherwise be expected, at least in the short term.

Family credit may also have an effect on what lone mothers can earn in the medium and longer term. This may be so if family credit jobs are 'poor' jobs, offering little or no opportunity to improve earnings, or to develop skills and experience that would permit a transfer to a better job for the same or different employer.[4] The availability of family credit to top up low wages may discourage employers from raising wages over time if they know that workers are unlikely to benefit a great deal.[5] Equally, family credit may have an indirect effect on weekly earnings through the hours recipients choose to work. The 'poverty trap', whereby recipients face high marginal deduction rates as earnings rise, may discourage workers from raising their hours or investing in their earning

---

4. That is, they are 'non-career jobs', to use Theodossiou's (1995) phrase.
5. Although family credit does not appear to affect employers' conscious wage setting behaviour (Callender et al, 1994), it is possible that wage supplements widely available to particular groups of workers could reduce earnings in the long run, for instance through a downward wage drift with employers failing to up-rate wages to the same degree.

potential, unless they can achieve earnings that push them beyond family credit.[6]

Work and family constraints

It is possible that all the working lone mothers in the sample may have experienced some constraints on their jobs from family responsibilities. Those with greatest care responsibilities (having younger and more children) may have experienced more constraints, adversely affecting their earnings. A high 'home orientation' might indicate a particularly high susceptibility to family constraint. For the present study, specific attitudinal variables capturing 'home-orientation' and 'work commitment' were derived[7] If family constraints have a cumulative effect over time, then time spent as a lone mother may have a negative impact on earnings. Conversely, (re)partnering may help overcome direct constraints if the man is unemployed and therefore has time to care, or if he works, improving the chances of paying for suitable childcare while both work. Children may also affect lone mothers' earnings indirectly through their impact on reducing the investments they make in wage-enhancing human capital.[8] This could occur through lower educational investments, the loss of work experience due to child-rearing, and the depreciation of human capital with time out of the labour market. Although having more children may lower effort at work (Becker, 1985), they may increase financial need and thus induce an increase in hours to make ends meet.

6. The concern that wage subsidies may be a disincentive to workers acquiring earnings-enhancing qualifications and training is one reason for the time-limiting of the wage subsidy in the Canadian self-sufficiency demonstration targeted at lone mothers (Card and Robins, 1996). Concerns that net income alters very little with extra hours while on family credit led the UK government to introduce a £10 family credit premium for those working 30 hours or more per week.

7. The two attitudinal variables used in the wages analyses were derived using factor analyses on 22 attitudinal questions asked at the first interview in 1991. 'Work commitment' is a scale running from 1 to 6, with respondents scoring an extra point every time they agreed to one of the following statements: (a) having almost any job is better than being unemployed; (b) if I didn't like a job I'd pack it in even if I had no other job to go to (reverse coding); (c) once you've got a job it's important to hang on to it even if you don't really like it; (d) a woman and her family will benefit if she has a paid job; and (e) a person must have a job to feel a full member of society. 'Home orientation' is a scale running from 1 to 5, with respondents scoring an extra point every time they agreed to one of the following statements: (a) it is just wrong for women with children under five to go out to work; (b) it is less important for a woman to go out to work than a man; (c) women with school age children should never work full time; and (d) if their child is ill and both parents work, the mother should take time off work.

8. Most studies indicate that children reduce women's earnings primarily indirectly by reducing labour force participation and the acquisition of human capital, rather than directly by lowering the productivity of otherwise similar women (Waldfogel, 1995).

ANALYSIS AND RESULTS

The discussion below is based on analyses of hourly and weekly net earnings in 1991 and 1995,[9] when the sample was last interviewed, and earnings changes during the survey period, 1991–5. It considers the medium term value of employment for the initial cross section of lone mothers. Half of those interviewed in 1995 were working, or had worked since the last interview in 1994. On average, they were earning £119 a week in 1995 prices, net of tax and benefit transfers, for a 28-hour working week.[10] The analysis is confined to those who had earnings data for 1991 and 1995[11] so that wage change over the period can be examined. These are the *persistent workers* who made up roughly half those working in 1991.

Dealing with potential sources of estimation bias

There are various possible sources of bias in estimating wage equations. First, labour market experience and job tenure are endogenous if labour supply is responsive to wages (Korenman and Neumark, 1992). This problem is minimised by estimating wage outcomes for 1995 and 1991–5 using work experience between 1991 and 1994. Second, fertility may be endogenous. The problem is minimised by using 1991 measures for household characteristics and children.

Third, women may be selected or self-select into different marital/ fertility states on the basis of unmeasured characteristics correlated with wages (such as career orientation). Results for cross-sectional analyses based on persistent workers are less likely to suffer from biases introduced by unobserved heterogeneity than analyses based on all workers because they are a more homogeneous group. In particular, they are likely to share a stronger work commitment, and the financial returns to working for this group are not severely disrupted by time out of the labour market.[12] The

---

9. A lone mother's worth in the labour market is best measured by hourly earnings (and to a lesser degree by the number of hours she is able to work). Weekly earnings are a better indicator of the resources available to the household than hourly earnings and, as such, may be more closely related to family welfare. Log wages were estimated using ordinary least squares regressions.

10. Earnings are net of deductions for tax, national insurance, pension contributions, union dues and so on, but including overtime, bonus, commission and other extra payments.

11. More precisely, it included those with wage data for current jobs in 1991 and 1995 plus those not working who gave wage data for a recent job. The 1991 wages include 55 wage observations for jobs going back to May 1988, and the 1995 wages include 12 observations for jobs going back to July 1994. These wages were up-rated to 1991 and 1995 levels respectively using the earnings index published in the *Employment Gazette*.

12. On average they had spent 84 per cent of the survey period in paid work. Their recent work experience may explain why their wages were higher than for all 1995 workers, averaging £138 a week.

inclusion of a lagged wage variable in the models for 1995 earnings and earnings progression over the survey period control for some unobserved heterogeneity. This is because observations of earnings at two points in time enable unobserved attributes to be 'netted out', provided they are fixed over the period. The use of this technique may substantially reduce the potential bias caused by unobserved heterogeneity in the sample.

Finally, there is the possibility of biased results if those in work are not representative of all lone mothers, that is the problem of sample selection bias. The persistent workers were not typical of the 1991 sample, or all workers in 1991. Compared with other workers they were better trained and qualified, and commanded higher wages. The standard technique is used to test for potential selection bias (Heckman, 1979).[13]

Testing the human capital hypothesis

The analyses confirm that investing in human capital is crucial in lone mothers securing higher wages: qualification levels, job-related training, recent work experience and age (a proxy for longer-term work experience) had significant, large effects on wages in 1995 and earnings progression over the survey period.

Age

Age, which is taken to stand for the value of experience, was a significant determinant of wages. Hourly wages continued to rise as women aged beyond 40, building up work experience as their children grew (Table 10.A3). However, when other factors are taken into account, the importance of age for weekly earnings peaked when lone mothers were in their thirties (Table 10.A1). This is because these women worked longer hours, on average, than younger and older workers.

Women entering their late thirties in 1995 experienced the most rapid growth in weekly earnings over the survey period, benefiting from increased hours and more work experience (Table 10.A2), whereas those aged forty and over by 1995 had experienced the fastest growth in hourly wages (Table 10.A4). It seems that, as hourly earning capacity rose, lone mothers were prepared to shorten their working week, a finding consistent

---

13. Full earnings equations are given in additional Tables 10.A1 to 10.A5 at the end of this chapter. All five models contain a Heckman sample selection bias correction term generated by a first stage probit regression in which participation in waged work at 1991 and 1995 was modelled for all 888 lone mothers in 1991. In the first four models it is not significantly different from zero, so sample selection bias is rejected. In the fifth model, estimating weekly earnings in 1991, the correction term is positive and significant at the 90 per cent level (t stat=1.71) indicating that the estimates are biased downwards by observable characteristics of workers versus non-workers.

with the idea that lone mothers seeking to balance work and family responsibilities prefer to trade some earnings for time at home when they can afford to do so.

Qualifications and training

One quarter of those working in 1991 and 1995 were unqualified in 1991. In 1995, they were earning £95 a week on average (£3.39 an hour), significantly less than those who had some form of academic qualification in 1991, after correcting for other characteristics and circumstances (Table 10.2). The 19 per cent of the sample who had achieved post-school and university qualifications by 1991 were earning between one-third and one-half more per week by 1995 than the reference group in row one of Table 10.2 (those with no qualifications in 1991). Their hourly rates were even higher relative to others.

Table 10.2:[14] *Variation in 1995 earnings by qualifications and training in 1991*

	% difference in weekly wage	% difference in hourly wage
Ref: No qualifications	—	—
Low school qualifications	ns	+17
Vocational qualifications	ns	ns
Advanced school qualifications	ns	ns
Post-school qualifications	+48	+63
University qualifications	+38	+46
Increased qualifications 1991–95	ns	ns
Job-related training	+31	+14

Although school qualifications had no significant effect on weekly earnings, hourly pay rates were one-sixth higher for lone mothers with low school qualifications than for similar lone mothers with no qualifications.

Over the survey period, 1991 qualifications had an even stronger effect on lone mothers' ability to improve their weekly earnings (Table 10.3). Their impact on hourly wage change over the period was very similar to their impact on hourly wages in 1995. It may be expected that those who were able to increase their qualification levels between 1991 and 1995 would be earning more than those who did not. However, controlling for

---

14. In the following tables the confidence level for significant differences is 10 per cent or higher. 'ns' means not significant at a 10 per cent level or above.

other factors, there was no significant difference in earnings. The policy
implications are clear: qualifications, particularly academic qualifications,
raise lone mothers' earnings. Those who have them see their earnings rise
more quickly than others. However, only a small proportion of lone
mothers possess the higher academic qualifications that bring the highest
rewards.

Table 10.3: *The impact of qualifications and training on changes in*
earnings, 1991–5

	% change in weekly wage	% change in hourly wage
Ref: No qualifications	–	–
Low school qualifications	ns	+19
Vocational qualifications	+23	ns
Advanced school qualifications	+73	ns
Post-school qualifications	+72	+63
University qualifications	+57	+49
Increased qualifications between 1991 and 1995	ns	ns
Job-related training, 1993–5	+31	+14

Table 10.4: *Proportion of workers receiving on-the-job training in*
1993–5

Professionals	Non-manuals	Service sector	Manual
73%	42%	56%	27%

There were substantial gains made from job-related training. Those who
had received job-related training at some point in their careers were
estimated to be earning nearly one-third more per week, and 14 per cent
more per hour, than those who had never received job-related training,
after correcting for other factors. Job-related training had similar effects
on earning progression during the survey period. It may be that those who
take up training are more highly motivated than others, which explains the
earnings increase, but a variable capturing work motivation is incorporated
in the analysis which should take account of this. It may also be the case
that on-the-job training is simply an indicator of being in a 'good
job', which also commands good wages. Table 10.4 lends some support to
this possibility: whereas professionals accounted for one-fifth of the

sample, they accounted for 31 per cent of those getting on-the-job training.

Nevertheless, since qualifications are taken into account in the analysis, it seems likely that lone mothers had been able to raise their wages having completed job-related training, regardless of the job they were in.

Recent work experience

On average, this sample had spent 70 per cent of their time between 1991 and 1994 in full-time paid work, and 11 per cent in part-time paid work of under 16 hours per week. Weekly earnings rose over the period with the time lone mothers had recently spent in full-time paid work. A rise of 10 per cent in the time spent in full-time paid work (equivalent to about ten weeks' work) was estimated to raise weekly earnings over the survey period by 6 per cent. Time in part-time employment had no effect on changes in weekly earnings over the period, and significantly reduced weekly earnings in 1995.

Recent work experience had no significant effect on hourly earnings in 1995, or changes in hourly earnings over the survey period. So, experience of full-time paid work did not raise lone mothers' labour market worth, as one might have expected. Instead, it simply indicated an increased likelihood of working longer hours in 1995. For instance, those who had spent all of their time in full-time employment between 1991 and 1994 were working an average of 34 hours per week in 1995, compared with 25 hours for the remainder of the sample.

Job tenure

These persistent workers had been in their jobs for a mean of 55 months by 1995. The median job tenure was 34 months. This suggests they may have acquired considerable expertise in carrying out their work efficiently and effectively. The time invested in these jobs was rewarded with higher hourly wages: a 10 per cent increase in job tenure (equivalent to about five and a half months in the job) raised hourly pay rates by 1 per cent. But job tenure had no significant effect on weekly wages in 1995, nor on changes in weekly earnings over the survey period. This implies that lone mothers sought to reduce their working hours as their hourly rates rose, preferring to spend more time at home when they could afford it.

The role of family credit

Those who received family credit in 1991 were earning £86 per week on average for a 32-hour week. Non-recipients were earning £117 for a 27-hour working week. However, with family credit payments averaging £35

per week, family credit claimants 'took home' £121 in earnings and benefits. In 1995, family credit recipients were getting an average of £87 in
wages and £52 in family credit, totalling £139 per week for 27 hours paid
work. Non-claimants were getting £156 for a 31-hour working week.
These crude figures suggest that family credit was bridging the gap in
weekly earnings between recipients and non-recipients.

A model estimating net weekly wages in 1991 confirms that the availability of family credit increased lone mothers' preparedness to take jobs at
lower wages (Table 10.A5).[15] Those with family credit entitlements earned
30 per cent less per week than might otherwise have been expected given
their other circumstances (including hours worked) and characteristics.
This may help explain family credit's effectiveness in raising full-time
employment probabilities (Bryson et al, 1997).

After accounting for the effects of other characteristics and circumstances, family credit receipt in 1991 appears to have had a detrimental
effect on earnings in 1995 and earnings progression during the survey
period (Table 10.5).[16]

Table 10.5: *Impact of family credit receipt in 1991 on earnings in 1995
and earnings change over the survey period*

Difference 1991 FC receipt made to 1995 weekly earnings	−16%
Difference 1991 FC receipt made to 1995 hourly earnings	−20%
Difference 1991 FC receipt made to change in weekly earnings, 1991–95	−16%
Difference 1991 FC receipt made to change in hourly earnings, 1991–95	−22%

The 23 per cent of persistent workers who had received family credit in
1991 were earning £107 per week in 1995, compared with £148 earned by
those who had not been on family credit in 1991. Their weekly earnings
were 16 per cent lower in 1995 than one would have expected given their
characteristics. Furthermore, the effect was not due to differences in the
hours worked by 1991 recipients and other working lone mothers. Receipt
of family credit in 1991 also reduced *hourly* earnings in 1995, by one-
fifth. Family credit recipients in 1991 saw their weekly earnings rise

---

15. It is not possible directly to estimate the impact of family credit receipt in 1991 on 1991 wages
because family credit receipt is dependent upon low earnings. That is, family credit receipt is
endogenous. This technical problem was overcome by incorporating into the model a continuous variable generated by a binomial probit model which captures the probability of family
credit entitlement if a mother worked 25 hours per week at her *predicted* hourly wage.

16. Because earnings through to 1995 could vary independently of the amount of family credit
received in 1991, it is possible to estimate the effect of actual family credit receipt in 1991 on
subsequent earnings.

during the survey period by 16 per cent less than one would have expected given their characteristics and circumstances, while their hourly earnings rose by one-fifth less.

The earnings effect of family credit may be due to family credit receipt encouraging people to take jobs below their earning capacity. This assumes that the individuals would have been employed regardless of family credit, whereas the benefit is intended to bring people into employment who would otherwise tend to be non-employed. Alternatively, the poorer paying jobs that family credit recipients occupied in 1991 may have held back these lone mothers' earnings relative to other workers, for reasons outlined earlier. It is also possible that family credit receipt in 1991 is a marker of labour market disadvantage not picked up by human capital variables, although this seems unlikely given the range of human capital variables used in the analyses.

These findings raise questions about the ability of lone mothers to prosper in paid work having entered or held on to low-paying jobs with the help of a wage top-up. Indeed, 42 per cent of the persistent workers who were on family credit in 1991 were still reliant on family credit in 1995. On the other hand, these women would have been substantially worse off working in these jobs if their earnings had not been supplemented by family credit.

Work and family constraints

As Waldfogel (1995) pointed out, family formation may have an impact on wages over and above its effect on human capital if family responsibilities interfere with paid working, or employers believe that they do.

In fact, the number and age of children had no direct significant effect on either weekly and hourly earnings in 1995, or on hourly earnings progression over the course of the survey;[17] nor did attitudes to home and work. Rather, the effect of children operated through their impact on work experience, and the number of hours worked each week. Job tenure, which raises hourly earnings, rose with the age of the youngest child and fell with the number of children. Time in full-time paid work, which boosts weekly earnings, also rose with the age of the youngest child, while time in part-time employment, which had a detrimental effect on weekly earnings, fell as the youngest child aged and rose with the number of

---

17. Those with a youngest child aged 16–18 in 1991 did experience higher weekly earnings growth over the course of the survey period, perhaps indicating that those leaving lone motherhood as their youngest child reaches adulthood may be able to devote more time and energy to their working lives.

children. Once the impact on work experience and weekly working hours are taken into account, the age and number of children had no significant, independent impact on 1995 earnings or change in hourly earnings over the survey period.

However, hourly earnings fell with the length of lone motherhood. A 10 per cent increase in the time spent as a lone mother up to 1991 – equivalent to 24 weeks – reduced hourly earnings in 1995 by 1 per cent (Table 10.A3). It had a similar effect on changes in hourly earnings over the survey period. These effects persisted even when account was taken of the origins of the lone motherhood. The finding suggests that long-term sole responsibility for childcare constrains lone mothers' ability to improve their earning capacity. This deficit can only be made good by working longer hours.

Improving childcare assistance for lone mothers is often identified as important in helping lone mothers to enter jobs; this analysis suggests it could also help lone mothers raise their earning potential.

Partnerships (re)formed during the survey period had a significant effect on what mothers earned. Those acquiring a non-working partner had higher weekly earnings than others by 1995, controlling for other factors, and they had raised their weekly earnings more over the survey period (Tables 10.A1 and 10.A2). Their hourly earnings were unaffected, the rise being due entirely to a substantial increase in the hours they worked. Over the survey period, their average working week increased from 24 to 33 hours, whereas others' hours had remained roughly constant at about 30 hours per week. This increase in hours may have been necessary to meet the extra needs occasioned by the arrival of a non-earner, or else they were freed to earn more by the availability of non-working partners to take over the household role.

Those acquiring a partner in full-time employment earned 30 per cent more per hour in 1995 than might have been expected given their other characteristics and circumstances, and their hourly earnings rose over the survey period by 31 per cent more than would otherwise have been the case. It may be that, with other earnings coming into the household, mothers can hold out longer for better paid jobs. Alternatively, 'better workers' may be attracted to one another, sharing some characteristics not otherwise accounted for in the analysis.

CONCLUDING REMARKS

This chapter indicates that lone mothers are no different from other groups of workers in that their earnings are largely determined by their work experience, qualifications and training. The big policy problem is the low levels of human capital that most lone mothers possess. Helping lone mothers to increase these resources would directly contribute to higher earnings, and hence also to higher employment rates. Children affected earnings in so far as they influenced these human capital variables and the hours mothers were able to work. However, there was evidence that lone mothers' earning capacity was limited by the experience of lone mother-hood, hourly earnings falling with the duration of lone motherhood.

The findings concerning the adverse effects of family credit on earnings progression suggest that the use of financial work incentives is not as straightforward as it may appear to be. Such incentives make it worthwhile for lone mothers to take jobs at wage rates below those they are capable of getting. This means that the advantage of helping more mothers to work is partly offset by the lower productivity of those receiving the benefit, including some who would have worked even without it.

Lone mothers working with family credit supplements had weekly earnings about 40 per cent lower (on average) than might have been expected given their circumstances and characteristics. Of course, employers may not have employed them at higher wages, or they them-selves might not have been able to reconcile longer hours or more demanding work with their domestic role. However, while the short-term trade-off may be to mothers' overall advantage, the long-term impact gives cause for concern. Family credit receipt at 1991 substantially reduced weekly and hourly wages at 1995, and earnings progression over this period was also relatively limited. It seems that lone mothers' ability to prosper in paid work is constrained, once they have entered or held low-paying jobs with a benefit top-up. Other policies are needed to carry on where family credit leaves off.

Greater opportunities for education and training offer the best prospects for lone mothers to increase earnings. Suitable policies might involve inducements to employers to improve training and childcare facilities plus statutory entitlements to training leave, allowing lone mothers to take-up training opportunities. Mothers would be better placed to take up learning opportunities if offered adult learning credits, a policy first suggested in the 1980s. These credits could be targeted at those in lower paying jobs who might benefit most from additional training or learning.

Table 10.A1: *Estimates for log net weekly wages in 1995*

Variables	Coefficients (*t*-stats in parentheses)
Human capital	
Age in 1991	
Ref: Under 25	–
25–29 yrs	0.1317 (1.04)
30–34 yrs	0.4189 (3.49)
35–39 yrs	0.1690 (1.34)
40+ yrs	0.2580 (2.07)
Highest qualification in 1991	
Ref: None	–
Low school qualifications	0.1207 (1.25)
Vocational qualifications	0.0283 (0.26)
Advanced school qualifications	0.2612 (1.69)
Post-school qualifications	0.3889 (3.09)
University-level qualifications	0.3228 (2.26)
Increased qualifications between 1991–5	−0.0230 (0.30)
Ever been on job-related training	0.2692 (4.05)
Months spent in 1995 job	0.0007 (1.18)
% time spent in full-time jobs, 1991–4	0.0056 (4.70)
% time spent in part-time jobs, 1991–4	−0.0034 (2.16)
Characteristics of 1991 job	
Log weekly wage	0.0894 (1.59)
Received Family Credit	−0.1800 (2.38)
Weekly hours	0.0077 (2.26)
Type of employer	
Ref: Other	–
Public sector	0.2886 (1.93)
Commercial	0.3556 (2.50)
Missing data	0.0619 (0.32)
Employer size	
Employs 10+ people	0.1695 (2.12)
Missing data	−0.1169 (0.55)
Trade union member	0.0634 (0.79)
Social characteristics of lone motherhood	
Attitudes to paid work and family	
Work commitment (1–6 scale)	−0.0384 (1.66)
Home orientation (1–5 scale)	−0.0239 (0.81)
Ever been on Income Support before 1991	−0.0357 (0.42)
Partnerships between 91–95	
Partner with no job, 93–94	0.3341 (2.92)

(*Table 10.A1 continued*) Variables	Coefficients (*t*-stats in parentheses)
Social background	
Brought up by both parents	−0.3330 (3.77)
Region in 1991	
Ref: Southeast	—
West	−0.3462 (2.74)
Wales	−0.2623 (1.56)
Midlands	−0.1253 (1.27)
East Anglia	−0.0312 (0.26)
Northeast	−0.2067 (2.06)
Northwest	0.0367 (0.36)
Scotland	−0.2998 (2.54)
Constant	3.4483 (8.24)
Heckman selection term	−0.1614 (1.28)
Number of observations	339
Adjusted R^2	0.58

Table 10.A2: *Estimates for change in log net weekly wages between
1991 and 1995*

Variables	Coefficients (*t*-stats in parentheses)
Human capital	
Age in 1991	
Ref: Under 25	–
25–29 yrs	0.1136 (0.86)
30–34 yrs	0.4370 (3.30)
35–39 yrs	0.1288 (0.89)
40+ yrs	0.1727 (1.15)
Highest qualification in 1991	
Ref: None	–
Low school qualifications	0.1629 (1.63)
Vocational qualifications	0.2086 (1.89)
Advanced school qualifications	0.5508 (3.59)
Post-school qualifications	0.5435 (4.30)
University-level qualifications	0.4473 (3.05)
Increased qualifications between 1991–5	–0.0185 (0.24)
Ever been on job-related training	0.2727 (4.02)
Months spent in 1995 job	0.0008 (1.23)
% time spent in full-time jobs, 1991–4	0.0058 (4.75)
% time spent in part-time jobs, 1991–4	–0.0023 (1.43)
Characteristics of 1991 job	
Log weekly wage	–0.9008 (15.73)
Received Family Credit	–0.1881 (2.45)
Weekly hours	0.0088 (2.53)
Type of employer	
Ref: Other	–
Public sector	0.2283 (1.51)
Commercial	0.2880 (2.00)
Missing data	–0.0539 (0.27)
Employer size	
Employs 10+ people	0.1745 (2.14)
Missing data	–0.1536 (0.70)
Trade union member	0.0569 (0.70)
Social characteristics of lone motherhood	
Attitudes to paid work and family	
Work commitment (1–6 scale)	–0.0141 (0.59)
Home orientation (1–5 scale)	–0.0462 (1.44)
Ever been on Income Support before 1991	–0.1032 (1.20)
No of dependent children at home in 1991	
Ref: One	–
Two	0.0146 (0.20)
Three or more	–0.1658 (1.55)

(*Table 10.A2 continued*) Variables	Coefficients (*t*-stats in parentheses)
Age of youngest child in 1991	
Ref: Under 5 years	—
5–10 years old	0.1306 (1.40)
11–15 years old	0.1747 (1.55)
16–18 years old	0.3636 (2.31)
Partnerships between 91–5	
Partner with no job, 93–4	0.3513 (2.97)
Region in 1991	
Ref: Southeast	—
West	−0.3832 (2.97)
Wales	−0.3295 (1.94)
Midlands	−0.1565 (1.57)
East Anglia	0.0033 (0.03)
Northeast	−0.2182 (2.15)
Northwest	0.0187 (0.18)
Scotland	−0.3258 (2.70)
Constant	2.6255 (6.64)
Heckman selection term	0.2113 (1.71)
Number of observations	339
Adjusted R^2	0.59

Table 10.A3: *Estimates for log net hourly wages in 1995*

Variables	Coefficients (*t*-stats in parentheses)
Human capital	
Age in 1991	
Ref: Under 25	–
25–29 yrs	0.0729 (0.75)
30–34 yrs	0.2149 (2.23)
35–39 yrs	0.4140 (4.00)
40+ yrs	0.4703 (4.31)
Highest qualification in 1991	
Ref: None	–
Low school qualifications	0.1564 (2.14)
Vocational qualifications	−0.0272 (0.31)
Advanced school qualifications	0.1911 (1.40)
Post-school qualifications	0.4877 (4.98)
University-level qualifications	0.3779 (3.57)
Increased qualifications between 1991–5	0.0662 (1.17)
Ever been on job-related training	0.1295 (2.68)
Months spent in 1995 job	0.0010 (2.27)
% time spent in full-time jobs, 1991–4	0.0001 (0.06)
% time spent in part-time jobs, 1991–4	0.0003 (0.26)
Characteristics of 1991 job	
Log weekly wage	0.1063 (2.37)
Received Family Credit	−0.2176 (3.94)
Weekly hours	−0.1241 (2.51)
Type of employer	
Ref: Other	–
Public sector	0.2279 (2.05)
Commercial	0.2991 (2.85)
Missing data	0.1161 (0.82)
Employer size	
Employs 10+ people	0.0525 (0.86)
Missing data	0.0076 (0.05)
Trade union member	−0.0078 (0.13)
Social characteristics of lone motherhood	
Duration of lone motherhood (months to 1991)	−0.0013 (2.20)
Route into lone motherhood	
Ref: Separated from cohabitant	–
Separated from marriage	0.0606 (0.79)
Single	0.0761 (0.75)
Divorced	0.0182 (0.26)
Widowed	−0.0519 (0.35)
Missing data	−0.4047 (1.34)

(*Table 10.A3 continued*) Variables	Coefficients (*t*-stats in parentheses)
Attitudes to paid work and family	
Work commitment (1–6 scale)	–0.0192 (1.02)
Home orientation (1–5 scale)	0.0037 (0.16)
Ever been on Income Support before 1991	0.0353 (0.48)
Maintenance entitled to in 1991	
Ref: None	–
Under £25 per week	0.0342 (0.63)
£25 and over per week	–0.1170 (1.80)
Partnerships between 91–5	
Partner in full-time job 91–92	0.2632 (3.46)
Social background	
Brought up by both parents	–0.3398 (4.74)
Housing tenure in 1991	
Ref: Owner occupier	–
Social renter	0.1591 (2.42)
Other forms of tenure	0.2490 (3.25)
Region in 1991	
Ref: Southeast	–
West	–0.0764 (0.83)
Wales	0.3404 (2.88)
Midlands	–0.1478 (2.05)
East Anglia	0.0784 (0.88)
Northeast	–0.0845 (1.19)
Northwest	–0.0684 (0.93)
Scotland	–0.1369 (1.57)
Constant	0.9891 (3.50)
Heckman selection term	–0.1534 (1.24)
Number of observations	336
Adjusted R^2	0.47

Alex Bryson

Table 10.A4: *Estimates for change in log net hourly wages 1991–95*

Variables	Coefficients (*t*-stats in parentheses)
Human capital	
Age in 1991	
Ref: Under 25	–
25–29 yrs	0.0811 (0.85)
30–34 yrs	0.2154 (2.27)
35–39 yrs	0.4160 (4.06)
40+ yrs	0.4716 (4.39)
Highest qualification in 1991	
Ref: None	–
Low school qualifications	0.1716 (2.39)
Vocational qualifications	–0.0147 (0.17)
Advanced school qualifications	0.2212 (1.64)
Post-school qualifications	0.4856 (5.03)
University-level qualifications	0.3953 (3.79)
Increased qualifications between 1991–5	0.0651 (1.15)
Ever been on job-related training	0.1299 (2.69)
Months spent in 1995 job	0.0010 (2.31)
% time spent in full-time jobs, 1991–4	0.0003 (0.30)
% time spent in part-time jobs, 1991–4	0.0005 (0.45)
Characteristics of 1991 job	
Log weekly wage	–0.8929 (19.81)
Received Family Credit	–0.2445 (4.43)
Weekly hours	0.0044 (2.20)
Type of employer	
Ref: Other	–
Public sector	0.2211 (1.99)
Commercial	0.3064 (2.91)
Missing data	0.1459 (1.02)
Employer size	
Employs 10+ people	0.0631 (1.04)
Missing data	0.0224 (0.15)
Trade union member	–0.0053 (0.09)
Social characteristics of lone motherhood	
Duration of lone motherhood (months to 1991)	–0.0011 (1.98)
Route into lone motherhood	
Ref: Separated from cohabitant	–
Separated from marriage	0.0576 (0.76)
Single	0.0582 (0.58)
Divorced	0.0114 (0.17)
Widowed	–0.0732 (0.51)
Missing data	–0.3893 (1.32)

(*Table 10.A4 continued*) Variables	Coefficients (*t*-stats in parentheses)
Attitudes to paid work and family	
Work commitment (1–6 scale)	–0.0143 (0.78)
Home orientation (1–5 scale)	–0.0004 (0.02)
Ever been on Income Support before 1991	0.0257 (0.35)
Maintenance entitled to in 1991	
Ref: None	–
Under £25 per week	0.0337 (0.62)
£25 and over per week	–0.1266 (1.95)
Partnerships between 91–5	
Partner in full-time job 91–92	0.2658 (3.47)
Social background	
Brought up by both parents	–0.3271 (4.64)
Housing tenure in 1991	
Ref: Owner occupier	–
Social renter	0.1530 (2.37)
Other forms of tenure	0.2454 (3.26)
Region in 1991	
Ref: Southeast	–
West	–0.0943 (1.02)
Wales	0.3536 (2.99)
Midlands	–0.1419 (1.96)
East Anglia	0.0874 (0.98)
Northeast	–0.0818 (1.14)
Northwest	–0.0590 (0.79)
Scotland	–0.1379 (1.58)
Constant	0.7261 (2.45)
Heckman selection term	–0.1276 (1.05)
Number of observations	336
Adjusted R^2	0.63

Table 10.A5: *Estimates for log net weekly wages in 1991*

Variables	Coefficients (*t*-stats in parentheses)
Human capital	
Age in 1991	
Ref: Under 25	–
25–29 yrs	0.1742 (2.63)
30–34 yrs	0.2936 (4.37)
35–39 yrs	0.2784 (4.02)
40+ yrs	0.2736 (4.31)
Highest qualification in 1991	
Ref: None	–
Low school qualifications	0.1093 (2.15)
Vocational qualifications	0.0882 (1.50)
Advanced school qualifications	0.1006 (1.12)
Post-school qualifications	0.2707 (3.48)
University-level qualifications	0.3876 (4.29)
Characteristics of 1991 job	
Weekly hours	0.0221 (8.69)
Type of employer	
Ref: Other	–
Public sector	0.0159 (0.34)
Employer employs 10+ people	0.0667 (1.39)
Trade union member	0.0782 (1.69)
Social characteristics of lone motherhood	
Attitudes to paid work and family	
Work commitment (1–6 scale)	–0.0223 (1.58)
Home orientation (1–5 scale)	–0.0038 (0.21)
Ever been on Income Support before 1991	–0.0446 (0.63)
Region in 1991	
Ref: Southeast	–
West	0.0116 (0.14)
Wales	–0.1080 (0.87)
Midlands	0.0053 (0.09)
East Anglia	0.0096 (0.10)
Northeast	–0.0482 (0.80)
Northwest	0.0279 (0.49)
Scotland	–0.0766 (1.11)
Probability of FC entitlement at 25 hours work	–0.3524 (3.00)
Constant	4.0614 (22.71)
Heckman selection term	–0.1237 (1.61)
Number of observations	527
Adjusted R^2	0.40

Chapter 11

Lone Parents on the Margins of Work
Louise Finlayson and Alan Marsh

More than almost any other large group of people of working age – realistically all except people with a disability – lone parents face the greatest circumstantial barriers to work. One in six has never had a proper job. Currently, less than a third of them have paid jobs that involve more than 16 hours a week – the hours that extinguish their entitlement to income support. Half these are supported in work by income-tested in-work benefits, mostly from family credit, though many receive housing benefit and council tax benefit as well (Marsh, Ford and Finlayson, 1997).

In this chapter,[1] we look at the role of such wage supplementation in improving lone parents' chances of getting and keeping paid work, particularly at the point when they are ready to re-establish themselves in the labour market. First, we discuss recent research on lone parents and paid work. We then look in detail at the financial incentive for lone parents to work and claim family credit. We end with a discussion of policy initiatives to help lone parents find paid employment, particularly the use of 'income-packaging'.

LONE PARENTS AND WORK

During the past six years, the DSS/PSI Programme of Research into Low-Income Families (PRILIF) has built up a detailed picture of Britain's lone-parent families in the early 1990s (Marsh and McKay, 1993b; Marsh, Ford and Finlayson, 1997).[2] The latest PRILIF cross-sectional survey was carried out in September to December 1994 using structured face-to-face interviews with a nationally representative sample of 880 of Britain's

---

1. This chapter is a shorter version of a report, 'Lone parents on the margins of work' (Finlayson and Marsh, 1998 forthcoming).
2. For a full description of the DSS/PSI Programme of Research into Low Income Families (PRILIF), see Marsh, Ford and Finlayson (1997).

lone-parent families, including widows and lone fathers. The survey confirmed that Britain's lone-parent families, financially and materially, often have a difficult time. But, the programme of research has shown much that is positive in benefit policy and lone parents' relationship to the labour market, at least at the margins:

- Family credit made a large contribution to lone parents' opportunities to enter and stay in paid employment.
- This impact of family credit had been increased by the reduction in the minimum qualifying hours rule from 24 to 16 hours worked each week.
- Receipt of maintenance payments made a small but significantly independent contribution to helping lone parents work, and one that seemed by 1994 to be gathering strength. The problem remained that only about 30 per cent of lone parents got any maintenance payments, a figure unchanged in 1994 compared with earlier surveys (Bradshaw and Millar, 1991), the introduction of the CSA notwithstanding.
- A link was established between the effects of family credit and the effects of maintenance payments by the introduction of a disregard of maintenance payments of up to £15 a week. Maintenance payments appeared to act alongside family credit as a kind of 'privatised in-work benefit' but one that had a far more favourable withdrawal rate against new earnings. Like family credit, it also permits short hours working. It particularly helps poorly-educated lone parents into work, if they can get any maintenance payments. Fewer than a fifth of them do.
- Crucially, lone parents working short hours, receiving family credit and maintenance payments together had levels of relative disposable income after housing costs that were 60 per cent greater than lone parents without work and receiving income support.
- The availability and cost of childcare remained a barrier to lone parents' entry to work, but by no means the only one.

Childcare apart (see Ford, 1996 and the following chapter here), the main influences upon lone parents' labour market participation are strikingly independent of one another. Combinations of seven key variables – housing tenure, prior marital status, experience of benefits, education and training, family composition, receipt of maintenance payments and family health – can together statistically explain large fractions of the variance in lone parents' chances of getting and keeping paid work. Typically, poorly-educated and occupationally inexperienced lone parents who are social tenants, who have young children and who cope with persistent ill-health will participate little in the labour market. In contrast, well-educated lone parents who are owner-occupiers and who have older children, participate a great deal in paid work, probably more than married mothers do.

Overall, the programme supports increasing incentives for lone parents to work through income packaging earnings, income-tested benefits and maintenance payments (Marsh, Ford and Finlayson, 1997). The more favourable the in-work benefit regime became, the more at least a minority of lone parents seemed able to overcome the significant barriers that lay in their path to work and to move towards earnings sufficiency, if not achieving complete independence, nor complete freedom from the risks of hardship. Actual movement into work, on the other hand, has been slow.

Between 1991 and 1993 there was a small rise in lone parents' employment rates (Table 11.1). This rise was associated with a change in family credit qualifying rules that lowered the qualifying hours of work from 24 hours a week to 16. There was significant entry into work between 16 and 23 hours a week and claiming family credit. In 1994, the proportion of lone parents in 'full time' work, using the pre-1992 definition of 24 or more hours a week, fell from a quarter to a fifth, the lowest figure of all the surveys, including the earlier Bradshaw and Millar figure (24 per cent). It is particularly disappointing in view of the significant drop in the proportion of the lone parent population, comparing 1994 with 1991, whose youngest child is preschool aged.

Table 11.1: *Employment characteristics of lone parent families*

	1991	1993	1994
(column percentages)			
Paid job, working 24+ hours	25	26	20
Paid job, working 16–23 hours	3	8	9
Paid job, less than 16 hours	10	8	10
Unemployed and seeking work	7	7	4
Economically inactive	56	51	57
	100%	100%	100%
(cell percentages)			
% economically inactive	43%	49%	43%
% of non-workers who have never had a job	15%	9%	11%
Base (weighted)	(938)	(849)	(833)

On the other hand, the proportions in paid work doing fewer than 24 hours a week held up, especially in the 16–23 hours slot opened up by the 1992 reforms, and just 4 per cent said they were 'unemployed and seeking work'. Thus, more than half of the 1994 survey were economically inactive: 57 per cent – much the same figure as in 1991 but significantly higher than in 1993 (51 per cent).

Overall, earnings contribute only a fifth of lone parents' total income and fewer than three in ten support themselves and their families primarily from earnings, while half rely on a wage subsidy from family credit averaging more than £50 a week. The rise in the proportion claiming family credit, from 10 per cent in 1991 to 16 per cent in 1993, held at exactly that figure in 1994, though it may have crept up a little to about 18 or 19 per cent since then (Table 11.2). Lone parents are now more than 300,000 of a total family credit caseload of about 700,000 (DSS, 1997a). The ratio of lone parents working and claiming family credit to those on income support is now three to ten compared with a figure of one to ten claiming family income supplement and supplementary benefit in 1979.

Table 11. 2: *Receipt of main income-tested benefits*[3]

	1991	1993	1994
(cell percentages)			
Proportion receiving:			
Income Support	68%	62%	65%
Family Credit	10%	16%	16%
as a proportion of lone parents who:			
work 16+ hours	35%	44%	48%
work 24+ hours	37%	37%	34%
Base (weighted)	(938)	(849)	(833)

The 1994 survey also contained measures that were intended to improve understanding of what additionally may help more lone parents get work. These measures concentrated more on the subjective and behavioural aspects of motivation and ability to work, to get at the fine details of what happens to lone parents when they try to find work. For example, the survey contained a self-assessed 'skills audit', and measures of self esteem, personal efficacy and well-being. The main points of the analyses are summarised below (Finlayson and Marsh, 1998 forthcoming):

• Of every ten lone parents, three worked at least 16 hours a week; three were ready to seek work, at least one actively; three will seek work one day, but not yet; and one believed she would never work. Most of these are unwell, though a few are well-off.

---

3. The 16 per cent of lone parents on family credit were of course more than 48 per cent of the 29 per cent who worked 16 or more hours a week. But 10 per cent of those receiving family credit had either reduced their hours below 16 a week during their current claim or had lost their jobs altogether.

- Whatever it is that keeps lone parents out of work, it is not unrealistic wage expectations. Reservation wages (the least they would settle for in a new job) remain low, little more than £100 a week among those currently out of work. But such wage expectations are fitted intuitively into an income package including in-work benefits.
- The majority of those looking for work expect to receive family credit in a job; half expect to claim on entry.
- The margin of incentive provided by family credit increased in real terms, despite shorter hours and lowered earnings, to £44 above out-of-work incomes (see in detail below). Over time, wage supplementation can mount up to substantial totals. The contribution to in-work income from benefit payments is about a third, though it runs at a level little more than half the corresponding support required out of work.
- There was a poor fit between the occupational profile of workers and non-workers. Paradoxically, many of those prepared to do the least skilled work found work hardest to find. There may be a barrier to manual work posed by low hourly rates that make short hours impractical, even with family credit.
- Lone parents' levels of educational qualifications are still much lower than other young women's.
- Half had ever undergone a programme of work training and only a third completed one. The cost of training was often cited as a difficulty and some had abandoned courses because of their cost.
- The skill base among out-of-work lone parents seems lowest in the key area of routine office skills. These are often built up in work rather than from pre-work training, but appropriate training would still help them find work too: a driving licence might help as much as anything.
- The relative morale of out-of-work lone parents is fragile, though less so among those most ready to work.

HOW LARGE IS THE FINANCIAL INCENTIVE FOR LONE PARENTS TO WORK AND CLAIM FAMILY CREDIT?

The first PRILIF survey undertaken to evaluate the effects of family credit in 1991 (Marsh and McKay, 1993b) found that lone parents receiving family credit would be about £30 a week worse off in total income if they were to lose their jobs and claim income support instead, other things being equal. Table 11.3 repeats this analysis for the lone parents in the 1994 survey, just three and a half years later.

If nothing had changed, we would expect the cash value of the gap between in-work and unemployed incomes to have risen a little with inflation to about £34. A good deal has changed, however, that might have influenced the size of the incentive-gap, in both directions. For example:

- It will have been reduced by the effect of the reduction in qualifying hours from 24 to 16 hours per week because this reduced the average hours worked by lone parents on family credit from 30 to 25 and so lowered the average wages they received. This in turn increased the size of the family credit award but will still have left their average final incomes in work lower than the previous average.
- It will have been increased by the introduction of a disregard of £15 a week of maintenance payments against assessable income for family credit but not for income support.[4]

Table 11.3 shows that both the level and the composition of in-work incomes had been affected by changes in the hours rule and by the introduction of the maintenance disregard. Wages have fallen from £87 to £81 whereas wage inflation (at constant hours) would have taken wages up to about £94 a week. Maintenance payments increased their contribution to total income across all lone parents from about £9 to £13 a week. Not all the £13 would be disregarded, of course, because only 40 per cent of the family credit recipients got any payments. Thus, they received typically about £32. Even so, lowered wages (against increased family credit entitlement levels) and more maintenance payments (about half of which was disregarded) resulted in greatly increased family credit payments, up from £34 in 1991 to over £50 in 1994 – half as much again. Increased rents and lowered wages also increased residual in-work entitlement to housing benefit, also more than a 50 per cent increase.

The result of these changes is that a typical lone parent on family credit in 1994 received about £175 a week, made up in round figures of £15 in maintenance payments, and £80 each from earnings and benefits – the benefit income comprising about £60 in income-tested benefit and £20 in child benefit.

Changes in the out-of-work income calculation are also a mixture of the expected and unexpected. Income support increased with up-rating from £61 to £72. Entitlement to help with mortgage interest increased a little, despite sharply reduced levels of interest rates in 1994 compared with 1991. The amount of housing benefit was reduced, despite higher rents. These two changes had the same cause: the 1994 sample of family credit recipients contained more owner occupiers and fewer tenants, and had more lone parents who lived in other people's households (often their own parents') and who were tempted into work at the new lowered hours.

The result is that the unadjusted difference between in-work and out-of-work incomes rose from £30 in 1991 to £44 in 1994. The adjusted

---

4. The weekly bonus payment of family credit for those working 30 or more hours a week, which is currently £10.55, had not been introduced by the time of the 1994 survey.

difference, deducting from in-work incomes the cost of travel and the (apparently increased) costs of child care, is £34 compared with £22 in 1991. Both these increases are larger than would be expected from a combination of benefit uprating and wage inflation. This is due largely to a combination of the effects of the maintenance disregard and lower average housing costs.

Table 11.3: *Average incomes of family credit recipients in work compared with their estimated incomes out of work (£s mean)*

	1991	1994
In work (actual)		
Net earnings	86.70	80.82
Maintenance	8.74	13.21
Housing benefit	5.60	8.93
Council tax benefit	0.90	0.76
Family credit	33.60	50.44
Child benefit plus one parent benefit	18.23	20.59
Other income	0.90	0.28
TOTAL	154.67	175.03
minus travel to work	4.20	4.93
minus childcare	3.10	5.84
REVISED TOTAL	147.37	164.26
Out of work (hypothetical)		
Income support rate[5]	61.07	71.43
Est'd Mortgage interest	8.10	10.52
Child benefit plus one parent benefit	18.23	20.59
Housing benefit	32.80	21.89
Council tax benefit	4.00	6.14
Other income (disregarded for income support)	0.20	0.28
TOTAL	124.40	130.85
Average net gain from work	30.27	44.18
Revised average net gain from work (deducting costs of childcare and travel)	22.97	33.41
Base (weighted)	91	119
Base (unweighted)	293	375

---

5. This amount remains constant against maintenance payments which are deducted pound-for-pound from entitlement to income support. Therefore, maintenance payments are not shown. Where they are shown above in the calculation of in-work incomes, the average amounts include all those who received none.

The effects of the childcare disregard are examined in detail in Ford (1996). Together, these measures are likely to have taken the average additional income in work for lone parents on family credit to over £50 above the corresponding estimate of their out-of-work incomes.

It should be noted that housing costs are held constant in the comparison between in-work and out-of-work incomes by adding mortgage interest payments and housing benefit to out-of-work incomes. These benefits, of course, have to be paid out again as interest or rent, just as the in-work calculation assumes that interest and rent are paid from the total in-work income, even though that too is raised by some residual entitlement to housing benefit (but not help with mortgage interest) in some cases. Also, the likely effects of non-dependent deductions are ignored. This is largely on the grounds that they are deducted on the assumption that the other adult member of the household causing the deduction is actually contributing to household income at least the value deducted. Of course, in practice this may not always be the case (Witherspoon et al, 1996).

It is also interesting to note that the change in contribution to incomes from income-tested benefits decreased from about £110 a week on income support (income support plus housing benefit plus council tax benefit) to about £60 on family credit (family credit plus housing benefit plus council tax benefit). The contribution in work therefore is about 55 per cent of the contribution out of work. Having a lone parent in work and on family credit instead of being out of work and claiming income support almost halves the total benefit bill.

The average or mean net gain from work in 1994 was £44.18 before adjustments for in-work costs and £33.41 afterwards. But this does not say how many people experienced a gain of the same magnitude. Some will have fared better or worse, and some may even have been worse off in work. To determine how representative the average gain is, it is necessary to look at the distribution across all respondents. This distribution is given in Figure 11.1. The sharp peaks at £40–£49 gain per week, and at £30–£39 for the revised gain suggest that the mean figures are quite representative. In fact, the medians and means almost coincide. The vast bulk of respondents experience between zero net gain and £110 per week gains, according to both revised and unrevised estimates. At the extremes, a handful appear to experience net losses or gains between £110 and £180. The losses are almost entirely accounted for by very high estimates of out-of-work income support entitlements, due to disability premia or mortgage interest payments.

At this point, it is also worth noting a different calculation made in an earlier report (Ford, Marsh and Finlayson, 1997) that compared the actual incomes of those in work and on family credit with those out of work.

Putting aside housing costs and controlling for the size of families, working lone parents claiming family credit who also managed to obtain the advantage of maintenance payments disregarded against their assessable income, were 60 per cent better off in real disposable income compared with those who depended solely on income support.

In all, Table 11.3 and Figure 11.1 provide an impressive picture of the extent of the wage supplementation that successive policy changes have wrought among working British lone parents. The British approach has been thought gradualist when compared, for example, with the American and Canadian programmes, and with the Australian JET schemes. These provide, in differing forms, some very substantial (though time-limited) wage supplements, combined with job-entry management and training. But the figures presented here suggest that the British approach provides a pound-for-pound match between earnings and benefit incomes, which when combined with other income from child benefit, for example, provides final incomes in work that are on average one-third higher compared with out-of-work income. And the British wage supplements are not time limited except by the duration of parenthood. Over a period of time, this implies a huge commitment of resources to lone parents in work.

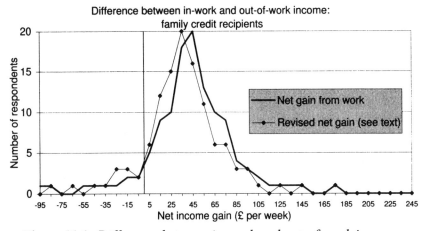

Figure 11.1: *Difference between in-work and out-of-work income: family credit recipients*

One further point needs to be considered. Those looking closely at the figures from Table 11.3 may ask why only £3 in 1991 (nearly £6 in 1994) is allowed for childcare in the adjusted figure. The answer of course is that only a minority of family credit recipients paid anything at all for childcare. The question then arises whether those who do pay anything for childcare end up making a loss from work.

Table 11.4: *Average incomes of family credit recipients in work
compared with their estimated incomes out of work: comparing those
who pay for child care and those who do not (£s mean)*

	Not Paying for childcare	Paying for childcare
In work (actual)		
Net earnings	79.30	86.57
Maintenance	13.56	11.86
Housing benefit	9.16	8.07
Council tax benefit	0.79	0.63
Family credit	52.70	41.92
Child benefit plus one parent benefit	20.56	20.70
Other income	0.36	0.00
TOTAL	176.43	169.75
minus travel to work	4.55	6.38
minus childcare	0.00	27.93
REVISED TOTAL	171.88	135.88
Out of work (hypothetical)		
Income support rate[6]	72.36	67.92
Est'd Mortgage rate	10.64	10.04
Child benefit plus one parent benefit	20.36	20.70
Housing benefit	22.10	21.10
Council tax benefit	6.22	5.83
Other income (disregarded for income support)	0.36	0.00
TOTAL	132.24	125.59
Average net gain from work	44.19	44.16
Revised average net gain from work	39.64	9.85
Base (weighted)	94	25
Base (unweighted)	285	75

Table 11.4 takes the 1994 figures and repeats the analysis given in Table
11.3 separately for those paying for childcare and those paying nothing.
On average, those paying for childcare – about a quarter of lone parents
receiving family credit – do not make a loss, though they come uncom-
fortably close to doing so. They clear £10 above their out-of-work
incomes on average, though three out of ten (29 per cent) of them actually
saw a negative gain from work. If they were out of work and managed to
earn the £15 a week disregard from income support without incurring
childcare costs, they would actually have been £5 a week better off. The

6. This amount remains constant against maintenance payments, which are deducted pound-for-
   pound from entitlement to income support. Therefore maintenance payments are not shown.

majority who payed nothing for childcare, in contrast, cleared a full £40 a week above their out-of-work income even after travel costs.

The disregard of childcare costs against family credit assessable income was introduced in 1994 specifically to counter this difficulty. Fewer than half would have been able to claim, however, because they did not employ 'professional' childcare. For lone parents claiming the childcare disregard, the incentive margin would have recovered (allowing for the 70 per cent rate of withdrawal) to an average of about £25 over their out-of-work income. This is a help, but the finding remains clear that lone parents on family credit would not want to work and pay for childcare for very long. Those free of childcare costs, on the other hand, stay well above their alternative income support levels.

For the majority of lone parents making their first move into work, additional help from family credit is the only way forward for them (Finlayson and Marsh, 1998 forthcoming). The more encouragement they get and the better the advice they are offered, the more they are likely to respond. Certainly, they can now be offered a confident 'better-off-in-work' prediction that they can see and understand, as demonstrated above. The difficulty remains with lone parents paying for childcare, who see a greatly reduced financial incentive to work and claim family credit, though still a positive one on average.

HELPING LONE PARENTS FIND PAID WORK

Since 1994, new modifications in the delivery of in-work benefits have been introduced. The 1994 data were gathered before the introduction of other measures that will have increased the gap between in-work and out-of-work incomes further:

- the childcare disregard that allows up to £60 a week paid to registered childminders or nurseries to be deducted from the assessable income of family credit applicants, presently helping about 7–8 per cent of lone parents claiming family credit with children under 11. From summer 1998, this will be increased to £100 for two or more children aged under 12 and £60 for a single child under 12;
- the additional weekly £10 credit (now worth £10.55) for those working more than 30 hours a week;
- the four-week continuation of housing benefit; and
- the new allowance that puts aside £5 each week of maintenance payments paid to those out of work to be repaid (up to a maximum of £1000) when entering work, and a similar allowance against small part-time earnings.

This gradualist approach to welfare-to-work policy – providing wage supplements to improve incentives and then taking successive nips and tucks in the system to make it work better – has been the basis of policy for some years. Research has shown the large contribution that family credit makes to lone parents' opportunities to enter paid employment (Marsh, Ford and Finlayson, 1997; Bryson, Ford and White, 1997). As a policy it has been sufficiently successful to overcome many objections to its use: low take-up among eligible families; high marginal disincentives; deterrent stigma and complexity; and inequity for non-claimants. None of these objections resisted close research scrutiny (Marsh, 1995).

On the other hand, the policy of wage supplementation for lone parents has clear drawbacks. Concern had been raised about the long-term impact of family credit on lone mothers' career progression and future earnings (see Chapter 10 here). As a policy, assisting lone parents off income support by supplementing low wages for low-skill, short hours work was never going to place many of them on to the first rung of the career ladder. As Alex Bryson notes, family credit recipients saw their weekly wages rise four years later by one-third less than would otherwise have been expected given their characteristics and circumstances. Another difficulty is likely to arise when their children grow up and former lone-parent family credit claimants remain stranded in their low-wage jobs.

A further drawback is that in-work benefits still do not attract enough lone parents into work. Lone parents in other countries tend to have far higher rates of labour market participation than British lone parents. In the United States, for example, nearly two-thirds of lone parents support themselves through their earnings compared with about a third in Britain, though they too can benefit from forms of assistance, more typically tax advantages, better after-school care, higher real wages and stouter anti-discrimination laws (Freeman and Waldfogel, 1995). Their rates of receipt of child support, however, are the same: still about 30 per cent despite similarly increased official effort to raise it.

Despite these levels of labour market participation, welfare provisions for US lone parents are changing sharply against their interests, with a two-year limit on continuous provision and a five-year lifetime limit on renewals. States have been charged with new roll-reduction briefs, which some places have taken up with enthusiasm. For example, in Wisconsin a newly-delivered lone mother must register for work 12 weeks after the birth.

Such initiatives have received close attention outside the Unites States. The questions that are likely to be raised for Britain are:

• How far is it feasible in Britain to try to move the boundary between work and non-employment beyond the one-third in work, which is broadly the present position, towards the two-thirds found in work in the United States or even further?

- How far should such a policy include coercion?

The research evidence seems to say two important things about this key middle third of 'work-ready' lone parents who might be the clearest target of welfare-to-work policies:

- Lone parents share with others out-of-work high levels of material hardship. This is likely to reduce their morale and limit their ambition. Equally though, it makes them sensitive to the potential improvements available in work;
- Lone parents want to work, though with varying urgency, and a third of them are actively looking for work. It is easy to forget that lone parents are typically low-paid workers who, like other low-paid workers, can spend quite a lot of time unemployed and seeking work.

Recent evidence shows that the cost and supply levels of childcare do not prohibit lone parents entering work but set practical limits on the amount of hours they can supply (Ford, 1996). It is a problem but it is by no means their only one. Lone parents try to limit their hours to weekly amounts that require only practical and affordable childcare, or ideally find work that fits neatly around school hours. It is important to them that any childcare used should be of a quality that, together with the advantages of the higher income from work, provides her family with a quality of life that is better than the bleak securities of life on income support.

Such a strategy responds well to the 'income package' available from wage supplementation: lone parents claiming family credit work only 25 hours a week on average – the five hours a day their children are at school. If lone parents have access to all three main sources of in-work income – earnings, benefits and maintenance – they exceed their equivalent out-of-work incomes by 60 per cent. No one is getting rich, of course. They typically raise their net incomes from about £90 to £150 a week. But when you consider the emphasis placed by a recent review of more than 30 studies of family poverty of the huge improvement that would follow increasing their incomes by just £15–£20 a week (Kempson, 1996), the extra £50–£60 transforms the lives of many who manage the transition.

CONCLUSION

So, again we must ask: why don't more 'work-ready' lone parents work and take advantage of the in-work income packaging that clearly helps many others to work, and what can be done to help them?

Why don't more lone parents work?

Again the evidence from research is that there is a discontinuity between the work experience of the minority of lone parents who had jobs and the prior work experience of the majority who were out of work (Finlayson and Marsh, 1998 forthcoming). The further from work they were, the greater the contrast between the relatively favourable occupational profile of the workers and the unfavourable profile of non-workers. Even those non-workers who had had some recent (post-1990) work experience showed a distinctly less favourable occupational profile compared with those who had entered or remained in work. They were half as likely to have been employed in the better-paid non-manual grades and correspondingly more than twice as likely to have been employed in the lowest-paid unskilled grades in catering and cleaning jobs.

Four out of ten of those not yet ready to contemplate a return to work reported a previous employment in these least skilled grades, compared with only 13 per cent of those with jobs actually working in these grades. A quarter of them had been cleaners, which may explain something of their reluctance to return to work. It may be hard to persuade women in this position that earning two or three pounds an hour as cleaners is more important than looking after their own children, however ingeniously their wages may be supplemented.

There may be a point when wage supplementation, especially if it also means claiming quite large amounts of housing benefit and even council tax benefit on top of family credit, has limited attractions viewed from this kind of position at the very bottom of the labour market. At rates of pay typically near to £2 an hour, lone parents would have to work 35 hours a week before they reached the maximum family credit threshold. That for most of them is too difficult, and the work itself is hardly congenial.

What can be done to help?

More could be done to improve the scope of in-work incentives. For example, improved maintenance payments would increase movement into work, especially small payments of £20–£30 a week to less-qualified lone parents on income support. Consideration could be given to building into family credit a time-limited underwriting of newly-committed maintenance payments. Those that fail to be paid (perhaps for perfectly understandable reasons) could be substituted at least for the six-month duration of the claim. This will increase confidence in a go-to-work strategy that, in effect, restores a divided family to the same two-earner status that is most other families' main protection against poverty. The additional housing costs will remain a problem for some.

The encouraging match between the increased incentive to work and the willingness to work among the 'work-ready' lone parents certainly gives support to the kind of encouragements planned under recent policy initiatives (DSS, 1997b). Though lacking the mandatory aspects of American schemes like GAIN in California (Riccio et al, 1994), the lessons from these experiences suggest that an emphasis on getting lone parents jobs, rather than prolonged periods of new education and training outside work, can be effective in the right labour market.

However, no discussion of welfare-to-work measures for lone parents in Britain can take into consideration any alterations in wage supplementation and the present rules of registration for work without at the same time considering the real state of the labour market that confronts them. The reason why the British incentives package has not moved the majority of lone parents into work must have a great deal to do with the weak bargaining position of workers entering the labour market in recent years. Entry level wages have fallen in real terms (Goodman et al, 1997). A great deal of the remaining problem lies outside the benefit system and even beyond the new encouragement that might be given to them. It lies in the labour market itself and in the kind of work lone parents can do.

We must remember that lone mothers face the same difficulties as many other women in the labour market. There is substantial evidence of gender discrimination (Wright and Ermisch, 1991) and occupational segregation by gender (Millward and Woodland, 1995) in the British labour market. Women are traditionally concentrated in occupational sectors associated with low pay and lack of career advancement – exactly the type of 'non-career' jobs family credit has been associated with (see Chapter 10 here). Recent policy emphasis away from lone parents towards lone mothers in particular should be noted: lone fathers are more likely to be in paid employment and the wages they can command in the labour market can spring them beyond the thresholds of in-work benefits altogether.

Increased mandates to work in the United States have been defended on grounds that the new rules are accompanied by new financial incentives. They are, and it is almost certainly the incentives and not the coercion that are reducing the welfare roles, together with a rising labour market. In Britain, we already have the incentives and, certainly for low-paid women, a rising labour market. We might need some more encouragement, help and facilitation too. We do not need coercion.

Chapter 12

Lone Mothers' Decisions Whether or Not to Work: Childcare in the Balance

Reuben Ford

Lone mothers in Britain have low and declining employment rates. Fewer than half are economically active and fewer than one in six secure enough earnings to clear the thresholds for entitlement to means-tested benefits. Two-thirds claim income support at a weekly cost to the exchequer of over £80 million. Yet, there is considerable evidence that most lone mothers currently out of the labour market want to work (Bradshaw and Millar, 1991; McKay and Marsh, 1994; Bryson et al, 1997). Most commentators point to problems with the cost and availability of childcare as a major barrier to work (Bradshaw and Millar, 1991; Bryson et al, 1997) or even as the major barrier (Bradshaw et al, 1996a; Holtermann, 1993).

Policy has been directed towards increasing financial incentives for lone parents to work. Since 1994, reducing the impact of childcare costs on final income has formed part of this policy, via an in-work benefit disregard.[1] The disregard will only be effective though if childcare costs are the only barrier to paid work for a significant number of lone parents.

Recently published evidence, collected as part of the DSS/PSI Programme of Research into Low Income Families (PRILIF), is used in this

---

1. The childcare disregard is intended to restore a financial incentive to work for parents with childcare costs. It is available to lone parents of children aged under 11 years, working 16 hours or more each week and who pay for childcare, provided care is sought from professional sources (registered childminders, after-school and holiday schemes and nurseries). Childcare costs (up to £60 each week) are deducted from income assessable for means-tested benefits (family credit, housing benefit and council tax benefit) available to those in work 16 hours or more each week. The effect this has on net income is to increase benefit entitlements, subject to the maximum amount of benefit payable, at any given level of earnings. In the budget of July 1997 it was announced that the disregard in childcare costs would be increased from £60 to £100 where there are two or more eligible children from the summer of 1998, and would cover children up to their twelfth birthday.

chapter to consider the role of childcare as a reason lone mothers give for taking up or not taking up paid work. A framework formalised elsewhere (Ford, 1996) is advanced, in which constraints such as childcare are assessed by lone mothers in terms of their contribution to the balance between financial and non-financial gains and losses in and out of work. It is suggested that different policy proposals be considered in terms of their impacts on this balance.

EVIDENCE ABOUT THE ROLE OF CHILDCARE

Evidence concerning the constraint childcare places on lone mothers' employment comes from many sources. Prima facie evidence includes the association between the probability of employment and age of the youngest child; and comparisons of UK lone mothers' participation with participation by mothers in couples, and with participation by lone mothers in other countries.

An example of prima facie evidence concerning children's ages appears in Figure 12.1, based on data from a cross section of 850 of Britain's lone parents, 95 per cent of them women, interviewed in late 1994. The graph shows that very few parents of preschool age children are in paid work. Among those who are, part-time hours are as likely as full-time. Once all children have attained school age, participation in employment reaches 40 per cent. Only by the time children are aged 13 years or more do the majority of parents work. Such patterns, observed persistently in surveys of lone mothers, offer evidence that the presence of young children acts as a constraint on participation (Bradshaw and Millar, 1991; Ford et al, 1995; Bryson et al, 1997).

Further prima facie evidence comes from comparisons between lone mothers and mothers in couples. Mothers in couples have much higher participation rates. Notably, mothers of preschool age children are more than twice as likely to participate in paid work if they have a partner than if they are a lone mother, even when observations are restricted to low-income families (Marsh and McKay, 1993b). The presence of partners can be taken as a proxy for wider family support, meaning mothers can draw on their partners or in-laws to provide childcare, or have more scope within their pooled household earnings to meet childcare costs.

Neither prima facie case is conclusive. They show that lone mothers of young children tend to stay at home rather than go out to work, but there are many plausible reasons to explain such behaviour, besides a lack of childcare. If the presence of young children is the major constraint on their parents' participation, this does not explain why three in ten mothers of children all aged 15 or over are out of work (Figure 12.1), and why fewer than half work full-time. Nor does it explain why parents of 13 and 14 year-olds are no more likely to engage in work of 16 hours or more each week than those of five and six year-olds.

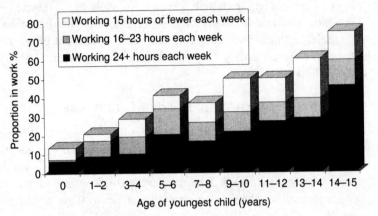

Figure 12.1: *Lone-parent employment participation by age of youngest child*

Any argument based on childcare comparisons between lone mothers and couples assumes women in couples and those bringing up children alone are similar but for the absence of a partner. Differences in participation might be explained by other factors – such as human capital, or discrimination – which in turn may be related to selection into lone parenthood as well as low levels of labour market participation.

Comparisons between lone mothers' employment rates in different countries (Bradshaw et al, 1996a) have identified childcare cost differentials as the single factor that discriminates unambiguously between countries with high and low participation. However, the estimates of childcare cost were made independently by local experts in each country, based on specified but not necessarily representative lone parent and childcare characteristics. The method did not ensure that cost estimates would correspond to the actual costs faced by parents. For example, the UK childcare cost estimate was based on fees for registered childminders, when the majority of lone mothers in work make use of informal care arrangements, if they use childcare at all. It is difficult to infer that non-working lone mothers would necessarily use such childcare sources and thus face such costs, if they were to enter work.

More sophisticated multivariate approaches have attempted to overcome selection effects. A multistage analysis of lone mothers' participation by Jenkins and Symons (1995) separately predicted individual level probabilities of incurring childcare costs, and (given the need to pay at all) of hourly costs. Childcare costs were found a significant disincentive to labour market participation. However, the effect was small. Reducing childcare costs to zero raised employment probabilities for a reference lone mother by just three percentage points. Age and number of dependent children still had a negative effect on employment participation, even after childcare costs were taken into account. As Jenkins and Symons (1995: 17) concluded, 'it appears that in the UK the impact of childcare costs is important, but perhaps rather less important than one might have expected from the emphasis in popular discussion.'

A problem in interpreting econometric models arises when family structure is not independent of the labour participation decision. As Connelly (1992) points out, parents may seek particular family structures because of their particular orientations to the labour market. If mothers who are less inclined towards paid work tend to have more children, then modelled employment activity is better explained by attitudinal differences rather than family constraints. Of course, due to birth intervals, mothers with more children will be over-represented among families with young children.

From the above studies, it is difficult simply to attribute participation differences to childcare constraints. Lone mothers face high childcare costs relative to their income; disproportionately more must pay for care of younger children, for whom costs are disproportionately high. Nonetheless, it does not hold that were this situation to change, perhaps through policy intervention, that lone mothers' participation would increase substantially. The barrier to lone mothers' labour market participation has still not been identified.

The remainder of this chapter concentrates on findings from a new study, which draws on accounts of how lone mothers themselves justify and rationalise their economic behaviour. Analysis has been directed specifically to determine the extent to which childcare costs and availability explain lone parents' low level of participation.

NEW RESEARCH INTO EMPLOYMENT DECISIONS

A new study of lone mothers set out to explore the role childcare plays in the decisions lone mothers made about work. The study formed part of the DSS-funded PRILIF programme at the PSI. It combined quantitative analysis of interviews with 850 lone mothers in late 1994 (the 'national' study) and qualitative analysis of follow-up depth interviews with 60 of the same lone mothers (the 'depth' study). The methods and findings are reported in full elsewhere (Ford, 1996).

In both the national and depth studies, parents in work and out of work were interviewed. This enabled a comparison between those who had entered work, with or without the use of childcare, and those who had yet to do so. The results presented here concentrate on the key barriers to employment lone mothers identify themselves, and on *how* these barriers are identified. The chapter is thus able to draw conclusions about how childcare weighs in to the decision about whether or not to work.

CURRENT AND ANTICIPATED USE OF CHILDCARE: THE NATIONAL STUDY

Before the role of childcare among constraints on employment is considered, it is useful to set the context of childcare decisions by looking at how childcare is used by lone mothers. Using data from the national study, Table 12.1 summarises both current use of childcare by parents working 16 or more hours each week, and anticipated use by those out of work 'if they were to take up work of 16 hours or more each week'.

Table 12.1: *Lone mothers'* current and anticipated use of childcare*

Source of childcare	A	B	C
Childcare multiple response			
Ex-partner	5	5	15
Parents (in-law)	29	17	41
Siblings	4	4	25
Other relatives/friends	14	17	69
Nursery/crèche	3	1	60
Nursery school/playgroup	2	2	100
Registered childminder	2	17	100
Unregistered childminder	4	3	100
Live-in/daily/shared nanny	1	1	100
After-school scheme	2	1	58
Non-childcare			
Only work during school hours	15	25	n/a
I take them to work	2	0	n/a
I work at home	2	0	n/a
Old enough to look after themselves	29	19	n/a
Base	(262)	(484)**	(142)

Notes: A = Currently working 16 or more hours each week (% using each source in term-time); B = Not working 16 or more hours who have sought work in past year, or who 'might look for a paid job one day' (% would use if in work); C = Among out of work, % giving source who feel they would have to pay for this care. *The national study interviewed lone mothers and lone fathers, the depth study just lone mothers. Lone fathers were just 4 per cent of the national sample, so the term 'lone mothers' is used throughout. **Includes 11 per cent 'Don't knows'.

The table divides arrangements between childcare and non-childcare sources. Those in work make extensive use of informal arrangements, while those out of work anticipate greater use of formal childcare sources, like childminders. Even so, only a minority plan to use formal sources of the kind that qualify for the in-work benefit childcare disregard.

A full quarter of those out of work anticipate working only during school hours, a rather higher proportion than found among those already in work, who typically have older children. This reflects a more general trend among the out of work to avoid childcare use. Two-thirds of those in work use some form of childcare, and just 42 per cent of these pay for their childcare. Among the out of work, just half anticipate using childcare, but two-thirds who would use it anticipate having to pay for it. It seems that a higher proportion of those out of work expect to pay for childcare than actually do pay among those found in work. The final column of Table 12.1 indicates which sources are most expected to incur costs. The formal sources, which more of the non-workers expect to use, are almost universally expected to charge. These observations accord with findings elsewhere (Jenkins and Symons, 1995; Connelly, 1992) that parents who have lower or no childcare costs (due to older or fewer children, access to relatives) are more likely already to be in work.

Perhaps more surprising are the high proportions who anticipate having to pay friends and relatives and even parents (in-law) to provide care. While such amounts may be nominal, or be expected to cover food, travel or other expenses, it suggests a restricted range of free childcare options for out of work lone mothers.

The high proportion of lone mothers out of work who anticipate using no childcare when working has an ambiguous interpretation. One view might be that if they do not plan to use childcare, then childcare cost or availability cannot be a major constraint on their employment comparison. Alternatively, childcare cost and availability may be so constraining that lone mothers cannot even contemplate using it. If they hold this view, childcare problems are indirectly a barrier to their employment. These lone mothers are out of work and cannot return until they can combine work with an arrangement for looking after their children, which does not involve childcare. The same finding thus simultaneously supports views that childcare is not the issue and that it is a constraint of the highest order preventing parents even considering a work-plus-childcare combination.

However, even the second view does not rule out other reasons besides cost and availability for not contemplating the use of childcare. We still cannot be certain that childcare is the barrier. The next question would seem to be what is it that lone mothers themselves see as keeping them out of the labour market? A more complete picture might be expected to emerge when lone parents themselves are asked directly what problems they face when considering work and when applying for jobs.

Reasons for not being in work

The national study directed questions to those out of work about the constraints – if any – they perceived on their ability to go out to work. Respondents gave answers in their own words (as many answers as they wished) which were allocated by interviewers to pre-codes on the questionnaire (listed in Table 12.2). Other answers were coded separately.

Table12.2: *Reasons for not working 16 or more hours each week at present among lone mothers not working 16+ hours in 1994*

Reason not working now	% giving reason (multiple response)	% giving this reason alone
Cannot afford childcare	36	5
No childcare available	13	2
Children too young	41	18
Illness/disability	11	6
No work available	15	4
Better off not working	26	9
No reason	6	5
Other	19	7
Base	(365)	(201)

Note: *excludes those who have sought work in the past 12 months and those who cannot see themselves looking for a paid job of 16 or more hours each week even 'one day'.

Among those who could see themselves returning to work 'one day', the most common reason given for not working at present was having children who were too young. If this answer is taken at face value it means these mothers felt their child was too young to be apart from their mother, or to use childcare. The answer could be associated in some cases with a lack of suitable childcare. Two-thirds of those who answered in this way had at least one child under five years. The next most common reason was not being able to afford childcare. This was the most common reason among those who had undertaken work of 16 or more hours in the recent past. However, mothers with children aged under five years were no more likely to give this reason than those whose youngest child was aged between five and ten years, and were *less* likely to state problems with the availability of care. This is further evidence that low participation rates among mothers of young children cannot be accounted for solely by childcare problems. Nearly one in five said that they were better off not working, rising to one in four among those who had spent more than three years out of work, and one in three among those whose youngest child was of secondary school age.

Although only one in five with recent experience of working 16 or more hours each week explicitly referred to the lack of a financial incentive, half said they could not afford childcare, suggesting many more might be in work if the financial rewards from work were sufficient to help pay for their childcare. The availability rather than the cost of childcare and, indeed, the availability of work itself, did not feature prominently among answers. Lone mothers tended not to envisage major problems finding work. Fewer than one in ten of those with preschool children or children of secondary school age saw finding work as a problem. One in four of those whose youngest child was aged between five and ten years did state such problems: perhaps a reflection of their (failed) attempts to find work of suitable hours once their children started school.

Lone mothers were able to give multiple answers to this question, and half gave more than one answer: 365 respondents gave a total of 611 reasons for not being in work. The second column of Table 12.2 shows the proportion who gave just one reason for being out of work. The reasons most commonly cited as a sole barrier to work were illness and disability, and having children who were too young. For only 5 per cent was the cost of childcare the *only* constraint on them entering work, and for just 2 per cent was it the availability of childcare. For 8 per cent either or both of these problems existed, but no other.

For six in every seven of those citing problems with childcare, there was also another problem, which would also have to be solved before the lone parent could enter work. This is evidence to suggest that solving lone mothers' childcare problems in isolation will not necessarily remove all barriers to their return to work. It would appear that overcoming the barriers posed by childcare cost and availability is a necessary condition for the return to work of almost half Britain's out-of-work lone mothers, but it is not a sufficient condition. Childcare needs to be placed in the context of other constraints.

Nonetheless, the boundaries between answers are subtle and open to interpretation. A lone mother who cannot afford childcare costs could argue that such costs meant it was not worth her while working. She might give both reasons but find her problems solved by a single solution: a change that made her able to afford her childcare. One who stated she could not work because her children were too young might say so because she could not envisage suitable childcare being available for her children.

These definitional problems arise because lone mothers can perceive objectively similar problems in different ways, and a single question on a pen and paper questionnaire cannot pick up the complexities of how each person arrived at their decision. One of the key objectives of the depth study was a more detailed analysis of this process.

THE DEPTH STUDY

The depth follow-up study was designed to learn more about how mothers reach their decision. Analysis of these interviews, exploring the intricacies of lone mothers' decisions, form the basis of a 200-page report (Ford, 1996). Mothers positioned themselves at various distances from the labour market, and explained how they viewed the different barriers preventing them from taking up paid work. These accounts cannot be summarised here. Instead, the focus is on the commonality of mothers' approaches in addressing these problems and particularly how childcare was positioned relative to other considerations. Examples are taken from the longer report.

There were few universals, but what was clear was that mothers could rationalise their behaviours: they had differing aspirations for themselves and their families and they differed in the extent to which they achieved these due to the different constraints they faced. But they justified their positions in relation to the labour market in similar ways. The image recurring again and again in accounts was one of a delicate balance between the demands of their family and the labour market and responsibilities to each. The balance was one that traded financial with non-financial gains. One working lone mother spoke of the separation from her children as a non-financial loss set against a financial gain:

> *I'd like to have more time with them. I think they would like more time as well, but they like all the luxuries that they get along with my working.*

The balance was a complex one because of the need to perform multiple roles. Respondents were conscious that as lone mothers they had sole responsibility for all adult roles in the house: breadwinner, child rearer and home maker:

> *Sometimes, I feel that housework, and job, and children: there aren't enough hours in the day. I can't keep on top.*

Though mothers were expected to fulfil three sets of responsibilities and tasks normally shared within a couple, external support for each role varies. The state is prepared to replace income the lone parent loses from being unable to fulfil the breadwinner role, but home-making and childrearing are not directly supported. Parents were thus conscious that were they to direct their efforts into earning a wage they might renege in areas of their responsibilities where less support was available. In general terms, any change in household economic circumstances could have implications for balancing their responsibilities. Paid employment required lone mothers to alter the focus of their time and efforts from their children to earning a wage. Such a transfer had financial and non-financial components:

It's not always the mother's fault that she's on her own, and she's the one that's caring for the children and sort of supporting them, loving them and bringing them up and to go out to work, you've got to give that up and I don't think it's fair on the children.

Others out of work were less sure of how the balance would tip, and would use a financial gain to balance a non-financial loss.

If we were going to be better off financially, then I don't really regard it would be that big a sacrifice for [my daughter] ... so she would have to put up with this, but she would get rewards for it, and I think she'd also have a saner mother. ... I don't think the time really matters, I think it's what we're going to do with the time that's important.

So this last example describes a situation where greater financial resources may actually improve the fulfilment of childrearing responsibilities, and substitute for the childrearing time lost to earning. As some other mothers perceived it, the balance tipped in favour of staying out of work.

You may be slogging your guts out 40 hours a week and still ending up with as little as you were getting on income support. Who's going to try? No one's going to try. I mean only for your own self-preservation, but for the actual love of work itself: I don't think anyone's going to put themselves out that much and miss out on their families growing up for the sake of it.

Although the system of in-work benefits is structured to maintain a financial differential between in-work and out-of-work incomes, parents may not perceive differences in this way. In depth interviews, respondents were asked how they would consider two hypothetical job vacancies with widely differing gross wage rates for a 35-hour week (£112 versus £250 per week). The critical factor in decisions about the attractiveness of each job was the wage rate itself. It was apparent that mothers were discouraged from taking the low-paid job, even though taxes and in-work benefits could narrow the difference between final incomes from the two jobs to within £20.

The balance analogy is a useful one for considering the role of childcare, since it permits the offsetting of financial with non-financial implications. On one side of the equation, childcare frees up time to devote to paid employment and it has the potential to provide an educational and developmental role for children. On the other side, it separates the mother from her family; it may take the children away from a familiar and secure environment; it can be inflexible; and it costs money. A mother with sole childrearing responsibility must decide whether their own care of the children is the best they can afford, or whether a 'work plus childcare' combination will better fulfil their responsibilities. How the balance is viewed depends on how mothers weight each of these gains and losses, and how their locally available childcare measures up to these benefits and disbenefits.

WHAT LONE MOTHERS MUST BALANCE

The decision to return to work is a difficult one for a lone mother whose children are not yet old enough to look after themselves at home. Of course, they must be able to find suitable employment for themselves and alternative care arrangements for their children. In addition, they must be motivated to work and feel that their time and effort is better invested in employment than in staying at home caring for their children. What is clear from mothers' own accounts is that childcare considerations comprise a subset of many competing factors that weigh in on alternative sides of the equation. These competing factors are set out in the form of an equation in Table 12.3.

Table 12.3: *Potential gains from employment (using childcare) and from remaining out of work*

	The in-work/out-of-work equation	
Gains from work	*Vs*	Gains from not working
Likely net wage from work (less in-work costs)		Out-of-work income/benefits
Social benefits from working		'Good' mothering
		Readjustment to lone parenthood
In-work benefits		Avoid hassle of juggling childcare and work
Child development		Avoid children's poor response to childcare

Gains from work

Potential gains from employment are summarised on the left hand side. These include the financial and non-financial returns from working to the mother (net wages, social network and self-esteem, in-work benefits) and returns to the child from using childcare (which could include accelerated educational development and socialisation). The child may also benefit from an improved standard of living and a more fulfilled mother, while she is a worker.

No element on the left-hand side of the equation is fixed. Childcare quality varies, as do the social advantages of employment. Each job vacancy will combine a requirement for hours and effort with short-term financial gains in the form of the current wage, and potentially long-term gains if it offers any form of progression (a higher future wage or future social benefits).

Lone mothers are restricted by their own skills to a subset of potential vacancies. Most appeared conscious of this restriction, which reduced the chances of achieving gains on the left-hand side of the equation. In considering the better-paying hypothetical job vacancy, one mother summed up how she viewed a 'skills' barrier to her employment. Her account is worth repeating at length, since she describes quite vividly how her low skills reduced her incentive to find work.

> *I'm not qualified or experienced enough to earn a decent wage, to come off the Social Security. No one's going to want to pay someone that's inexperienced. Even after a three-month trial period, and training, I've got to be doing a good job, and I've got to be really good at that job, to pick up a minimum £160 a week. 'Cos, straightaway, dentist bills, prescriptions, school meals, rent, rates. All that. I probably wouldn't have to pay all of it, but even half of each, of everything, would mount up. And it's no good paying for all that, and then finding out I'm worse off. ... Because I've got no experience behind me, and I can't ever see myself gaining any experience, to stay in a good job, and to get a good wage, it is off-putting. I don't want to go on the government pay-roll for the rest of my life.*

While the immediate prospects for attractive financial gains to the low-skilled from work appear poor, the equation suggests that other non-financial gains could offset a poor financial incentive to seek employment. Lone mothers placed a strong emphasis on the social gains from work, and these contribute to the left-hand side of the equation. As the sole parent with a low income, fulfilling family demands can become repetitive and tedious:

Everywhere you go, you've got to have two kids around.

Employed mothers would talk about the social gains from employment
in the same breath as the financial ones. Two mothers on family credit had
slightly differing perspectives about why they worked:

> *It's a break off the kids: money, mostly money. It's time to get away
> from the kids for a wee while, definitely. Sometimes I go insane 'cos it's
> my day off. I thought: 'How could I cope?'*

> *It's not really the money. Though it does help and it makes the world
> go round doesn't it, but with me it keeps my sanity going.*

So, although the left-hand side of the equation contributes positive
elements to the incentive to work, these are by no means all financial. Two
final examples emphasise this point. One mother valued the contribution
of her childminder to her children's upbringing and wanted to increase her
hours so that her children could benefit from spending longer with her
childminder. Another worked because she wanted to contribute to her
children's development by giving them a role model.

> *I wanted them to think that Mum was there, at home, doing the home. But I
> also wanted them to think that there was a breadwinner in the family.*

In such cases, 'good' mothering requires participation in paid employment
in addition to time spent caring for children at home. This view can be
contrasted with those of other lone mothers who align 'good' mothering
with a more traditional home-based role (see below).

Gains from staying at home

On the right-hand side of Table 12.3 appear the potential gains from staying at home. The financial returns are rarely anything other than benefit,
which for the majority will correspond to the income support rate. Other
factors are non-financial and will vary with the mother's perception of her
family role. Like other women in couples, some lone mothers subscribe to
a 'traditional' family role and would be expected to place a premium on
staying at home with their children as such behaviour accords with their
beliefs about what constitutes 'good motherhood'. Alternatively, the lone
mother may find that her social environment (parents, neighbours, friends)
discourages her from spending time apart from her children, regardless of
her own views. In some sections of the community, her behaviour in going
out to work may not be reinforced:

> *It annoys me because you can't win. If you stay at home all day, and
> live off the state, you get criticised. If you go out, and try and make*

things better for yourself, you get criticised the same. You can't win, really. It's just hard, 'cos you've got to play two roles.

Others – recently separated from their partners – may find that the task of adapting to lone motherhood cannot be shared with participation in paid employment. It may be difficult for mothers of children who have recently seen their fathers leave the household, to leave them themselves, to go out to work, or to pass them on to a new carer.

I think that's the worst of it. It does take a long time to get used to being on your own, and being able to cope with children on your own.

Table 12.3 lists two other benefits of staying at home relative to going out to work and using childcare. The first is the problem of time management in maintaining attendance to fixed hours at work alongside each child's attendance at their childcare provider. Complicating factors include term-time and holiday differences in childcare needs, child illness, shift work and unpredictable, varying working hours. Aligning these many elements may be found (or at least perceived as) stressful and contribute to the disbenefits of working.

You think 'Wow, he's got a place at nursery' and nursery finishes at half past eleven. What do you do with them at half past eleven? The sheer business of: you then have to get a child from the nursery to whatever other arrangement you've made. When you are not in a situation where you can repay that. You can't say 'You do it on Monday and I'll do it on Tuesday' because you are supposed to be working. So you end up having to pay somebody to take the child from the nursery to somewhere else.

The second problem is the child's response to childcare. Children may take time to readjust to their care arrangements or even refuse to take them up. Placing children in arrangements that cause them distress, however temporary, will prove difficult for mothers. Some care arrangements may be perceived as detrimental to the child(ren) – making the child development element on the left hand side of the equation negative.

It was stressful, really stressful. Paying for it was fine. It was just the rushing about, and him clinging to me when I was going and I had to sneak off. I just felt really devious and horrible. ... Everywhere I left him he was just upset all the time. So that was upsetting me as well.

A lengthy discussion with each lone mother about the type of childcare available locally revealed many mothers to be distant from both the childcare and labour markets. Their perceptions of the sorts of care available to their children could be coloured by one-off events and media hearsay.

It always fears me because you see these programmes on the telly about these childminders that battered the kids and it puts me off it. Like these childminders that have sexually abused the children they've been minding, that have been registered. No, I couldn't have a registered childminder. No.

I've watched one woman in the area with some younger kids and they're always trailing behind her and ... sometimes I look and think 'Thank God that's not my toddler she's watching'.

Even if misconceived, such views will help tip the balance away from the use of childcare, in favour of working only school hours, or not at all. In the national study, nearly one in five out-of-work lone mothers said they would *never* consider using a registered childminder. Evidently, childcare quality is an issue for lone mothers. It is one that not only requires carers to achieve known and acceptable standards of care, but for those standards to be seen to be achieved.

As children grow older, they too become entitled to a judgement about the acceptability of childcare. Children will wish to become more independent of their parents and thus deny their parents the option of spending time with them. Alternatively, they may reject certain types of care provision. In both situations, parents must weigh up their responsibilities with the net benefits of working to decide the best course of action.

In most circumstances, lone mothers will bear sole responsibility for any decision to change the family's status quo. Given the complexity of the decision, and the far-reaching consequences of the outcomes, they are likely to vacillate.

Making the decision whether or not to work

A lone mother contemplating work and taking up childcare will value different elements of the equation in Table 12.3 differently. She may be motivated largely financially, or she may seek social rewards for her efforts. In contemplating the return to work, she will not have perfect information about all elements of the equation, and cannot know exactly how it will balance. Even in the context of a single vacancy, she is unlikely to know how well her childcare arrangements will work, or what gains work will offer besides the wage. Without professional advice about in-work benefit entitlements, she is unlikely to be able to estimate the financial element of the equation, let alone its non-financial elements. As a lone mother, she suffers the additional disadvantage relative to a couple in having no partner with whom to gather information, discuss and rationalise decisions.

So, even if the lone mother perceives the equation to balance in favour of taking up work, there will still be some risk attached to the decision. The risk is posed not only to her financial security, but to her and her children's emotional wellbeing and even to her social support network. If the mother is risk averse, she may choose to err on the side of caution and remain out of work, even given the risks of long-term dependence on out-of-work benefits. Many of the in-work risks may be misconceived due to a poor understanding of the benefit system, poor information or biased perceptions.

It is worth noting that the equation described in Table 12.3 does not specifically mention childcare costs, quality or availability. Childcare arrangements, like other facilitators of the transition to work (travel arrangements, clothing, social support) interact on both sides of the equation. It is the relative impact of specific arrangements that helps tip the balance one way or the other.

For example, childcare fees act as in-work costs and reduce the net wage from work, but they may qualify the parent for a childcare disregard in in-work benefits, which alters the balance again. Childcare arrangements may interleave well or poorly with work schedules, may be well or poorly received by children, and may hold out the prospect of benefiting or disadvantaging the child's long-term development. Childcare availability determines the limits of the arrangements available. Their quality is relative to the mother's and child's needs. The balance of in-work to out-of-work income determines their affordability. It may be possible for the lone mother to determine the value of a particular vacancy plus childcare arrangement, but it will be difficult to know whether any other permutation of work with childcare would prove more or less valuable.

Parents cannot know all they need to arrive at a perfect decision. Some information will be specific – a specific job vacancy, a specific childcare provider – and some will be based on estimates and generalisations – how much in-work benefit they will receive, how their children will react to care. Lone mothers differ in their familiarity with different elements of the equation, and thus in what combination of specifics and generalities they use to base their decisions about whether or not to work. In interviews, mothers intending to work divided on whether finding childcare or the job vacancy came first. One contributor to the division was the degree of confidence mothers had in locating either. Another factor was the relative importance parents placed on their different roles: child rearing or working. It was the aspect upon which most restrictions were placed that was arranged first. Mothers who would only consider a certain type of childcare would seek work with this source in mind. Mothers who felt restricted in the types of work they could do, or were likely to be offered, prioritised the job search. The evidence above suggests that some are closer to the decision than others, but the elements are constantly changing, as are mothers' perceptions of them.

WHAT DOES THIS MEAN FOR POLICY?

The equation implies that factors that increase the gains on the left-hand side and diminish the gains on the right-hand side will aid movement into work. Good quality, low-cost or subsidised childcare will obviously improve returns from work, but so will increasing the level of in-work benefits, or even the social value and self-esteem that employment offers. Likewise, increasing the likely net wage from work – through lower taxes, equal pay, or improving human capital and thus earning potential – or increasing access to vacancies – through equal opportunities legislation – will have the same effect.

The relative gains from working would be increased through a reduction in out-of-work income, relative to that available in work. Likewise, structures that coordinated employment with childcare opportunities and ensured quality standards would support a decision to enter paid employment. Women might also have less doubt about the validity of their decisions if they were the subject of fewer prevailing ambiguities about their role as mothers. A more explicit family policy would help here.

But, some children will never accept childcare, or childcare will never accept them. *And*, some parents in the aftermath of a traumatic separation will simply be unable to contemplate any decision. A period of adequate (perhaps even targeted) financial support needs to be allowed for this so that these mothers are not forced into actions that are inappropriate for their own or their children's futures. At the same time, absence from the labour market will reduce the range of potential vacancies and earnings levels available to her. Targeted reskilling or induction programmes may be necessary after any period out of the labour market.

Nobody's interests are served by poor quality decisions. There is little advantage in encouraging entry into work that fails to match expectations. Parents will just be dissuaded from further attempts. As one mother put it:

> *I'm determined now. I've tried [returning to employment] and it didn't work, so.*

More generally, the promotion of better informed decisions requires better decision makers. While a reduction in out-of-work benefits may force the balance in favour of employment, it may increase hardship and thus reduce lone mothers' ability to make a well-informed decision. Hardship has been found independently to reduce lone mothers' chances of labour market participation (Bryson et al, 1997). There would appear limited returns to reductions in out of work benefit.

CONCLUSION

There is no conclusive evidence that childcare cost or availability is the sole barrier to paid employment for a substantial proportion of out-of-work lone mothers. Cost and availability certainly comprise *a* barrier, identified by half those out of work, but only one in twelve identify them as the only barrier. There are many other factors influencing the decision whether or not to work. A complex equation of competing gains and losses has been described to aid explanation of how childcare and other factors can influence the decision. The device may help evaluation of policy options intended to increase lone mothers' labour market participation. What is clear is that any proposed change in economic, childrearing or home role of the mother is relative, not absolute. Lower childcare costs will have a positive impact on participation only if all else remains equal. It would be ineffective to lower costs simultaneously with quality, for example.

Cost-effective policy will need research inputs to quantify these rela-tivities. Wholesale investment in free childcare at point of use may be less cost effective in achieving a policy aim of increasing the income security of lone parents than investment in young women's skills. The evidence from this study suggests either approach is valid. They are both part of the same equation.

Chapter 13

The Origins of Child Support in Britain and the Case for a Strong Child Support System
Mavis Maclean

In this chapter I give my account of the setting up of the Child Support Agency (CSA), put the case for a strong child support system and summarise my reasons for continuing to defend this unpopular creation. These centre on the recognition in the Child Support Act of the need to treat all children living apart from a parent in the same way; on the need to recognise the hidden costs of child rearing for the parent with responsibility for care, which is entirely separate from any obligation between two partners who have shared a relationship or household in the past; and, finally, on the need for a system to assess, modify and collect the money due, given the likelihood of reduced access to the courts in the near future over such matters.

The 1991 Child Support Act has few friends. It has been denigrated for putting the interests of the Treasury before those of children, for failing to reduce poverty for children living apart from a parent or to help lone parents into work. Not surprisingly, it has failed to bring the men of Britain to their senses and stop them from fathering more children than they can afford, as Mrs Thatcher had hoped it would Nevertheless, I argue for its continuation and for additional resources to strengthen its implementation, despite all the imperfections in administration and the complexity of the formula.

HISTORICAL CONTEXT

British policy traditionally permitted an absent parent to support his present family while the first family was supported by the state through social security. Lone parents during the 1960s and 1970s received reasonably generous welfare provision. Mothers were not required to register for work until the youngest child reached school leaving age and, though little help was provided for childcare (as Hilary Land and Jane Lewis point out in their chapter here), there were many passported benefits and access to subsidised public housing. However, the court system for assessing and awarding maintenance did not work well. Any resources available for transfer between men and women after divorce were arranged under the heading of wife support. Although, in practice, transfers were almost always made to a parent with the care responsibility, these payments were thought of as wife support. Orders for children were low and rarely paid in full. During the 1980s, interest increased in children as capable individuals with rights, and research began to show how their interests were being ignored in the battles between men and women after divorce. Children's life chances were shown to experience more disruption than had been realised, and the issue of support for children began to be discussed more widely.

At the same time, the Thatcher administration, under economic pressure, became increasingly impatient with what it perceived as the 'nanny state culture of dependency' and worked to promote the value of participation in the labour market as the way out of poverty for various groups and particularly lone parents. In 1990, Mrs Thatcher announced that she was 'looking at ways of strengthening the system for tracing an absent father and making arrangements for recovering maintenance more effective'. The cost of benefits paid to lone parent households was estimated to have increased from £1750 million in 1981 to £3600 million in 1990 (Kiernan and Wicks, 1990). Compliance with court maintenance orders was low, and furthermore it was clear that courts were sometimes maximising the value of social security payments to the parent with care responsibility, even if they needed to keep maintenance payments low to achieve this. If a registrar thought that an absent parent on a low income would be unlikely to comply with a child support order and that irregular payment might prejudice the caring parent's entitlement to ongoing payment of mortgage interest by social security, he was liable to make a nominal award in the interest of the child. The problem was highlighted in the case of *Delaney v Delaney* (2 Fam 457, 1990) in which the judge reduced a maintenance award in order to enable an absent father and his new partner to get started on their new life, leaving the first family on social security.

Children Come First

All these developments came to a head at a time when knowledge was beginning to spread in the UK about the 'magic' formulas for child support being used first in Wisconsin and then in Australia. An interdepartmental group was set up to review maintenance for lone-parent families. There was strong governmental support for the formula concept, but unfortunately complex problems are rarely amenable to simple solutions. The choice of a formula was the simplest of many decisions involved in preparing the UK Child Support Act. Progress was rapid, from the first policy announcement in 1990 to the introduction of legislation in February 1991. Consultation was brief, but it is possible to identify the various interests that provided the impetus for change. The Prime Minister sought to strengthen parental responsibility on moral grounds. The Department of Social Security (DSS) was concerned about the rising weekly payment to lone parents whose liable relatives might be able to pay more. This view was of course supported by the Treasury. Meanwhile, the Lord Chancellor was in the middle of a review of family justice, which aimed to promote the interests of children. But the Lord Chancellor's Department was also concerned about rising costs and pressure on the courts of publicly funded legal services, and was therefore amenable to an administrative solution provided that an equitable and effective outcome could be achieved.

The chosen solution presented in *Children Come First* reflects a balance of these concerns. Following the legislation, the CSA was set up as a semi-privatised 'next steps agency' within the DSS, for this department had a national network of offices with good experience of collecting information and dispensing cash. The agency is responsible for both assessment and enforcement of child support. The aim was to exclude the courts from the basic child support assessment process, except in exceptional cases. This is in marked contrast to the American schemes, which produced guidelines to be used in courts, and the Australian system, which made the scheme compulsory at first for benefit recipients but optional for others.

Out of court

This move of child support out of the courts is a radical change. It has been compared with the setting up of the special procedure for undefended divorce, whereby what had been a matter for court became in practice an administrative procedure. There are many difficulties in taking a matter out of court. The agency and its tribunals have the characteristics of a system where the individual is seeking money from the state, his/her claim is investigated by the state, and a decision is made. It is not a structure that is well equipped to deal with the conflicting interests of two parties.

In addition to this kind of structural difficulty, there were certain features of the design that offended various interest groups. The lawyers disliked the apparent retrospectivity of the scheme in that, initially, when making current child support assessments, it disregarded any previous financial settlements, which might have included the disposal of the family home. A man who had left the house to his wife on the understanding that this represented his contribution to the child's needs might find himself asked to pay a substantial ongoing support order. The act also changed the traditional balance between the claims of first and second families. First families are now put first in the order of claims to an absent parent's resources, and again an assessment could happen some time after both families had established a new way of life. The scheme did not include any incentive to the parents with the care responsibility to use the agency, as had been the case in Australia, with the result that any maintenance paid often benefits the state rather than the lone parent household. Protection for stepchildren was minimal.

Housing costs

A key feature of the payer's position was that the allowances given before income is deemed available for assessment included actual housing costs. Housing remains the critical and intractable problem at the heart of this and all alternative post-separation schemes in the UK. Home ownership has spread far down the income scale, following the selling of publicly-owned and rented housing, and the virtual disappearance of private rented housing, so that we now have a significant property owning welfare population. The family home now represents the credit worthiness as well as the actual property of the couple, which neither can replicate separately. The home represents, if left with the mother, compensation for her loss of earnings and pension entitlements, a substitute for wife support and even child support. For people on income support, the state still largely meets ongoing mortgage repayments. The family home forms the core of solicitors' and registrars' approach to making financial arrangements on divorce. It is feared that the child support cash payments under a rigid formula may be endangering the complex packaging of resources that takes place, with the possibility of serious knock-on effects on the groups of owner occupiers now divorcing. Permitting the man to protect his housing costs may go some way towards enabling him to leave the family home to the first partner, and still rehouse himself, but he has no incentive to do so. If he leaves the house, forgoing his capital, his periodical payments will not fully reflect this transfer.

THE IMPACT OF THE CHILD SUPPORT ACT ON FAMILIES

Preliminary findings from a study of the operation of this much criticised scheme by Davis, Young and Wikely (1996) indicated that 72 per cent of women were neither better nor worse off as a result of the scheme, 8 per cent were worse off and 20 per cent better off. This was compared with the impact on men and on the public purse. Of the men, 15 per cent were better off, 38 per cent worse off and 47 per cent the same. In 37 per cent of cases, the Treasury was better off, in 12 per cent worse off and in 51 per cent the same. These were preliminary findings, which may be revised, but they indicate an entirely predictable result. There were no 'pots of gold' out there to be discovered, but it was possible to get some absent parents to pay a little more. When this was the case, these payments did in some cases make it possible for a parent with the responsibility for care to return to work even on a low wage. The cases where there was a negative effect merit serious attention, and have received it from the research community. However, we note that it is a very small group.

THE IMPLICATIONS OF THE CHILD SUPPORT ACT FOR ALL CHILDREN

This legislation marks the emergence of the right of a child to financial support from both parents irrespective of their legal relationship, namely whether they are or have been married, whether they have ever lived together, or whether they had no common household. The link between financial responsibility and biological parenthood rather than established social parenthood is a harsh one, but we should remember that in practice it is only men who have the choice to distinguish between the two. For women, biological parenthood is almost always coterminous with social parenthood.

The CSA has transformed what in the past was a claim for support for the child, which often took last place in the ordering of competing claims on resources after a divorce, into the primary call on the absent parent's resources, and has extended this right to *all* children with one resident parent.

At the same time, it offered recognition of the economic cost of parenthood for the resident parent and differentiated this cost from the concept of spousal maintenance, which had been losing ground with women's increased participation in the labour market, with no fault divorce, and in the context of women's claims to equality. The allowance in the formula for this purpose is small, hardly more than a token. But it does recognise that whoever cares for children has reduced real income either as a result of curtailed hours and experience if taking care of the child, or through the effect of having to pay others to provide childcare if not.

Finally, the legislation was designed to bypass the courts as the mechanism whereby women in the past had sought to claim financial support for their children, and have been able to do so largely through making use of the legal aid fund. Legal aid paid the immediate costs of legal advice and representation, though contributions may be payable and the costs of the case recoverable from any settlement made even after a period of time under the statutory charge on property. The CSA legislation came on to the statute book just as the legal aid budget came under scrutiny. This budget still is not capped, and after meeting the eligibility criteria, which in effect reduce availability to those living at benefit level, and a test of reasonableness for the case, the woman seeking help is likely to receive it.

But, towards the end of the 1980s, this demand-led budget was coming under pressure, and the Lord Chancellor was seeking ways to control legal aid expenditure and to ensure value for money. We still do not have legal aid legislation, but reform of the system is being actively discussed. It can be only a matter of time before a cap is set. When this happens, it will be difficult to protect the civil legal aid budget that covers family matters, for legal aid for criminal cases will take priority. The government is bound to provide legal help for those at risk of losing their liberty or risk further censure in Strasbourg. It is therefore unlikely that the present relatively generous provision of legal aid to women seeking financial support will continue. Without legal advice, it will be difficult for women either to obtain an order from the court for child support, or, and equally importantly, be able to modify or enforce it.

In sum, the Child Support Act gives all children the right to a share in both their parents' incomes, when these parents do not share a household, and recognises for the first time the economic burden of child rearing.

ACCEPTANCE OF THE CHILD SUPPORT ACT

The principles underlying this part of the act seem to have fairly widespread support, (see Maclean and Eekelaar, 1997). It is when we turn to the implementation of the act and the processes of assessment, modification and collection of child support that serious difficulties have emerged. But, even here, we should be careful to compare the CSA with what went before it as well as with what we would like to see as a preferred outcome. Before the act, even with widespread legal aid, child support payments were irregular, infrequent and low. Payments that were made were largely restricted to the children of divorcing parents. If we had retained the system and lost the legal aid input, the continuation of any child support payments would have become problematic. Under the CSA, awards are available to never-married and separating cohabitants in the same way as divorcing parents. The system will survive radical reform to the legal aid system and it would not be difficult to amend the formula to remove some of the complex detail, for example regarding actual housing costs, and to continue to improve the administrative procedures. The commonest causes of complaint are linked to delay. With a hybrid system midway between the detailed investigation of individual circumstances by a benefit agency and the two-party situation more often found in court procedure, where each party must be given the opportunity to comment on the facts put forward by the other, it is not surprising that changes of circumstance occur during the process and that the whole business of assessment and collection is prolonged.

CONCLUSIONS

I expect the hostility to the scheme to diminish as it has done in Australia, and the benefits to remain in the form of an expectation that child support will be paid as a right and not debated as a claim, and that the amount involved will be somewhat higher than under the previous regime. There will be no immediate eradication of poverty in one-parent households. This could only be achieved through either draconian measures against the absent fathers or by state generosity. Given the political realities, the CSA makes a reasonable attempt to increase public awareness of the costs of parenthood and the need to distribute them more equitably between men and women. With legal aid women were doing badly. Their prospects without it, or with more limited access, must be worse. An administrative mechanism open to revision and improved performance is the only choice we have. (For a full account of the development of the CSA, see also Maclean 1994.)

Chapter 14

Supporting Children? The Impact of the Child Support Act on Lone Mothers and Children

Karen Clarke, Caroline Glendinning and Gary Craig

The social problems resulting from the substantial growth in lone parenthood over the past 20 years are well documented and are comprehensively summarised in Chapter 1 here. Policy concern in recent years has focused on a particular aspect of the lone-parenthood problem – the increasing dependence of lone mothers on welfare benefits and the rapidly escalating costs to the state of their support. The 1991 Child Support Act, in conjunction with changes to the rules for family credit, was intended to address this problem by shifting as much responsibility as possible for the financial consequences of family breakdown and lone parenthood on to the parents themselves, by ensuring that as many absent parents[1] as possible pay maintenance to their former partner and by encouraging lone mothers to support themselves as far as possible through paid employment. The formula for the calculation of child support obligations and the establishment of the Child Support Agency (CSA) to implement the new system for child support were intended to create a system that was fair, efficient and responsive to changes in the circumstances of parents. The act also had a clear moral agenda, which was to create a greater sense of responsibility towards children on the part of absent parents through the enforcement of what were presented as the universal financial obligations of biological parenthood (and paternity in particular).

The act and the preceding white paper, 'Children Come First', thus concentrated on a limited aspect of the social problems associated with lone parenthood. It looked primarily at the problems the welfare dependency of

---

1. The terms 'absent parent' and 'parent with care' are used in official documents; we have followed that convention without necessarily endorsing the terminology.

lone parents creates for the Treasury and did not address the main problem to flow from this dependency as far as lone parents themselves are concerned, namely poverty. Similarly, the government's concern to ensure greater responsibility on the part of absent parents is viewed through the lens of financial responsibility only, without regard to other crucial aspects of how the exercise of parental responsibility may be experienced by parents and children: the meeting of social and emotional responsibilities through contact between absent parents and their children. The Child Support Act was not therefore primarily concerned with addressing the principal problems lone parents and their children may feel themselves to face, but rather with another set of problems relating to the role of the state and the burden of lone parent support on public expenditure.

In this chapter, we examine the effects on lone mothers and their children of the implementation of the Child Support Act, drawing principally on a part-longitudinal qualitative study of lone mothers on benefits carried out between March 1993 (just before the act was implemented) and March 1995. Interviews with a sample of 29 lone mothers on benefits before the act came into effect examined its anticipated impact on them (Clarke, Craig and Glendinning 1993). A larger sample of 54 lone mothers (including six who were interviewed in 1993) who had had some contact with the CSA was interviewed early in 1994 to explore what effects the act had had on their situation (Clarke, Glendinning and Craig 1994). A further sample of 53 lone mothers, including 41 interviewed in one or both of the first two stages of the study, was interviewed between January and March 1995 in order to look at some of the longer term effects of the legislation (Clarke, Craig and Glendinning 1996a). We also drew on a small pilot study that examined children's views on child support and on the impact on them of the Child Support Act. This was conducted in 1995 and involved interviews with 12 of the children of the lone mothers included in the final stage of our study (Clarke, Craig and Glendinning 1996b).

We focus here on two aspects of the act's impact on lone mothers and children: its effects on the financial circumstances of lone mothers dependent on means-tested benefits, who constitute the overwhelming majority of all lone mothers, and its effects on relationships between lone mothers, absent fathers and children.

FINANCIAL IMPACT ON LONE MOTHERS OF THE ACT

Lack of financial gain from child support

While the payment of child support by absent parents has resulted in substantial savings in social security expenditure (estimated at £1740 million from April 1993 to December 1996) (House of Commons Social Security

Committee Fifth Report, 1997, para 9), financial gains to lone mothers and their children are less evident. Lone mothers on income support have child support deducted from their benefit on a pound for pound basis and therefore can only gain financially if their income from child support lifts them off income support altogether. However, the only lone mother in our qualitative study for whom this was the case had actually lost financially because of the loss of passported benefits associated with income support (Clarke et al,1996b: 20).

Lone mothers on family credit are entitled to keep the first £15 a week of maintenance and therefore potentially stand to gain financially from child support payments. However, maintenance payments for family credit recipients are not guaranteed by the CSA and the extent to which lone mothers on family credit gain from maintenance awards in practice depends crucially on the regularity with which the former partner makes his child support payments either directly or through the agency. Where payments are made via the CSA, lone mothers' financial security is dependent on the promptness with which these payments are then passed on to her. The lack of direct coordination between the CSA and the procedures for assessing family credit adds further to financial uncertainty for lone mothers on family credit. Because family credit is only reassessed every six months, any change in the circumstances of the absent parent leading to a reduction in the amount of child support paid cannot be adjusted for in her family credit entitlement in the interim. Our study found that four of the 15 mothers on family credit had lost financially because payments were being made erratically or not at all, and also because of insufficient coordination between the assessment of family credit and the assessment of child support (Clarke et al, 1996: 20).

Despite the extensive powers of the CSA to enforce payment of child support through the use of attachment of earnings orders, the amount of maintenance unpaid by absent parents remains very substantial. In December 1996, £438 million was outstanding on full maintenance assessments, of which £271 million was being repaid by instalments, leaving £167 million to be collected (House of Commons Social Security Committee Fifth Report, 1997, para 11). The non-payment of maintenance does not reduce the income of lone mothers on income support, for payments are guaranteed by the CSA. However, for lone mothers who are on family credit or who are wholly dependent on child support for their income, the lack of any guarantee of payment places them and their children in a financially vulnerable position. This was recognised by Ann Chant (then chief executive of the CSA) in her evidence to the Social Security Committee's fifth enquiry into the agency (House of Commons Social Security Committee Fifth Report, 1997, paragraphs 24-5).

However, the committee stopped short of recommending that the CSA be given funds to allow all maintenance payments to be guaranteed, noting (paragraph 24): 'We accept that there would be an element of risk to the taxpayers if the Agency had its own funds and that this would be a major policy change which Ministers would need to consider carefully.'

The principal group for which enforcement of maintenance payments remains a problem is that of the self-employed. In our own study, one mother reported that her ex-partner had changed his employment status to self-employment in what she thought was a deliberate attempt to make assessment and collection of maintenance more difficult. This may change because of new regulations giving scope for investigation by the agency if there is a major discrepancy between declared income and lifestyle. However, other studies have shown the difficulties and delays encountered in trying to assess the income of the self-employed (Corden, Eardley and Smellie, 1993) and this is likely to remain a problem for lone mothers whose former partner is self-employed.

In relation to the agency's own role in making payments, the speed with which payments are passed on to parents with care has undoubtedly increased in the time since our studies were carried out – the latest report from the Social Security Committee shows that 98 per cent of payments were passed on to parents with care within ten working days in 1995/6. However, it is important to note that what may be an acceptable level of speed and efficiency to a large bureaucracy such as the CSA may nonetheless still constitute an unacceptable delay to lone mothers living on very low and precarious levels of income from a number of different sources. A two-week delay (ten working days) in receiving a payment of £40 per week (the average full assessment for an employee in February 1997), potentially represents a quarter of total weekly income of a lone mother on family credit with one child under five. The disjuncture between the priorities and perceptions of CSA staff and those of lone parents were noted in a recent study involving parents, their legal advisers and agency staff (Bennett 1997: 11–12)

Those mothers on benefits who are subject to a reduced benefit direction have lost a substantial proportion of their income under the Child Support Act. At the time of our studies, this was set at 20 per cent of the adult income support rate for six months and 10 per cent of the adult rate for a further twelve months. A reduced benefit direction can be made either if a lone mother refuses to cooperate with the CSA by completing the maintenance application form, or if the agency does not accept her claim to be exempted from cooperation for 'good cause' (on the grounds that she or her child would suffer 'harm or undue distress'). The agency has taken the view that the 'good cause' exemption was being abused and used to conceal fraud, in the form of undeclared payments from absent parents. While it is true that some lone mothers may have used the good cause exemption as a way of protecting undeclared financial arrangements between themselves and former partners, it is important to recognise that this may not be the only reason why lone mothers do not wish to cooperate. One lone mother in our study had suffered ten years of physical and emotional abuse. Although she could have claimed good cause, she had refused to cooperate and had had the benefit penalty imposed, in order to avoid the humiliation of having to explain her reasons:

> *I didn't want money from him ... and (they are) the last people I want to turn to and ... tell them the gory details of my rotten marriage. ... I don't want to go into the office and have them telling me 'your husband should be keeping you,' which one of them did.*

Refusal to cooperate may also arise from a wish to preserve a delicate set of arrangements involving not only financial support but also other forms of support for children. This will be discussed further below.

Since October 1996, the benefit penalty has been set at 40 per cent of the adult income support allowance for a period of three years, renewable indefinitely. This amounts to a reduction in weekly income for a lone mother on income support of almost £20. Further measures are to be introduced from September 1997 to compel early cooperation with the CSA by making entitlement to benefit conditional on assisting with seeking child support (House of Commons Social Security Committee Fifth Report, 1997, paragraph 22). Both these changes will clearly result in very severe hardship to lone mothers who feel unable to cooperate for some reason, and to children living in such households.

There is an assumption underlying much of the discussion of lone parents' refusal to cooperate with the agency, that this is because of fraud. The Social Security Committee noted with apparent satisfaction that the CSA had reported: 'Between April and December 1996 over 33,500 parents with care withdrew their benefit claim within four weeks of CSA action, realising savings of £115 million.' There is no recognition by the CSA or by the Social Security Committee that withdrawal of a claim may occur for reasons other than the original claim being fraudulent. For example, one mother in our study withdrew her claim for family credit because of the potential effects on her relationship with her former partner and his new family, which she wanted to preserve in the interests of her daughter's continuing contact with her father. Savings achieved in this way, which result in increased financial hardship to families already on very low incomes, are not in the interests of children, or, arguably, ultimately in the long-term interests of society.

The Child Support Act therefore appears to have brought little or no direct financial gain to lone mothers who are dependent on income support and been of dubious benefit to lone mothers on family credit. It also appears, so far at least, to have been unsuccessful in achieving the objective of increasing the extent to which absent parents are contributing to the support of their children through the payment of maintenance. The proportion of lone mothers receiving regular maintenance payments, 30 per cent, is the same as the proportion who were receiving regular maintenance before the introduction of the act (Marsh et al, 1997). The amount paid in maintenance may have increased as a result of the introduction of a formula for calculating children's maintenance requirements, but Marsh's findings suggest that this is because those who are paying are paying more, rather than an increase in the extent to which absent parents are paying child support.

The CSA's own figures on child support payments make it clear that shifting the focus from the state to absent parents as the source of lone parent's income is failing, not only because of absent parents' unwillingness to pay, but also because of their inability to do so. Some 40 per cent of absent parents assessed by the agency in November 1996 were dependent on income support, job seekers allowance or disability benefits and were therefore liable to pay either £4.80 per week or nil (depending on their circumstances).

Indirect losses

The (re)assessment of child support may cause losses to lone mothers and their children other than financial ones. For example, they could lose various forms of help formerly provided in kind, such as assistance with holidays, buying children's clothing or presents, or providing treats for them. These contributions were highly valued by mothers as direct contributions to their children's standard of living, for they were things she could not afford out of her own income. This was also the kind of material support from absent parents of which children were most aware, and it therefore contributed to their sense of being provided for by their father. From children's own accounts, it was clear that such support in kind was often provided in the context of contact and was an important way in which fathers could have some involvement in their daily lives (Clarke et al, 1996b,: 17).

About one-third of the lone mothers in our study reported that such forms of hidden subsidy to them from former partners had ceased or been significantly reduced as a consequence of the initiation of the maintenance assessment process, leaving lone-parent families worse off overall where, if they were on income support, there was no financial gain from the receipt of (or an increase in) child support payments. Such help in kind provides not only an important form of additional material help to lone mothers and their children living on very low incomes, but also carries emotional significance for children in terms of their feeling supported and cared for by their father. Several mothers reported that their children could not understand why their father was unable to make this kind of contribution any longer:

> *[Ex partner] used to buy a lot of clothes and take them on holiday but that's all cut down now, can't take them away on weekends, give them sweets ... he's struggling to give them much at all. ... I feel pretty sick because we had a good agreement and the kids got the best out of everything, the best we could do.*

Children's own accounts of the impact on them of the act also reflected a sense of injustice that they had lost out materially. One child who had experienced a reduction in informal support from her father, because he was having to pay increased maintenance, commented on the paradox of families suffering an overall loss where fathers were paying increased maintenance:

> *Dads have to pay more money for their kids to make the children well off, but it isn't working. We're worse off. We're not getting as much stuff as we used to because dad's giving mum more money than he used to.*

Another child commented:

> *[It] should be making it better for children – but it doesn't – it makes it just the same.*

Enforcement of the Child Support Act has relied almost entirely on the use of penalties against those who do not cooperate in seeking maintenance and has provided no positive incentives for cooperation for the majority of lone parents on means tested benefits – those on income support – in the form of some immediate financial gain. The lone mothers in our study who had completed a maintenance application form and not yet received notification of the assessment of maintenance had all been waiting for over 12 months to hear the outcome of their application. However, those on income support had no reason to contact the CSA to find out what had happened to their claim because an assessment would make no difference to their financial situation unless they were to move into work and off income support. Fathers who want to support their children also have no positive incentive to do so through the agency, since none of the money they pay in child support to a former partner on income support will bring material gains to the child and, as we have seen, the resources put into formal maintenance may mean there is little or nothing left to provide other forms of material support. Cooperation by both parents would, it would seem, be encouraged if the emphasis on coercion was balanced by offering some rewards to cooperating parents.

The payment of child support brings with it not only material but also emotional consequences. Lone mothers interviewed both before and after the implementation of the act believed that the payment of maintenance brought with it a right to contact and could also be used by a former partner to exercise control over them by withholding payments or by demanding accountability for the way in which the money was used. A change in child support arrangements could therefore have important effects on relationships between parents and between children and absent parents. We turn now to examine how family relationships had been affected by the implementation of the act.

EFFECTS ON RELATIONSHIPS

The term lone-parent family implies a homogeneity of experience that in reality does not exist. There is an enormous variety of relationships between lone mothers, children and their ex-partners/fathers. The range includes relationships that ended before the child's birth and involved little or no further contact between the father and the mother or child, through relationships that ended because of violence to the mother, child or both, with no subsequent contact, to situations where there is frequent and regular contact and relatively amicable relationships between the adults and children. In some cases, these relations are further affected by subsequent relationships entered into by one or both parents. The impact of the Child Support Act on relationships within families depends on the history of the relationship between the parents. We examine how the implementation of the act had affected parents and children in each of these groups in turn.

Parents with a history of no contact or very limited contact

In our interviews with lone mothers before the act was implemented, there was considerable anxiety on the part of mothers who had had little or no contact with their child's father that a maintenance (re)assessment might provoke a renewal of interest in contact with the child by the father. The mothers felt that contact renewed on this basis was unlikely to be sustained and would ultimately be damaging to the child (Clarke et al, 1993: 60–1).

However, interviews with mothers in this situation subsequent to the act's implementation revealed no evidence of serious attempts to re-establish contact in response to a maintenance (re)assessment. In fact, in a high proportion of cases where there was no contact, no maintenance was being paid at the time when the lone mother was contacted by the agency and the CSA appeared to have been relatively unsuccessful in contacting and assessing the father. The same was true for lone mothers whose contact with their former partner was very infrequent. There was thus no evidence from our studies to support the anxiety that contact might be renewed as the quid pro quo for money and no indication that a broader sense of parental responsibility had been prompted by a requirement to pay child support. It is important to point out that at the time of our studies the CSA's financial targets had resulted in a policy of targeting absent parents who were already paying maintenance, were in contact with their children and were therefore easy to trace. Fathers who were not in contact and not paying maintenance were a low priority and it is not clear what the response of this group will be when they are more actively pursued.

Lone mothers with no contact because of violence

A substantial minority of lone mothers whom we interviewed had suffered violence from a former partner. While some women had successfully claimed good cause exemption, a number had been put under considerable pressure by CSA staff to cooperate, despite there being a known history of violence in the relationship. Mothers described how they felt they had 'no option' but to complete the form or said they had been told 'it was against the law for me not to sign it', despite having described a long history of violence in the relationship, involving criminal proceedings for assault. Others had felt indirect pressure to do so because of fear of the benefit penalty.

Most mothers with a history of violence who had completed a maintenance application form were still awaiting notification of the outcome of the (re)assessment, or appeal, more than 12 months after completing the form. It was therefore not yet clear what effect, if any, it would have on the relationship with the former partner. This period of protracted uncertainty had been stressful for mothers who were worried about a violent response from their ex-partner. In a number of instances there had been hostile responses from former partners to mothers completing the maintenance application form. Two women had suffered threats and abuse, with serious effects on their health, and in a third case the former partner had threatened to seek contact with his son, in what the mother felt was in fact an attempt to intimidate her. She was subsequently able to withdraw her authorisation to the agency to pursue maintenance, but only after she had been hospitalised as a result of her distress.

Since our studies were carried out there has been a substantial increase in the benefit penalty and a move to interpret the good cause exemption more narrowly. Among the 'encouraging developments' reported by the Social Security Committee in its fifth report on child support (paragraph 22) was the fact that:

> *Since September 1996 there has (also) been a decrease in the number of Good Cause accepted decisions and an increase in the number of Good Cause not accepted decisions. This reflects the more probing investigative approach now being adopted by the Agency.*

Without further evidence on the effects on families of these developments, it is difficult to judge whether they are in fact encouraging or simply represent an increase in the pressures experienced by some lone mothers.

Parents and children with regular contact

In just over one-third of the families interviewed for our study, the absent parent was in regular contact with the mother and child(ren). These former partners were also more likely than others to be paying regular and significant sums in maintenance. Ironically, it was in these circumstances that the CSA's involvement was most likely to have resulted in acrimony between the parents and adverse effects on the children. This increased friction between former partners was the result of a number of factors:

- the overturning of a mutually agreed and satisfactory set of arrangements covering maintenance, property and contact;
- men's apprehension about the amount they might be required to pay, especially where the man was in a new relationship;
- feelings of grievance at being targeted by the government when the father had in his view (and that of his former partner) been meeting his financial obligations

Some mothers in this group had successfully argued that they should be exempt from the requirement to cooperate on the grounds that the parents' relationship or the father's relationship with the child would be adversely affected. However, the more rigorous interpretation of the good cause provisions, following the government and the agency's concern that good cause was being claimed fraudulently, suggests that such a broad interpretation of what constitutes 'good cause' would be less likely to succeed now. This is supported by monitoring evidence from the National Council for One Parent Families, which indicates that an increasingly narrow view is being taken by the CSA of what constitutes 'harm and undue distress', with a very substantial reduction in the proportion of such claims being accepted (Bennett, 1997: 10). Such a narrow definition of what constitutes good cause gives a perverse incentive to absent parents for violence, or the threat of it, against their former partner as a way of avoiding an assessment by the CSA.

Despite the fact that cooperation with the agency in seeking maintenance is compulsory for all lone mothers on benefit, former partners' anger was directed against the lone mother rather than the CSA because, according to the formal assessment process, she was nominally the instigator of the claim:

> *before ... we treated each other with respect. Now there was no conversation – it was like he thought that I was behind all this and they had said to him in a letter that I had applied for this.*

In several families, the friction between the parents prompted by the maintenance assessment process resolved itself with time, as the assessment turned out to be less than feared or as men adjusted to the change, but in others the former partner's reaction was extreme and had caused more permanent damage to the parents' relationship.

The adverse effects on relationships were not confined to friction between parents. Children inevitably witnessed the conflicts over maintenance between their parents:

> *we couldn't bear to be in the same room as each other, there was such an atmosphere, whereas before [father] would come and he could have a cup of tea and [son] could feel at ease to show him things, but that stopped. He knew he had to get his shoes on and get out quick.*

In some cases children were drawn in more directly to the hostility between the parents, which the assessment process and its outcome provoked:

> *They've [ex-partner and new wife] made the children feel under pressure, saying their resources are limited because of having to pay me ... the children have picked this up along the way, to a certain extent blaming me.*

The frequency and quality of contact between children and their fathers was affected either because fathers could not afford to see their children so often or because their activities when they were together were restricted because of lack of money. Some kind of adverse effect on parent–child relationships was found in a quarter of the families in our study where children had contact with their fathers.

Six of the twelve children interviewed in the pilot study on children's experience of the act were in contact with their fathers and a number of them had been distressed by the effects on both their parents of the agency's assessment. One 14-year-old girl said, 'I don't think they realise what a state families are in.' She was concerned that her relationship with her father might be affected because of the act's financial impact on him:

> *Dad says he'll have to move away for work. [He] says I'll get closer to mum. We'll see him less often when he sells the house.*

Another girl whose father had been paying maintenance before the implementation of the act, felt her father had been unfairly targeted:

> *They shouldn't be asking my dad, they should be asking fathers who don't pay. ... He tries hard. ... He's picked on. ... My dad has been very upset.*

It could be argued that this kind of friction, hostility and distress is unavoidable under the difficult circumstances that follow parental separation, that it was as likely to have occurred under the previous court-based system and that the act and the agency were simply convenient scapegoats for the emotional upheaval and difficulties these families were suffering. Children's and parents' distress is unavoidable under these circumstances, but arguably one of the objectives of policy in relation to lone parents should be to minimise the negative emotional impact on children and encourage conciliation between the parents. The 1996 Family Law Act introduces a compulsory 18-month conciliation period for divorcing couples with children and yet the Child Support Act significantly reduces the scope for conciliation by its inflexible specification of child support obligations. There are a number of features of the Child Support Act, which, we would argue, significantly increase the scope for exacerbating tensions between parents and creating difficulties for children's relationship with the absent parent:

- the compulsion on all lone parents on benefits to seek maintenance through the CSA, with very restricted grounds for exemption. This makes it impossible for parents to make their own mutually satisfactory arrangements;
- the separation of the issue of maintenance from the settling of other issues, such as contact and property, so that there is less scope for reaching agreement on the situation as a whole;
- the use of a formula to determine child support obligations, with very limited scope for departure from the formula to take into account individual circumstances;
- the high level at which the formula is set and the lack of financial gain to children in households on income support; and

- the failure to make provision adequately for couples who had reached an agreement on a property and maintenance 'package' prior to the implementation of the act.

Amendments to the legislation and the regulations under the act have addressed the latter three points by allowing departures from the formula for reasons that include the cost of maintaining contact; by setting a ceiling on the proportion of an absent parent's income that can be paid in child support; and by allowing the transfer of capital assets to be offset against the maintenance assessment. However, these are all modifications that are intended to accommodate the problems faced by absent parents but that do nothing to address the problems lone mothers and children experience.

Wider family relationships

It is important, in looking at the effects of the act on children in lone-parent families to consider the wider impact of the act on new families formed by either parent and the implications of this for children's continuing relationships with both the absent parent and with new step-parents in either household. The formula for calculating child support allocates a higher proportion of the absent parent's income to the children of the 'first' family than was generally the case when courts had responsibility for determining child support. This is a potential source of friction between 'first' and 'second' families, affecting both adults and children in all the households involved.

There is relatively little evidence on this question from our own studies, but it is an issue that merits further investigation. Some lone mothers in our study who had formed a new relationship thought that their new partner's financial obligations to a former partner and children might make the formalisation of the current relationship harder:

> *If we ever got married or anything like that it'd be hard for him because if they catch up with him and make him pay ridiculous amounts ... that would give us no chance at all.*

> *If you've got children from a previous marriage, it doesn't give any incentive to settle down, not when you've got the Child Support Agency yapping at your heels for all your money. Because with what they're taking ... you'd just be putting yourself on the poverty line.*

There is also a danger that the act may discourage fathers from acknowledging paternity and meeting their responsibilities towards children:

*You would find that most women and men [will do] what my friend did –
the father's page is a blank and she is still with the father – they are not
actually living together but they are still going out together ... because of
this [the Child Support Act] the new baby now had a birth certificate with
no father on it ... and the mothers have to say 'Well it's because of the
government, we couldn't put your dad on the birth certificate.*

Lone mothers also reported negative effects of maintenance (re)assess-
ments on fathers' new relationships. The second marriage of the ex-partner
of one lone mother had eventually broken up because of arguments
following the father's receipt of a maintenance evaluation form. In another
case, the father had temporarily separated from his new partner after
difficulties in their relationship while maintenance was being assessed. In
both cases, the children involved had been affected by the difficulties in
their father's new relationship. Since we did not interview absent parents
or new partners, we cannot be sure that the lone mothers' accounts are
accurate and complete, or that the attribution of blame to the Child Support
Act is correct. Evidence from other studies carried out before the
introduction of the Child Support Act shows that second marriages are
more likely than first marriages to end in divorce, and that the more
complex the household created by the second marriage, the more likely
this is to be the case (Kiernan and Wicks, 1990). However, any evaluation
of the act needs to consider whether it has further added to the difficulty of
forming new long-term relationships for either parent, particularly since
remarriage has in the past offered one obvious route out of the poverty of
lone parenthood.

The act attempted to alter the balance in the allocation of resources
between 'first' and 'second' families in favour of the 'first' family, to the
point where stepchildren in 'second' families have no claim on the
resources of their stepfather. Our own studies, and others that have interviewed absent fathers and women and men involved in cross-household
parenting, all find that there is widespread consensus about obligations to
children in 'first' families – a view also echoed by the children in our pilot
study. However, such obligations are not seen as unconditional. The
degree of financial obligation is seen as affected both by mothers' and
fathers' current circumstances and the history of the parents' relationship
(Bennett 1997: 23–4; Clarke et al, 1996a: 32–5). Child support in a
broader sense than simply financial support for children, entails the maintenance of good relationships with both parents. This in turn requires that
the impact of financial obligations on both the material well-being of
'second' families and on the feelings of new step-parents and of step and
half siblings towards children of the first family need to be taken into
account. This is an important area for future research.

CONFLICTING INTERESTS: STATE, MOTHERS, FATHERS AND CHILDREN

Policies towards lone parents and their children have to try to balance a highly complex and, to some extent, mutually incompatible set of interests – those of the state, of lone mothers (parents), absent fathers (parents) and of the children of each parent's past and present relationships. As we have seen, current policy, in the form of the Child Support Act, is dominated by the government's wish to minimise the financial implications of lone parenthood for public expenditure 'in the interests of the taxpayer'. It must be pointed out, however, that it cannot be taken as axiomatic that the interests of the state and of taxpayers (who include past, present and future lone and absent parents) are best served by minimising state support for lone parents and their children. A broader and longer-term view of lone parenthood, which acknowledges it as a phase in the life-course of many families, might give the state a greater role in their support in the interests of reducing poverty and family conflict and so serving the long-term interests of children. Our research suggests that the Child Support Act has done little to serve the interests of lone mothers and children in terms of reducing their vulnerability to poverty or in attempting to promote their welfare in a wider sense by facilitating the maintenance of contact and of good relationships between the various parties concerned.

Current policy on family responsibilities is marked by contradictions between the two key pieces of recent legislation in this area (Leigh, 1992). The 1989 Children Act gives paramount consideration to the welfare of the child and adopts the principle of minimising state intervention in families. The act is informed by the assumption that parents can and should be trusted to make arrangements between them that will be in the interests of their children, and that the role of the state should as far as possible be limited to providing support for parents where this is needed, with state intervention in families used only as a last resort (Fox Harding, 1991). The act takes a broad view of who can and should have parental responsibility for children, which allows for the formal acknowledgement of a variety of social arrangements in which children live. Although biological status is the basis for mothers' parental responsibility, for other adults it derives from social (including legal) relationships between adults and children, rather than from biological ones. The Children Act is therefore able to accommodate the changing family circumstances in which children may find themselves in the course of their childhood, when they may move from living with two birth parents to living with one and then to living with one birth parent and a step-parent, or even alternating between two such situations.

This is in marked contrast with the Child Support Act where, at least for lone parents on means tested benefits, state intervention in the financial arrangements between separated parents is mandatory, with no scope for parents to come to their own arrangements. There is no provision for considering whether child support payments serve to promote the welfare of children and, unlike the Children Act, children's views and wishes have no place in the implementation of the act. The Child Support Act takes a rather rigid and static approach to parents' financial responsibilities, which derive from their biological status and which are not seen as in any way contingent on the particular social circumstances of either parent, either in terms of the history of the parents' relationship or their current circumstances.

Finally, the two pieces of legislation take very different views of what constitutes 'support'. The Children Act (s.17) gives the state an obligation to provide services for 'children in need', in the form of family support. Such support can take the form of a wide variety of services providing different kinds of help for both parents and children in order to serve the interests of children and can also be provided in the form of financial assistance to families. The Child Support Act addresses the support of children purely in terms of the private financial obligations of parents and in isolation from any consideration of other forms of support, either private – in the form of parents' material and emotional support of their children – or public – in the form of services to support children and parents.

Policy options

How then might child support policy be amended in the future in order to serve the interests of children and parents better? A number of short-term changes could be made that would help address some of the issues we have identified.

First, lone mothers on income support could be given a disregard on child support payments. This would both acknowledge the poverty they experience on income support and provide an incentive to cooperate with the CSA in seeking child support. It might also increase the willingness of absent fathers to pay if there were some material gain for the child and, to some extent, would compensate for any loss of other material support, which the channelling of increased resources into cash payments makes difficult or impossible for absent parents. From a broader perspective on family poverty more generally, however, such a disregard might be seen to create inequities between two-parent and one-parent families on income support.

Second, income security and work incentives for lone mothers on family credit could be increased by the guaranteeing of child support payments (as already happens for income support claimants). This would help to support women making the difficult transition from a low but secure income on income support to greater financial independence in relation to both the state and a former partner through paid work. Such a measure would clearly be in the long-term as well as the short-term interests of women in terms of their labour market prospects and the level and security of their income in old age (Joshi et al, 1996), as well as in the immediate material interests of children.

A maintenance guarantee would also benefit women by reducing the extent to which they are dependent on a former partner, and thereby reducing the extent to which they experience themselves as remaining under his control.

There is no way of avoiding the fact that, because of their joint responsibility for children, parents remain tied together in a relationship for the period of their children's dependency. Because of this dependency, their financial support has to be mediated by the parent with care and that in turn necessarily involves a form of financial dependency of the parent with care on the absent parent, if he is contributing financially to their support. However, the extent to which this is felt to be the case depends crucially on what mechanisms are used to make the contribution, the closeness of the link between the absent parent's level of financial liability and the amount received by the parent with care, and the impact of the absent parent's contribution on the lone parent's income. The more indirect the contribution and the more 'invisible', the less likely it is to create feelings of dependency and accountability on the part of the lone parent and, arguably, to contribute to friction between the parents and hence emotional conflict for children. This is the structure of the more radical approach to the financial needs of lone parents and children proposed in the Finer Report (DHSS, 1974), which would have provided a common guaranteed maintenance allowance for all lone parents with recovery of a contribution from the absent parent. The Finer proposal thus severed any direct link between the absent parent's resources and the lone parent's income and, by proposing a universal benefit for lone parents, rendered the absent parent's contribution relatively invisible.

Third, the removal of the requirement for lone parents on means-tested benefits to cooperate with the CSA would allow parents to decide whether, on balance, maintenance as assessed and collected through the CSA would be damaging to relationships and/or other financial and capital settlements. Lone parents who are not dependent on benefits are not required to cooperate and the only justification for this difference in treatment is therefore a fiscal one.

Voluntary cooperation with the agency would enable lone parents, who have the day-to-day responsibility for their children's welfare, to assess all the relevant considerations, including both the material circumstances and the quality of the relationship between the child and the absent parent, in their particular case. Such an approach would be consistent with that taken in the 1989 Children Act, which assumes that parents will act in their children's interests unless there is clear evidence to the contrary.

The narrow focus of the Child Support Act on maximising the cash transfers from absent parents to lone-parent families and on maximising the savings to the state takes insufficient account of the complex web of post-separation arrangements of which child maintenance is only one part. It also fails to acknowledge the emotional significance of financial transfers, particularly under what are often very difficult emotional circumstances. If there were some material gain to lone mothers, this might compensate them and their children for some of the emotional difficulties caused by the higher levels of child support payable under the act. As it is, the lack of any financial gain to mothers on income support and the continuing financial insecurity of lone mothers on family credit, combined with the difficulties created in relationships by the implementation of the act, cannot be seen as being in the interests of children or contributing to child support in a broader sense.

Chapter 15

Lone Parenthood and Future Policy
Jane Millar and Reuben Ford

The rise in lone parenthood is one of the most striking demographic and social trends of the last 25 to 30 years. The growing social acceptance of a separation of sex, marriage and parenthood has created a situation in which lone parenthood is increasingly coming to be seen as another stage in the family life cycle, rather than as an aberration from 'normal' family patterns. This is true not just in the UK, but throughout western industrialised countries. Changing social attitudes and behaviour are everywhere creating more diverse patterns of family structure: cohabiting couples, first marriages, remarriages, lone-parent families, step-families, children who live sometimes with one parent and sometimes with another. With these more complex families come more complex ties of family love, support, exchange, duty and obligation.

Lone parenthood is the most visible face of these new family patterns. In the eyes of some, it is the most problematic. How can we provide better support for children in lone-parent families without encouraging such families? How can we reduce public expenditure without driving poverty up even higher? These questions have no easy solutions, but a knowledge and understanding of the lives and circumstances of lone parents can help inform policy, generate ideas for policy options and provide guidance for their evaluation. In this final chapter, we briefly summarise some of the key research findings discussed at the seminar and outlined in the various contributions here and consider their implications for future policy directions.

CONTINUITIES AND CHANGES IN LONE PARENTHOOD

The number of lone parents grew from just over half a million at the beginning of the 1970s to nearly one million by the beginning of the 1980s, largely driven by a rise in divorce. As John Haskey shows, there was a moderate rise during the 1980s, followed by a marked rise during the 1990s. The latest, provisional estimate is about 1.7 million. The number of children in these families has risen to nearly three million. Part of the reason is demographic – the generation of baby boomers born in the early 1960s has now entered the modal age of lone parenthood. This contribution to the numbers of lone parents is temporary and, in the absence of other influences, may decline in the next decade.

There are two main routes of entry into lone parenthood: relationship breakdown and the birth of a child outside marriage. There are also two main routes out: repartnership and children growing up. All lone parents ultimately cease to be lone parents as their children grow up, but repartnership appears to be becoming less popular and so 'exit rates' from lone parenthood are falling. Thus, not only are there more people becoming lone parents but those who do are staying lone parents for longer.

One of the factors that has caused much recent comment and concern is the fact that the fastest growing group among lone parents are now single, never-married mothers. This is seen by some as a direct challenge to family values and a reflection of the 'perverse incentives' offered by state support for single mothers. However, the statistics here are somewhat misleading, for two main reasons. First, there is confusion caused by the rising numbers of couples living together without marriage. Women who separate from a cohabiting relationship are usually counted as single, but could more accurately be described as separated. About 38 per cent of all lone mothers are defined as 'single', but overall only 21 per cent report that they have never lived with a partner. This proportion has changed little since the 1960s. Second, there have been changes over time in the way in which people respond to a pregnancy outside marriage. In the 1960s and 1970s such a pregnancy would often lead to a 'shotgun wedding'. These marriages had a very high rate of divorce and so these women would subsequently turn up in the statistics as divorced lone mothers. Today, a pregnancy to a single woman may lead to cohabitation but rarely leads to marriage, and so these women – in broadly the same situations – now turn up in the statistics as single lone mothers.

The analysis by Stephen McKay and Karen Rowlingson shows that if we divide lone mothers into two groups – ex-partnered women who become lone mothers as a consequence of relationship breakdown and solo women who are single and have never lived with a partner – then there are some important differences between them. As Kath Kiernan (who acted as one of the discussants at the seminar)[1] pointed out, the evidence suggests that:

---

1. Other discussants were Fran Bennett, Rosalind Edwards, Robert Walker and Ruth Lister. We have drawn extensively on their comments and contributions in writing this chapter (and in the JRF Foundations, published in June 1997) and we are very grateful to them for allowing us to use their material in this way.

'women who are poor become solo mothers while separated mothers become poor.' Single women who come from poor socio-economic backgrounds, live in social housing, are black and who live in areas of high local unemployment are most likely to become solo mothers. Their economic prospects are already poor and so are those of the men living in the same areas. Solo motherhood is rarely the result of a planned pregnancy, but, having become pregnant, the women do not necessarily see this as a 'problem' requiring a 'solution'. If they could, they might have chosen a different timing and maybe a different relationship, but motherhood is for them, as it is for most women in our society, a desirable and valued goal. By contrast, separated lone motherhood is less linked to prior social disadvantage than solo lone motherhood. Although women who are pregnant at marriage, or who marry or cohabit at a young age, are most at risk of separation, the risk of marital or relationship breakdown is now quite widespread and brings in many different types of people. However, after separation their experiences are similar: most separated women, and their children, suffer a significant and sudden decline in their incomes and living standards. They often experience high levels of economic stress. As Sarah Jarvis and Stephen Jenkins show, their former partners, by contrast, are typically able to maintain their incomes and living standards.

Quality of life and resources

When examining the quality of life of lone parents and their children, a mixed picture emerges, as the chapters in this book by Eileen Evason and her colleagues, John McKendrick, and Sue Middleton and Karl Ashworth show. On the one hand, there is poverty, debt and material hardship. Parents suffer this more than their children. Lone parents spend as much on their children as married parents. Those living on income support are the most constrained in their spending, the most personally deprived and the most stressed by their financial circumstances. Other negative aspects of life as a lone parent include feeling a heavy burden of responsibility as a consequence of not having a partner with whom to talk and share decision making. Social networks, with friends and families, may also be restricted as lone parents feel uncomfortable at being unable to return favours and support. Those with very young children, those with problems of ill-health (their own or their children's), and those who have recently become lone parents are particularly vulnerable, both economically and emotionally.

On the other hand, their lives have many positive aspects. Their family, particularly their children, are a source of great love and pride to lone parents and most put family life at the top of the list of things that are important to them. Many lone mothers say they particularly value their independence and autonomy as lone parents and describe their former relationships as unequal partnerships, characterised by a lack of sharing – of time, money, household tasks, child care and so on. 'Access to a job, to decent housing, and to childcare all contribute to a better quality of life.' A job provides an income and social contacts, decent housing provides a very important feeling of security, access to childcare helps parents feel more in control and opens up other choices to them.

Historical and comparative contexts

Historically, Britain has witnessed a shift in the way lone mothers have been treated in policy, as discussed by Hilary Land and Jane Lewis. Until the 1960s, most lone mothers were largely invisible to public policy: they lived at home with their parents and often worked full time while their mothers looked after the children. They may have come into contact with social services, but not with other government departments. From the late 1960s onwards, however, lone mothers became increasingly visible on the national policy agenda. They gained access to public housing and to social security benefits, although they were not generally helped with childcare. This combination meant that, throughout the 1980s, lone mothers were living in housing that was increasingly costly as rents were pushed up to market levels, on benefits that were low and so made budgeting, penny-pinching and worrying about money an ever-present feature of life, and had to be available to provide full-time care for their children at all times. The 1980s' labour market, with its high rates of unemployment and often only low-paying jobs available, further exacerbated their difficulties. Not surprisingly, the proportion in employment fell and the proportion dependent solely on income support rose.

Changing views of 'motherhood' have also played an important role, both in policy and in how lone mothers perceive themselves and their obligations. Does a 'good mother' stay at home to look after her children? Or does she go out to work to try to provide for them? Or does she do both? The dominant view emerging is that good mothering is not simply full-time mothering, but does also include some paid work, especially once children get to school. Lone mothers are also very aware that they are *sole* parents and that this makes their choices more complicated. Some feel that because they are the only parent available, their children need more of their time, making paid work difficult. Negative images of lone motherhood, which have been so prevalent in recent years, make them sensitive to accusations of neglect and failed parenting.

The way in which lone mothers define their mothering role also varies with personal characteristics, such as class, race, age and age of children. Black Caribbean lone mothers, for example, are much more likely than white lone mothers to perceive of good mothering as including full-time paid work. Where lone mothers live and the attitudes held by their friends and families are also important, as is past experience. Lone mothers who have never had access to childcare are more likely to be suspicious of the quality of such care and so prefer to stay at home and care for their children themselves.

Although there has been much concern that if benefit levels are too 'high' they discourage lone parents from working, it is clear that things are more complicated than that. Employment rates are not solely, or even mainly, the consequence of the level of state benefits and services. They also reflect attitudes and values on the one side, and job opportunities on the other. This is apparent when we examine the situation in other countries. There are a number of countries with less generous state support for lone parents where employment rates are indeed higher. But there are others with more generous state support where employment rates are also higher. Jonathan Bradshaw's cross-national study of labour market conditions and earnings, education and training services, attitudes to lone mothers' employment, daycare, tax, benefits and maintenance in more than 20 countries concluded that no one model could explain variations in employment rates, though childcare support was important everywhere. The availability of childcare opens up opportunities and its lack of availability acts as a significant constraint. Reuben Ford's analysis tends to confirm this: access to childcare is a necessary, but not by itself a sufficient, condition for lone parents to work.

Cross-national comparison also suggests that lone mothers do best, in terms of relative incomes and living standards, in countries where they are treated in the same way as married mothers and where all mothers – or indeed all parents – are supported to be both parents and paid workers, not one or the other.

POLICY GOALS: CURRENT POLICY AND FUTURE OPTIONS

Three main sources of income are available to lone parents – their own earnings, state benefits and family transfers. Until recently, these have generally been treated in policy as alternative, rather than complementary, sources of income. For example, lone parents on income support have not been required to seek employment and receipt of maintenance from former partners has been fully deducted from state benefits. As a consequence, lone parents tended to be either completely dependent on state support or in full-time employment, for the option of combining part-time work with some additional support from benefits was difficult to achieve. However, this approach to policy has increasingly given way to the idea that the incomes of lone-parent families can, and should, involve combinations of these different sources.

Supporting employment and supplementing wages

Family credit – the means-tested benefit payable to low-income working families – has been central to recent policy. It has two main goals: to encourage paid work by providing a financial incentive, and to keep low-paid working families out of poverty. It has had some success on both counts. It does provide a financial incentive to work; it overcomes the stigma and complexity of other benefits; lone parents prefer it to income support; it is largely taken up by those who need it; it lifts them out of the worst effects of poverty and it provides a guaranteed basic income for six months before eligibility is reassessed. It works even after controlling for other key markers of labour market disadvantage, such as housing tenure, prior marital status, experience of benefits, education or training, maintenance and family health.

However, there appear to be two major problems with family credit. First, it only helps one in six lone parents to work. Most remain on income support. The barriers to work for lone parents are formidable. They include the attitudes of employers; the organisation of work; scarcity of jobs; lack of transport; lack of skills; current hardship and the constraints that it imposes; lack of access to childcare, both formal and informal; lack of confidence and work experience; low pay and insecure jobs; concern about meeting housing costs; and the complexity of the benefit system, particularly in respect of moving from out-of-work to in-work benefits. Any policy intended to increase employment rates must begin to address this complex mix of factors. As Louise Finlayson and Alan Marsh show, not all lone mothers are equally 'work-ready'. They find that three in ten already work near full-time hours, three in ten are ready to work now, three in ten will work one day and one in ten will never work.

Second, many lone parents have a low skill base, which is reflected in their low hourly wage. As such, they are prone to unemployment. Keeping them in work may require continuous support and lone mothers are very likely to be long-term recipients of family credit. But, among such long-term recipients, there is emerging evidence that receipt of family credit is associated with lower wages. The principal determinants of lone mothers' wage rates are human capital, family constraints and family credit. In 1991, weekly and hourly wages were lower for those on family credit with every other potential influence on wages held constant. By 1995, among the same people, those on family credit received about one-third less in wages than those working without family credit. Thus, wages rose less quickly when combined with family credit. Taking family credit jobs may be making it difficult for lone parents to improve their wages and may mean that the state is paying wage supplements for longer than might otherwise have been the case. Lone mothers who improve their skills through additional training or education do see improvements in their hourly wage rates.

Supporting children in cash and kind

The financial consequences of marital separation are unequivocally worse for women and children than for men. Under the courts-based system, child support payments were irregular, infrequent, low and largely confined to the children of divorcing parents. The Child Support Act was intended to overcome the disadvantages inherent in the court-based system and, as Mavis Maclean argues, it does have many advantages over the previous system. In particular, it treats the needs of all children living apart from parents in the same way; and, in a situation when access to the courts is becoming more difficult, it ensures that lone mothers have a chance to pursue claims for child support. However, as Karen Clarke, Caroline Glendinning and Gary Craig discuss, in the years since the Child Support Agency (CSA) began to operate there has been no noticeable increase in the proportion of lone parents receiving child support and the policy itself has created new difficulties and problems. These include:

- a two-tier system has evolved between the benefit claimant-dominated customers of the CSA, and non-claimants who have the option of not involving the agency;
- the formula is complex, perceived to be too rigid, and certain features of it are very unpopular;
- the lack of a guarantee to child support alongside family credit makes in-work income potentially less stable than out-of-work income;
- the loss of informal help from the absent parent as a consequence of the formal assessment is felt keenly by some parents and children, and is not compensated for by increased financial returns if the family is on income support; and
- the requirement to name the absent parent did not cause lone mothers problems in the early stages of operation, but it seems that lone mothers are increasingly being required to cooperate in inappropriate circumstances, sometimes under threat of, or actual, violence.

Most importantly, there are limits as to what any CSA could ever achieve. Marital breakdown occurs disproportionately among less well-off parents whose wages pre-split, let alone post-split, may be inadequate to support a family. Even those who do have reasonable incomes cannot usually support two households at an adequate level at the same time. The CSA cannot increase the resources available to these families.

Support for children in kind – through childcare provision or subsidy – is an issue that has come more centrally on to the policy agenda in recent years. This has been driven at least in part by a growing recognition of the needs of parents, particularly mothers, who are in paid employment. But childcare, as both Reuben Ford and John McKendrick show, is not simply an issue that relates to labour market participation. Childcare provision helps lone parents to take up paid work, but childcare is just one element, albeit an important one, in the decision about whether or not to seek work. Access to childcare services may help lone parent and their children in other ways too. It provides a point of social contact and could make lone mothers feel less restricted and more in control of their lives. The way in which childcare is currently subsidised – through the family credit system and so only for those currently employed – may therefore not be the most effective way of reaching all those who could benefit. The exclusion of non-formal care from this subsidy (the childcare disregard only applies where children are in registered childcare) also means that those who choose to use informal childcare, for example grandparents, are not given any financial help towards this. But, for many lone parents, informal care and formal care are not alternatives. Both are necessary and it is only by putting together a 'package' of care (such as grandparents caring for children to bridge the gap between the end of the school day and the end of the working day, or caring for children when they are sick) that effective childcare support can be created.

FUTURE POLICY DIRECTIONS

It is essential to move away from the negative image of lone parenthood that has dominated debate and constrained policy options in the UK. In the vast majority of cases, lone parenthood is not a selfish and wilful choice; lone parents are not feckless, unreliable and undependable; children living in lone-parent families are not neglected and undisciplined. In thinking about future policy options, there are three important principles to recognise:

1. Lone parenthood is a life-cycle stage, just as parenthood is, but it is a time when there are particular needs and pressures.

Lone-parent families have a legitimate claim to some collective support. However, that support should not necessarily be available only to lone-parent families. Families have many needs in common, whether there are one or two parents. Policies to help all families, all children, all mothers will also help lone-parent families, and do so without stigmatising them and without setting their needs in opposition to others.

2. Support for lone-parent families should not be separated from issues relating to support for all families with children.

Support is required across a broad front and this means developing a much more integrated approach to policy. We should look closely at the inter-actions between income maintenance policy, childcare policy and housing policy, and also consider two key areas: the level and nature of support for children; and the level and nature of support for parents to help them reconcile work and family life.

3. Policy should be integrated across the areas of income support, housing and childcare.

There are also a number of specific areas of policy that should be taken forward. These include the following:

1. education, training and job prospects for young people. These can be effective barriers to early parenthood – for both young women and young men;
2. the adequacy of the level of income support for families should be reviewed. This should include consideration of the age-related benefits for children. There is no case for abolishing the one-parent benefit or the lone-parent premium on income support;
3. the quality of childcare cannot be ignored in efforts to increase availability. High quality care may be needed to compensate some children for a poor home environment. Demonstration projects should be used to help overcome concerns about childcare quality;
4. the 'new deal' for lone parents, whereby lone parents with school-age children are asked to take part voluntarily in interviews with employ-ment advisors, represents a welcome shift in policy emphasis. How-ever, not all lone parents are in a position to take up immediate paid work and neither could the labour market absorb them all. A policy of compulsion would be both difficult to implement and counter-productive. Non-employed lone parents receiving income support are more likely to become 'work-ready' sooner if they are not so poor and demoralised, and if they are already using childcare services;
5. improving the employment prospects of lone parents is an important policy goal. This will require action on a number of fronts. Employers need convincing that lone parents are worthwhile employees and that flexible employment patterns can suit the needs of workers as well as employers;

6. just like other workers, lone parents need access to education and training. If they can improve their human capital they can improve their long-term prospects significantly. Lifetime learning and higher education are important routes to higher incomes, yet lone parents are the worst off among undergraduates, make most use of hardship funds and loans and are more likely to drop out of courses due to cost;

7. there should be some caution in adopting the 'any job is better than none' approach. Lone parents who take jobs with low pay and top up their wages with family credit may find themselves locked into a low-pay, low-skill job market while the state continues to support them with long-term wage subsidies. A statutory minimum wage may help prevent this. Strenuous efforts to promote gender equality and equal pay would also help;

8. in-work benefits should be kept to a minimum number, to reduce complexity. Housing benefit is a particular source of problems and there is a case for a more general review of alternative ways to deliver support for housing costs;

9. lone-parent families are in need of strong social networks. It is inappropriate to place them in temporary housing that requires them to be frequently mobile and that – because it is in the private sector – carries a higher cost; and

10. the CSA should be reviewed and consideration given to removing the requirement to cooperate, introducing a small disregard of child support payments in income support, and guaranteeing child support for family credit claimants as it already is for income support claimants.

Lone parents and their children are one of the poorest groups in our society. The social, economic, political and personal changes that have brought these families into such prominence are beyond the reach of government to 'fix', even if this were thought to be a desirable goal. But governments can act to prevent, alleviate and eliminate poverty, and child poverty must have a particular claim on collective responsibility. A key policy goal should be the elimination of child poverty, regardless of the type of family in which children find themselves living at a particular time. This involves support for all children, all parents, all families.

References

Abel-Smith, B and P Townsend (1965) *The Poor and the Poorest*, London: Bell

Atkinson, A B (1987) 'On the measurement of poverty', *Econometrics*, vol 55, pp 749–64

Banks, J and P Johnson (1993) *Children and Household Living Standards*, London: Institute for Fiscal Studies

Becker, G S (1981) *A Treatise on the Family*, Cambridge, Mass: Harvard University Press

— (1985) 'Human capital, effort and the sexual division of labor', *Journal of Labor Economics*, vol 3, no 1, S33–S58

Bell, T L (1984) 'Places rated almanac: flawed but pedagogically useful', *Journal of Geography*, pp 285–90

Bennett, F (1997) *Child Support: Issues for the Future*, London: CPAG

Berthoud, R and S Beishon (1997) 'People, families and households', in T Modood, R Berthoud, J Lakey, J Nazroo, P Smith, S Virdee, and S Beishon, *Ethnic Minorities in Britain*, London: Policy Studies Institute

Berthoud, R and R Ford (1996) *Relative Needs: Variations in the Living Standards of Different Types of Households*, London: Policy Studies Institute

Bittles, A H and D F Roberts (eds) (1992) *Minority Populations: Genetics, Demography and Health*, London: Macmillan Press in association with the Galton Institute

Bowlby, J (1951) *Maternal Care and Mental Health*, Geneva: World Health Organization

Bradshaw, J (1989) *Lone Parents: Policy in the Doldrums,* London: Family Policy Studies Centre

— (1996) 'Family policy and family poverty', *Policy Studies*, vol 17, pp 93–106

Bradshaw, J and J Millar (1991) *Lone Parent Families in the UK*, Department of Social Security, Research Report 6, London: HMSO

Bradshaw, J, J Ditch, H Holmes and P Whiteford (1993) *Support for Children: A Comparison of Arrangements in Fifteen Countries*, London: HMSO

Bradshaw, J, S Kennedy, M Kilkey, S Hutton, A Corden, T Eardley, H Holmes and J Neale (1996a) *The Employment of Lone Parents: A Comparison of Policy in 20 Countries,* London: Family Policy Studies Centre

— (1996b) *Policy and the Employment of Lone Parents in 20 Countries: The EU Report*, DGV and the Social Policy Research Unit, University of York

Bradshaw, J, C Stimson, J Williams and C Skinner (1997) 'Non-resident fathers in Britain', Paper to the ESRC Programme on Population and Household Change Seminar at PSI: 13 March 1997, Unpublished conference paper

Brown, J (1988) *In Search of a Policy,* London: National Council for One Parent Families

— (1989) *Why Don't They go to Work? Mothers on Benefit*, Social Security Advisory Committee, Research Paper 2, London: HMSO

Bryson, A, R Ford and M White (1997) *Making Work Pay: Lone Mothers' Employment and Wellbeing*, York: Joseph Rowntree Foundation

Buhmann, B, L Rainwater, G Schmauss and T M Smeeding (1988) 'Equivalence scales, well-being, inequality, and poverty: sensitivity estimates across ten countries using the Luxembourg Income Study (LIS) database', *Review of Income and Wealth*, vol 34, pp 115–42

Burghes, L (1994) *Lone Parenthood and Family Disruption: The Outcomes for Children*, London: Family Policy Studies Centre

Burkhauser, R V, G J Duncan, R Hauser and R Berntsen (1990) 'Economic burdens of marital disruptions: a comparison of the United States and the Federal Republic of Germany' *Review of Income and Wealth*, vol 36, pp 319–33

— (1991) 'Wife or frau, women do worse: a comparison of men and women in the United States and Germany after marital dissolution', *Demography*, 353–60

Cairns, E (1988) 'Social class, psychological wellbeing and minority status in Northern Ireland', *The International Journal of Social Psychiatry*, vol 33, no 3, pp 231–6

Cairns, E and R Wilson (1985) 'Psychiatric aspects of violence in Northern Ireland', *Stress Medicine*, vol 1, pp 193–201

Callender, C, G Court, M Thompson and A Patch (1994) *Employers and Family Credit*, DSS Report no 32, London: HMSO

Card, D and P Robins (1996) *Do Financial Incentives Encourage Welfare Recipients to Work: Evidence from a randomised evaluation of the self-sufficiency project*, Working paper no 5701, Cambridge, MA: National Bureau of Economic Research

Caterall, Peter and Virginia Preston (1995 and 1996) *Contemporary Britain: An Annual Review*, London: Institute of Contemporary British History

Central Statistical Office (1997) *Social Trends 27*, London: HMSO

Cherlin, A (1992) *Marriage, Divorce, Remarriage*, London: Harvard University Press

Clarke, K, G Craig, and C Glendinning (1993) *Children Come First?* London: Barnardos

— (1994) *Losing Support. Children and the Child Support Act*, London: Children's Society

— (1996a) *Small Change: The Impact of the Child Support Act on Lone Mothers and Children*, London: Family Policy Studies Centre

— (1996b) *Children's Views on Child Support: Parents, Families and Responsibilities*, London: Children's Society

Clarke, L (1996) 'Demographic change and the family situation of children', in J Brannen, and M O'Brien (eds) *Children in Families: Research and Policy*, London: Falmer Press, pp 66–83

Cmd 9684 (1956) *Report of the Royal Commission of Marriage and Divorce*, London: HMSO

Cockett, M and J Tripp (1994) *The Exeter Family Study: Family Breakdown and its Impact on Children*, Exeter: University of Exeter Press

Cohen, B (1988) *Caring for Children: Services and Policies for Child Care and Equal Opportunities in the United Kingdom*, London: Commission of the European Communities

Connelly, R (1992) 'The effect of childcare costs on married women's labour force participation', *Review of Economics and Statistics*, vol 24, pp 83–90

Corden, A, T Eardley and R Smellie (1993) 'Assessment of self-employed earnings for family credit', *Public Money and Management*, vol 13, no 1

Coulter, F A E, F A Cowell and S P Jenkins (1992a) 'Differences in needs and assessment of income distributions', *Bulletin of Economic Research*, vol 44, pp 77–124

— (1992b) 'Equivalence scale relativities and the extent of inequality and poverty', *Economic Journal*, vol 102, pp 1067–82

Crowe, Grahame and Michael Hardey (eds) (1991) *Lone Parenthood: Coping with Constraints and Making Opportunities*, Hemel Hempstead: Harvester/Wheatsheaf

Davis, G, G Young and N Wikely (1996) 'Preliminary findings from child support study', Southampton: Sociological Studies Association Conference

Dennis, N and G Erdos (1992) *Families without Fatherhood*, London: Institute of Economic Affairs

Department of Health and Social Security (1974) *Report of the Committee on One-Parent Families (Finer Report)*, Cmnd 5629, London: HMSO

— (1986) *Social Security Statistics 1986*, London: HMSO

— (1988) *Social Security Statistics 1988*, London: HMSO

Department of Health and Social Services (NI) (1995) *Northern Ireland Social Security Statistics 1994*, Belfast: HMSO

Department of Social Security (1993) *Social Security Statistics 1993*, London: HMSO

— (1994) *Social Security Statistics 1994*, London: HMSO

— (1995a) *Social Security Departmental Report*, London: HMSO

— (1995b) *Households Below Average Income 1979–1992/93*, London: HMSO

— (1996) *Households Below Average Income: A Statistical Analysis 1979–1993/4*, London: HMSO

— (1997a) *Social Security Statistics, 1996*, London: The Stationery Office

— (1997b) 'Historic new deal for lone parents launched', DSS press release, 21 July

Ditch, J, H Barnes, J Bradshaw, J Commaille and D Eardley (1995) *A Synthesis of National Family Policies in 1994*, SPRU/DG5

Ditch, J, H Barnes and J Bradshaw (1996) *A Synthesis of National Family Policies in 1995*, SPRU/DG5

Dobson, B, A Beardsworth, T Keil and R Walker (1994) *Diet Choice and Poverty: Social Cultural and Nutritional Aspects of Food Consumption among Low-Income Families*, London: Family Policy Studies Centre

Donnison, D (1982) *The Politics of Poverty*, Oxford: Martin Robertson

Dowler, E and C Calvert (1995) *Nutrition and Diet in Lone-Parent Families in London*, London: Family Policy Studies Centre

Doyal, L and Gough, I (1991) *A Theory of Human Need*, London: Macmillan

Duncan, A (1991) 'Taxation, social security and lone parents', *Benefits*, Issue 2

Duncan, G J and S D Hoffman (1985) 'Economic consequences of marital instability', in M David and T M Smeeding (eds) *Horizontal Inequity, Uncertainty and Well-being*, Chicago: University of Chicago Press

Duncan, S and R Edwards (1997) 'Single mothers in Britain: unsupported workers or mothers?', in S Duncan and R Edwards (eds) *Single Mothers in an International Context: Mothers or Workers?* London: UCL Press, pp 45–79

Duskin, E (1990) *Lone-Parent Families: The Economic Challenge*, Paris: OECD Social Policy Studies, no 8

Eardley, T, J Bradshaw, J Ditch, I Gough and P Whiteford (1996) *Social Assistance Schemes in the OECD Countries: DSS Research Report*, London: HMSO

Edwards, R (1993) 'Taking the initiative: the government, lone mothers and day care provision', *Critical Social Policy*, pp 36–50

Eilers G M and T K Swanson (1994) 'Women's satisfaction with Norplant compared to oral contraceptives', *Journal of Family Practitioners*, pp 596–600

Employment Committee (1990) *Part-Time Employment: The 38th Report of the Committee* (HC249, 1990/91), London: HMSO

Equal Opportunities Commission (1986) *Childcare and Equal Opportunities: Some Policy Perspectives*, London: HMSO

Ermisch, J (1986) *The Economics of the Family: Applications to Divorce and Remarriage*, Discussion Paper 140, London: EPR

— (1991a) *Lone Parenthood: An Economic Analysis*, Cambridge: Cambridge University Press

— (1991b) *The Economics of Lone Parenthood*, London: National Institute for Economic and Social Research

— (1995) 'Pre-marital cohabitation, childbearing and the creation of one parent families', *Working Papers of the ESRC Research Centre on Micro-social Change*, Paper 95–17, Colchester: University of Essex

— (1996) 'The economic environment for family formation', in D Coleman (ed) *Europe's Population in the 1990s*, Oxford: Oxford University Press

Ermisch, J F and R E Wright (1991) 'Welfare benefits and lone parents' employment in Great Britain', *Journal of Human Resources*, vol 26, no 3, pp 424–56

Esam, R and R Berthoud (1991) *Independent Benefits for Men and Women*, London: Policy Studies Institute

Evandrou, M and J Falkingham (1995) 'Gender, lone parenthood and lifetime income', in J Falkingham, and J Hills (eds) *The Dynamic of Welfare: The Welfare State and the Life Cycle*, Hemel Hempstead: Prentice Hall, pp 167–83

Evason, E (1980) *Just Me and the Kids: A Study of Single Parent Families in Northern Ireland*, Belfast: EOCNI

Evason, E, A Allamsy and R Woods (1989) *The Deserving and Undeserving Poor*, Northern Ireland: Child Poverty Action Group

Evason, E and G Robinson, (1995a) *Lone Parent Study: Literature Review*, Report to DHSS (NI), University of Ulster

— (1995b) *Lone Parent Study: Focus Groups Project*, Report to DHSS (NI), University of Ulster

— (forthcoming) 'Lone parents in Northern Ireland: the effectiveness of work incentives', *Social Policy and Administration*

Evason, E and R Woods (1995a) 'Poverty, deregulation of the labour market and benefit fraud', *Social Policy and Administration*, vol 29, no 1

— (1995b) *Poverty, Charity and Doing the Double*, Aldershot: Avebury

Evason, E, G Robinson and K Thompson (forthcoming) *Lone Parents in Northern Ireland: Final Report*, Ulster: University of Ulster

Finlayson, L and A Marsh (1998 forthcoming) *Lone Parents on the Margins of Work*, London: The Stationery Office, DSS Research Series

Finnie, R (1993) 'Women, men, and the economic consequences of divorce: evidence from Canadian longitudinal data', *Canadian Review of Sociology and Anthropology*, vol 30, pp 205–41

Ford, R (1996) *Childcare in the Balance: How Lone Parents Make Decisions about Work*, London: Policy Studies Institute

Ford, R, A Marsh and S McKay (1995) *Changes in Lone Parenthood*, Department of Social Security, Research Report No 40, London: HMSO

Ford, R, A Marsh and L Finlayson (1998 forthcoming) *What happens to Lone Parents*, London: The Stationery Office, DSS Research Series

Fox Harding, L (1991) 'The Children Act 1989 in context: four perspectives in child care law and policy', *Journal of Social Welfare and Family Law*, pp 179–93, 285–302

Freeman, R and J Waldfogel (1995) 'Dunning delinquent dads: effects of child support enforcement policy', paper read to the conference on Social Security Policy and the Labour Market, Exeter College, Oxford

Garfinkel, I and S McLanahan (1986) *Single Mothers and their Children: A New American Dilemma*, Washington: Urban Institute Press

George, V (1975) 'Why one-parent families remain poor', *Poverty*, no 31, pp 6–12

Gibson, C S (1991) 'The future for maintenance', *Civil Justice Quarterly*, vol 10, pp 330–46

Glendinning, C and J Millar (eds) (1987) *Women and Poverty in Britain*, Hemel Hempstead: Harvester/Wheatsheaf, second edition 1992

Goldberg, D P (1972) *The Detection of Psychiatric Illness by Questionnaire*, Maudsley Monograph no 21, Oxford: Oxford University Press

Goodman, A, P Johnson and S Webb (1997) *Inequality in Britain*, Oxford: Oxford University Press

Gregory, J and K Foster (1990) *The Consequences of Divorce: The Report of the 1984 OPCS Consequences of Divorce Survey carried out on behalf of the Lord Chancellor's Department*, London: HMSO

Greve, J (1964) *London's Homeless*, London: Bell

Haskey, J (1990) 'The children of families broken by divorce', *Population Trends*, vol 61, pp 34–42

— (1991) 'Estimated numbers and demographic characteristics of one-parent families in Great Britain', *Population Trends*, vol 65, pp 35–47

— (1993) 'Trends in the numbers of one-parent families in Great Britain', *Population Trends*, vol 71, pp 26–33

— (1994) 'Estimated numbers of one-parent families and their prevalence in Great Britain in 1991', *Population Trends*, vol 78, pp 5–19

— (1997) 'Children who experience divorce in their family', *Population Trends*, vol 87, pp 5–10

Hastings, D (1997) 'Household and family data from the Labour Force Survey: recent improvements in approach', *Labour Market Trends*, June, pp 209–16

Heckman, J J (1979) 'Sample selection bias as a specification error', *Econometrica*, vol 47, pp 153–61

Hodgkin, R and P Newell (1996) *Effective Government Structures for Children*, London: Calouste Gulbenkian Foundation

Holden, K C and P J Smock (1991) 'The economic costs of marital dissolution: why do women bear a disproportionate cost?', *Annual Reviews of Sociology*, vol 17, pp 51–78

Holtermann, S (1993) *Becoming a Breadwinner: Policies to Assist Lone Parents with Childcare*, London: Daycare Trust

— (1995) *All our Futures*, Ilford: Barnado's

House of Commons Social Security Committee Fifth Report (1997) *Child Support*, House of Commons Session 1996–7, HC 282

Hoynes, H W (1996) 'Work, welfare and family structure: a review of the evidence', *Institute for Research on Poverty Discussion Paper*, pp 103–96

Jarvis, S and S P Jenkins (1997) *Marital Splits and Income Changes: Evidence for Britain*, Working Paper 97–4, Colchester: ESRC Research Centre on Micro-Social Change, University of Essex

Jenkins, S P (1991) 'Poverty measurement and the within-household distribution', *Journal of Social Policy*, vol 20, no 4, pp 457–83

— (1992) 'Lone mothers' employment and full-time work probabilities', *The Economic Journal*, vol 102, no 411, pp 310–20

Jenkins, S P and F A Cowell (1994) 'Parametric equivalence scales and scale relativities', *Economic Journal*, vol 104, pp 891–900

Jenkins, S P and E Symons (1995) *Childcare Costs and Lone Mothers' Employment Rates: UK Evidence,* Working Papers of the ESRC Research Centre on Microsocial Change. paper 95–2, Colchester: University of Essex

Jenkins, S P, J Ermisch, and R Wright (1990) 'Adverse selection features of poverty amongst lone mothers', *Fiscal Studies*, vol 11, no 2, pp 76–90

Jones, A and J Millar (eds) (1996) *The Politics of the Family*, Aldershot: Avevury

Joshi, H (1996) 'The opportunity costs of childbearing: more than mothers' business', paper presented at the British Society for Population Studies annual conference at the University of St Andrews, September 1996

Joshi, H, H Land, and A Dale (1996) *The Tale of Mrs Typical*. London: Family Policy Studies Centre

Kempson, E (1996) *Life on a Low Income*, York: Joseph Rowntree Foundation

Kempson, E, A Bryson and K Rowlingson (1994) *Hard Times? How Poor Families Make Ends Meet*, London: Policy Studies Institute

Kiernan, K and M Wicks (1990) *Family Change and Future Policy*. London: Family Policy Studies Centre

Kiernan, K, H Land and J Lewis (forthcoming) *Lone Mothers in Twentieth Century Britain: From Footnote to Front Page*, Oxford: University Press

Koven, S and S Michel (1995) *Mothers of a New World,* London: Routledge

Korenman, S and D Neumark (1992) 'Marriage, motherhood and wages', *Journal of Human Resources*, vol 27, no 2, pp 233–55

Lampard, R (1993) 'An examination of the relationship between marital dissolution and unemployment', in D Gallie, C Marsh and C Vogler (eds) *Social Change and the Experience of Unemployment*, Oxford: Oxford University Press

Land, H (1980) 'The family wage', *Feminist Review*, vol 6, pp 55–7

— (1986) 'Women and children last: reform of social security?', in M Brenton and C Ungerson, *Yearbook of Social Policy in Britain 1985/86*, London: Routledge & Kegan Paul

— (1996) 'The crumbling bridges between childhood and adulthood', in J Brannen and M O'Brien (eds) *Children in Families: Research and Policy*, London: Falmer Press, pp 189–201

Land, H and J Lewis (1997) *Lone Mothers and Policy in the Twentieth Century: Findings*, York: Joseph Rowntree Foundation

Leibenstein, H (1974) 'An interpretation of the economic theory of fertility: promising path or blind alley', *Journal of Economic Literature*, pp 457–79

Leigh, J (1992) 'The Child Support Act 1991: its relationship with the Children Act 1989', *Journal of Child Law,* vol 4, pp 177–80

Lewis, J (1989) 'Lone parent families: politics and economics', *Journal of Social Policy*, vol 18, no 4, pp 595–600

— (1992) 'Gender and the development of welfare regimes', *Journal of European Social Policy*, vol 3, pp 159–73

— (1995) *The Problem of Lone Mother Families in Twentieth Century Britain*, STICERD (London School of Economics) Paper WSP/114

Mack, J and S Lansley (1992) *Breadline Britain in the 1990s*, London: Harper Collins

Mack, S and S Lansley (1985) *Poor Britain*, London: Allen & Unwin

Maclean, M (1994) 'Child support in the UK: making the move from court to agency', *Houston Law Review*, vol 31, no 2, pp 515–36

Maclean, M and J Eekelaar (1997) *The Parental Obligation, A Study of Parenthood across Households*, Oxford: Hart

Marsden, D (1969) *Mothers Alone: Poverty and the Fatherless Family*, Harmondsworth: Penguin Press

Marsh, A (1995) 'Lowering the barriers to work', in R Bayley, A Condy and C Roberts (eds) *Policies for Families: Work, Poverty and resources*, London: Family Policy Studies Centre

Marsh, A and S McKay (1993a) 'Families, work and the use of child care', *Employment Gazette*, August, pp 381–90

— (1993b) *Families, Work and Benefits*, London: Policy Studies Institute

— (1994) *Poor Smokers*, London: Policy Studies Institute

Marsh, A, R Ford, and L Finlayson (1997) *Lone Parents, Work and Benefits*, Department of Social Security, Research Report No 61, London: The Stationery Office

McCashin, A (1997) *Employment Aspects of Lone Parenthood in Ireland*, Dublin: Department of Social Studies, Trinity College

McKay, S and A Marsh, (1994) *Lone Mothers and Work: The Effects of Benefits and Maintenance*, London: HMSO

McKendrick, J H (1983) *In What Sense Lone Parent Migration*, Paper presented to the Department of Geography, Kingston University, 24 May

— (1994a) *The quality of life of a deprived population group: lone parents in Scotland*, Unpublished Ph.D. thesis, Department of Geography, University of Glasgow

— (1994b) 'Lone parents, migration and the quality of life', Paper presented to the Population Group of the Institute of British Geographers, University of Nottingham, 4 January

— (1995) *Lone Parenthood in Strathclyde Region: Implications for Housing Policy*, Spatial Policy Analysis Working Paper 30, School of Geography, University of Manchester

McLanahan, S and Sandefur, G (1994) *Growing Up with a Single Parent: What Hurts, What Helps*, London: Harvard University Press

McCormick, J and C Philo, (1995) 'Where is poverty? The hidden geography of poverty in the UK', in C Philo (ed) *Off the Map: The Social Geography of Poverty in the UK*, London: CPAG

Middleton, S, K Ashworth and R Walker (1994) *Family Fortunes: Pressures on Parents and Children in the 1990s*, London: Child Poverty Action Group Ltd

Middleton, S and K Ashworth (1997) *Small Fortunes: Spending on Children, Poverty and Parental Sacrifice*, York: Joseph Rowntree Foundation

Middleton, S and N Croden (1997) 'Children's work and children's pay', in *Children and Work: Rethinking the Debate'*, London: Child Poverty Action Group Ltd and Save the Children Fund

Millar, J (1987) 'Lone Mothers', in C Glendinning and J Millar (eds) *Women and Poverty in Britain,* Hemel Hempstead: Harvester/Wheatsheaf, pp 159–77

— (1989) *Poverty and the Lone Parent: The Challenge to Social Policy*, Aldershot: Avebury

— (1992) 'Lone mothers and poverty', in C Glendding and J Miller (eds) *Women and Poverty in Britain: The 1990s*, Hemel Hempstead: Harvester/Wheatsheaf, pp 129–48

— (1997) 'Family policy', in P Alcock et al (eds) *Students Companion to Social Policy*, London: Blackwells/Social Policy Association

Millar, J and J Bradshaw (1987) 'The living standards of lone-parent families', *Quarterly Journal of Social Affairs*, vol 3, no 2, pp 233–52

Millward, N and S Woodland (1995) 'Gender segregation and male/female wage difference', in J Rubery and J Humphries (eds) *The Economics of Equal Opportunities*, London: Equal Opportunities Commission

Mitchell, D and J Bradshaw (1993) *Lone Parents and their Incomes: A comparative study of Ten Countries*, York: University of York

Morgan, P (1995) *Farewell to the Family?* London: Institute of Economic Affairs

Murray, C (1994) *Underclass: The Crisis Deepens,* London: Institute of Economic Affairs

National Association of Citizens Advice Bureaux (1994) *Child Support: One Year On*, London: NACAB

O'Brien, M (1997) 'Missing Mavis', *Communicating with Users and Beneficiaries of the Children 5–16 Programme*, mimeo, pp 43–5

O'Brien, M and S Dench (1996) *The Out of School Childcare Grant Initiative: A Second Evaluation*, London: HMSO

Organization for Economic Cooperation and Development (1993) *Breadwinners or Child Rearers: The Dilemma for Lone Mothers*, Paris: OECD

Parker, H (1995) *Taxes, Benefits and Family Life*, London: Institute of Economic Affairs

Polachek, S W (1995) 'Earnings over the life cycle: what do human capital models explain?', *Scottish Journal of Political Economy*, vol 43, no 3, pp 267–89

PPRU (1992) *MONITOR, no 1, 1991/1992*, Belfast: Policy Planning and Research Unit

Price, S and McKenry (1988) *Divorce,* London: Sage Publications

Renvoize, J (1985) *Going Solo: Single Mothers by Choice*, London: Routledge & Kegan Paul

Riccio, J, D Friedlander and S Freedmam (1994) *GAIN: Benefits, Costs and Three-year Impacts of a Welfare-to-Work Program*, New York: Manpower Demonstration Research Corporation

Robertson, I M L (1984) 'Single parent lifestyle and peripheral estate residence', *Town Planning Review*, vol 55, pp 197–213

Rogerson, R (1989) 'Measuring quality of life: methodological issues and problems', *Applied Population Research Unit Discussion Paper 89/2*, Glasgow: APRU, University of Glasgow

Roll, J (1992) *Lone Parent Families in the European Community: The 1992 Report to the European Commission*, London: European Family and Social Policy Unit

Rose, N E (1995) *Workfare or Fair Work: Women, Welfare, and Government Work Programs*, New Brunswick: Rutgers University Press

Rose, D and C Le Bourdais (1988) 'The changing condition of female single parenthood in Montreal's inner-city and suburban neighbourhoods', *Urban Resources*, vol 3, pp 45–52

Rowlingson, K and S McKay (1997) *The Growth of Lone Parenthood: Diversity and Dynamics*, London: Policy Studies Institute

Rowntree, B S (1902) *Poverty: A Study of Town Life*, 2nd edn, London: Macmillan

Sanderson, I and J Percy-Smith (with Ann Foreman, Melissa Wraight, Liam Murphy and Pat Petrie) (1995) *The Out-of-School Childcare Grant Initiative*, Sheffield: Employment Department

Select Committee of the European Communities (1982) *Part-Time Work* (HL216, 1980/81), London: HMSO

Selman, P and C Glendinning (1996) 'Teenage pregnancy: do social policies make a difference?' in J Brannen and M O'Brien (eds) *Children in Families: Research and Policy*, London: Falmer Press, pp 202–18

Sen, A K (1983) 'Poor, relatively speaking', *Oxford Economic Papers*, vol 35, pp 153–69

Shaver, S and J Bradshaw (1995) 'The recognition of wifely labour by welfare states', *Social Policy and Administration*, vol 29, no 1, pp 10–25

Silva, E (1996) *Good Enough Mothering?* London: Routledge

Smart, C (1991) 'Securing the family? Rhetoric and policy in the field of social security', in M Loney, R Bocock, J Clarke, A Cochrane, P Graham and M Wilson (eds) *The State or the Market: Politics and Welfare in Contemporary Britain,* second edition, pp 153–68

Song, M and R Edwards (1997) 'Comment: raising questions about perspectives on black lone motherhood', *Journal of Social Policy*, pp 233–44

Tate, P (1997) 'Data on households and families from the Labour Force Survey', *Labour Market Trends*, March, pp 89–98

Taylor, A (1994) 'Appendix: sample characteristics, attrition and weighting', in N Buck, J Gershuny, D Rose and J Scott (eds) *Changing Households: The British Household Panel Survey 1990–1992*, Colchester: ESRC Research Centre on Micro-Social Change, University of Essex

Taylor, M F (ed) (1996) *British Household Panel Survey User Manual. Introduction, Technical Reports and Appendices,* Colchester: ESRC Research Centre on Micro-Social Change, University of Essex

Theodossiou, I (1995) 'Wage determination for career and non-career workers in the UK: is there labour market segmentation?', *Economica*, vol 62, pp 195–211

Townsend, P (1985) 'A sociological approach to the measurement of poverty: a rejoinder to Professor Amaryta Sen', *Oxford Economic Papers*, vol 37, pp 657–68

Utting, D (1995) *Family and Parenthood: Supporting Families, Preventing Breakdown*, York: Joseph Rowntree Foundation

Waldfogel, J (1995) 'The price of motherhood: family status and women's pay in a young British cohort', *Oxford Economic Papers*, vol 47, pp 584–610

Walker, R with K Ashworth (1994) *Poverty Dynamics: Issues and Examples*, Aldershot: Avebury

Whiteford, P and J Bradshaw (1994) 'Benefits and incentives for lone parents: a comparative analysis', *International Social Security Review*, vol 47, nos 3–4, pp 69–89

Whiteford, P and L Hicks (1992) *The Costs of Lone Parents: Evidence from Budget Standards*, Working Paper 16, Family Budget Unit, York: University of York

Wilson, W (1994) *Lone Parents and Housing*, House of Commons Research paper 94/11

Witherspoon, S, C Whyley and E Kempson (1996) *Paying for Rented Housing*, DSS Research Report no 43, London: HMSO

Wright, R E (1992) 'Single parenthood and poverty: what the data tell us', *Discussion Papers in Economics No 9211*, University of Glasgow, Department of Political Economy

Wright, R E and J E Ermisch (1991) 'Gender discrimination in the British labour market: a reassessment', *The Economic Journal*, vol 10, May, pp 508–22

Young, M and P Wilmott (1973) *The Symmetrical Family*, London: Routledge & Kegan Paul

Index

Family Resources Survey (FRS), 24–5
Finer Committee, 1, 147–8, 155
Finer Report, 22, 143, 249
Finland, 155–6, 165
Finlayson, Louise, 3, 256
Ford, Reuben, 4, 7, 16, 79, 82, 87, 90, 95, 100, 128, 140, 170, 200, 255, 258
Fowler reviews, 1, 15
France, 141, 155–6, 158–9, 164–5

GAIN, 207
general health questionnaire (GHQ), 68, 75–6
General Household Survey (GHS), 24–7, 36
George, V, 1
Germany, 104, 155–8, 161, 164–5
Gibson, C S, 17
Glendinning, Caroline, 4, 5, 257
Greece, 156–8, 165
Gulbenkian Foundation, 12

Haskey, John, 2, 6, 59, 167, 251
Hodgkin, R, 12
House of Lords Select Committee on Children, 12
Housing Act, 16, 151
housing benefit, 69, 114–15, 153, 159, 166, 168, 193, 198–200, 202–3, 206, 260

income support, 1, 6, 9, 13–17, 19, 21, 43, 50, 58–66, 68–70, 75–7, 113–14, 116, 119, 124–6, 130–40, 148–51, 153, 159, 164–8, 170–1, 184, 186, 189, 191–4, 196–206, 208, 217, 220, 229, 235–9, 244, 248–50, 253–7, 259–60
Institute of Economic Affairs, 165
International Year of the Family, 8
Ireland, 155–6, 158, 164–5; *see also* Northern Ireland
Irish Labour Force Survey, 155
Italy, 155–8, 164–5, 167

Japan, 155–7, 167
Jarvis, Sarah, 3, 107, 253
Jenkins, Stephen, 3, 107, 210–11, 253
JET schemes, 201

Joseph Rowntree Foundation, 118, 141

Kiernan, Kath, 252

Labour government, 148–50
Labour Force Survey (LFS), 24–5, 155–6
Land, Hilary, 3, 12, 50, 80, 254
legal aid, 231–2
Lewis, Jane, 3, 12, 50, 80, 227, 254
Lister, Ruth, 252n1
Lone Parent Survey, 56, 89
Lord Chancellor, 228, 231
Luxembourg, 155–8, 165
Luxembourg Income Survey, 161–3

Mack and Lansley index, 68, 72–4
McClements equivalence scale, 106, 110–13
McKay, Stephen, 2, 45–6, 79, 126–7, 252
McKendrick, John, 3, 55, 80, 101, 253, 258
Maclean, Mavis, 4, 257
Marsh, Alan, 3, 126–7, 238, 256
Middleton, Sue, 3, 253
Millar, Jane, 4, 58, 63, 78–9, 82, 90, 100, 140, 170, 195

national assistance, 21
National Assistance Act (1948), 145
National Assistance Board, 150
National Council for One Parent Families, 242
Netherlands, 155–8, 164–5
New Deal for Lone Parents, 82, 102–3
New Jersey, 11
New Zealand, 155–8
Newell, P, 12
Northern Ireland, 2, 58–60, 63, 65, 68–9, 73–7
Norway, 155–7

Omnibus Survey, 34, 58

Parliament, 149
Poor Law, 144
Portugal, 155–6, 158, 164–5, 167

Robertson, I M L, 101